T0261026

Digital Twin Technology

Scrivener Publishing
100 Cummings Center, Suite 541J
Beverly, MA 01915-6106

Publishers at Scrivener
Martin Scrivener (martin@scrivenerpublishing.com)
Phillip Carmical (pcarmical@scrivenerpublishing.com)

Digital Twin Technology

Fundamentals and Applications

Edited by
Manisha Vohra

Scrivener
Publishing

WILEY

This edition first published 2023 by John Wiley & Sons, Inc., 111 River Street, Hoboken, NJ 07030, USA and Scrivener Publishing LLC, 100 Cummings Center, Suite 541J, Beverly, MA 01915, USA
© 2023 Scrivener Publishing LLC
For more information about Scrivener publications please visit www.scrivenerpublishing.com.

Wiley Global Headquarters
111 River Street, Hoboken, NJ 07030, USA

For details of our global editorial offices, customer services, and more information about Wiley products visit us at www.wiley.com.

Limit of Liability/Disclaimer of Warranty
While the publisher and authors have used their best efforts in preparing this work, they make no representations or warranties with respect to the accuracy or completeness of the contents of this work and specifically disclaim all warranties, including without limitation any implied warranties of merchantability or fitness for a particular purpose. No warranty may be created or extended by sales representatives, written sales materials, or promotional statements for this work. The fact that an organization, website, or product is referred to in this work as a citation and/or potential source of further information does not mean that the publisher and authors endorse the information or services the organization, website, or product may provide or recommendations it may make. This work is sold with the understanding that the publisher is not engaged in rendering professional services. The advice and strategies contained herein may not be suitable for your situation. You should consult with a specialist where appropriate. Neither the publisher nor authors shall be liable for any loss of profit or any other commercial damages, including but not limited to special, incidental, consequential, or other damages. Further, readers should be aware that websites listed in this work may have changed or disappeared between when this work was written and when it is read.

Library of Congress Cataloging-in-Publication Data

ISBN 978-1-119-84220-0

Cover image: Pixabay. Com
Cover design by Russell Richardson

Set in size of 11pt and Minion Pro by Manila Typesetting Company, Makati, Philippines

Printed in the USA

10 9 8 7 6 5 4 3 2 1

Contents

Preface

The various capabilities of digital twin technology make it a powerful tool that can be used to effectively boost different sectors of the health-care, automotive, and construction industries among others. Although this technology has been making its way into various sectors, unfortunately it has yet to receive the kind of exposure necessary to increase awareness of its potential in these industries. Therefore, a better understanding of digital twin technology is needed to promote its use in different sectors to help them grow. When properly implemented in industrial sectors, such as healthcare, automotive, etc., it will not only greatly benefit them, but will also bring about a tremendous positive transformation in them. Therefore, this book was designed to be a useful resource for those who want to become well acquainted with digital twin technology. Briefly stated, it explains the fundamentals of digital twin along with its applications and various other aspects. A brief description of the information covered in each chapter follows.

– Chapter 1: Digital twin technology is opening doors to various possibilities in different sectors which will prove to be very fruitful. This chapter provides an overview of digital twin, including explaining what it is, a discussion of how this technology began, how it works, its features, etc.
– Chapter 2: Digital twin has entered the limelight in recent years. Even though this powerful technology has only gained notability recently, it dates back to the 1960s. In this chapter, digital twin is introduced. In addition to its history, its concept is also explained.
– Chapter 3: In this modern world, technology is used everywhere in almost each sector. Among the many technologies already in use, with many more still to come, digital twin is gaining popularity. In this chapter, insight into digital twin technology is provided. This technology is explained in detail along with different aspects of digital twin, including how it works, its types, traits and advantages, etc. Some real examples of the application of digital twin are also given.

– Chapter 4: A digital twin simulates the state and behavior of a physical object in real time. This work primarily focuses on digital twin solution architecture and how the digital twin can be designed to deliver common use cases. In this chapter, the authors first review how the physical object can be connected to the digital twin through the internet of things (IoT) and then show a layered view of the digital twin solution architecture. Digital twin solution architecture is explained from various viewpoints, including data stores, user experience, integration with external applications, application programming interface (API) and cybersecurity. Concepts involved in digital twin solution architecture are illustrated through examples from the world of discrete manufacturing.

– Chapter 5: In today's scenario, digital technology is gaining prominence in different sectors like business, healthcare, education, security, aerospace, construction, automotive, etc. This chapter discusses the novel digital twin technology. It presents generic applications of the digital twin and the role of digital twin technology in the medical sector.

– Chapter 6: Construction is a broad term that refers to the formation or creation of structures. The construction industry is involved in the installation, preservation and renovation of buildings and other immovable structures, as well as that of roadways, amenities, etc., which form the fundamental components of structures necessary for the structure's complete development and usage. This chapter discusses the role of digital twin technology in the construction industry. In the context of construction-related work, it provides an understanding of how digital twin technology can be used as a game-changing technology that could transform the construction industry. It also analyzes different perspectives of the role of digital twin in this industry.

– Chapter 7: Because digital twin is an efficient technology, various sectors can benefit from its evolution. In this chapter, a literature survey is presented on the different applications of digital twin found in the healthcare sector. A real-life example of its healthcare application is also briefly discussed and explained, along with the challenges digital twin faces in the healthcare sector.

– Chapter 8: Digital twin (DT) as a scientific paradigm offers extraordinary supremacy and dexterity both to the physical objects/systems and its digital counterparts against the backdrop of an Industry 4.0 environment. In this chapter, an attempt is made to explain the applicability of DT in structural health monitoring systems (SHMS). The DT paradigm and its related application in SHMS are discussed in this chapter, which offer useful insights in relation to damage identification in infrastructure (such as dams, bridges, etc.) and their structural health monitoring dimensions.

– Chapter 9: The emergence of a high level of focus on utilizing simulation via digital twin to assist operational choices should be welcomed by simulation and automation experts. However, it is believed that critical concerns like usability, maintainability, sustainability, effectiveness and all other aspects should be seen and evaluated if the entire potential of digital twins is to be achieved. This chapter discusses digital twin technology and explains its role in relation to the oil and gas industry by conducting a literature survey.

– Chapter 10: Digital twin is swiftly making its way into numerous applications and is evolving at a fast pace. Any technology is basically used to simplify things, make work easier, provide as many advantages as possible, etc. In short, each technology works towards helping the application in which it is applied. Digital twin technology also does the same. In this chapter, the application of digital twin in smart cities is discussed. The different ways in which the digital twin can help in the development of smart cities are presented. Its benefits are also discussed.

– Chapter 11: Digital twin technology can be useful in the pharmaceutical industry. Since it is one of the most important industries directly connected to healthcare, this chapter explains the application of digital twin in the pharmaceutical industry with examples. The advantages of its use in this industry are also discussed.

– Chapter 12: A digital twin is a virtual copy of an entity. It is a duplicate copy of a product, process or a system that is updated from real-time data that simply bridges the gap between the physical world and digital arena. Digital twin is not only used to understand the present but also helps to predict the future. In this chapter, different digital twin applications are explained and their importance is also stated.

– Chapter 13: Digital twin technology can be used in the development of products in organizations. This chapter discusses and analyzes its role in relation to the development of these products, along with the implications of its use. Since digital twin technology is a digital representation of physical products or processes, it facilitates the decision-making process in product development. It enables cost reduction and maximization of the benefits of the products in the competitive environment of organizations. The digital twin is an ideal technology as it allows obtaining all the information on a product or production process, thereby gaining great insights which can be applied to the physical world product or process on which the best decisions can be based. As illustrated in this chapter, the implication of adopting digital twin technology to develop products in organizations is found to be encouraging.

‒ Chapter 14: Digital twin technology is one of the fastest emerging concepts. Since digital twins are virtual replicas of real-world objects, they are extremely useful for predicting future problems in real-world objects or products. Digital twin technology can be used in many applications in different sectors, including aerospace, construction, smart city development, etc. In this chapter, after the digital twin technology concept is introduced, different possibilities afforded by digital twin in the automotive, aviation and supply chain sectors are discussed.

‒ Chapter 15: In this fast-moving world, the use of technology is of great importance. Therefore, more new technologies are continuously being sought that will be of great help in different sectors. Be it any sector like health, education, automotive, aviation, etc., it is a known fact that new technologies can benefit the whole sector. Digital twin is a technology that can match the expectations of different sectors at a high level. In this chapter, the pros and cons of using digital twin technology are presented along with an example of the real-world application of digital twin technology.

In closing, the editor would sincerely like to thank Martin Scrivener of Scrivener Publishing and all the chapter contributors for making this book possible. I hope this book will be a great resource for those who want to become well acquainted with digital twin.

Manisha Vohra
October 2022

Overview of Digital Twin

Manisha Vohra

Independent Researcher, India

Abstract

Digital twin is a technology which is opening doors to various possibilities in different sectors which will shall prove to be very fruitful. Digital twin basically means a replicated digital model of any device or product. It has great abilities which can benefit various sectors when applied in those sectors. This technology is growing with great pace. It has some really amazing and useful advantages. This chapter is all about the basics of digital twin which includes understanding what it is, discussion regarding the beginning of this technology, its working, features, etc. In this chapter an entire overview of digital twin is provided.

Keywords: Digital twin, digital twin technology, digital model, technology, mirror worlds, virtual environment, National Aeronautics and Space Administration (NASA)

1.1 A Simplistic Introduction to Digital Twin

Digital twin, a technology named in two words is a technology with great abilities. It is a technology which is very powerful. It is powerful enough to replicate real world devices, products and processes virtually. Digital twin works in a virtual environment. Digital twin in simple words is a virtual representation of real world devices, products or process. This is one basic way of how digital twin can be defined. Another basic and brief definition and explanation of what is digital twin will be stated further on in the chapter.

Digital twin can run simulations, it can predict the possible errors which could turn up or occur in a device, product or process.

Email: manishavohra94@gmail.com

Manisha Vohra (ed.) Digital Twin Technology: Fundamentals and Applications, (1–18) © 2023 Scrivener Publishing LLC

In today's world, virtual environment plays an important role in various sectors. For example, in healthcare sector, use of telemedicine. In use of telemedicine option, consultation via video conferencing is done in a virtual environment. In education sector, curriculum classes are also nowadays carried out in a virtual environment via video conferencing. Likewise, in different sectors, virtual environment is playing an important role and is being very helpful.

Digital twin is also a technology which works in a virtual environment. Its utilization in different sectors like global industry, healthcare, engineering, etc. can be the key to a whole lot of advantages and benefits for those sectors.

Digital twin does not remain static in nature. It changes in accordance to the changes in the real object it is replicating. The input of the real-time data it can receive from the original object which it is replicating is truly helpful. It will update itself in accordance with changes in the object. Whenever there is any change in the original object, that particular change will occur in the digital twin model as well. This in itself is a huge plus point.

To bring some innovation in any new product or device, one might try to experiment while working on it. Even while working on an existing product, for coming up with a new version of it as there are chances for its improvement and betterment, one might experiment, alter and bring changes to it in this case as well. Even after careful intervention during the attempt of trying to experiment with all necessary measures and precautions taken be it in a new product's case or existing one, there can be multiple scenarios as resultants.

This move of trying to experiment could either go right, benefitting the product hugely or could have some adverse effects which could damage or hamper the product early or in the later stages of the product lifecycle. Well, in the case, that the experiment is successful then there's no problem but if something turns out wrong then it could damage or hamper the product in the early or later stages of the product lifecycle as mentioned above. Here, one needs to be having something like a technology which could in advance inform regarding the issues, hurdles that the product could probably face in any stage of its lifecycle, thus preventing it from occurrence in reality. For such instances and situations, digital twin could be the best fit option.

It can provide prediction in advance on what issues could arise in a product. So before they come in reality they can be predicted by using digital twin. Through this kind of prediction, digital twin can help to prevent any issues or hurdles from arising and occurring not just in a product but be it a system, process, etc. Hence, it can be rightly told that digital twin has the capability to keep problems at bay.

The concept of digital twin is decades old, despite this fact, its real impact has only come into being in recent years [7]. Currently, industry 4.0 is a popular term to describe the imminent changes of the industry landscape, particularly in the production and manufacturing industry of the developed world [13]. The design of a manufacturing system is not simple. It is a complex and critical activity [4].

Digital twin technology is nowadays being developed and commercialized to optimize several manufacturing processes [2]. Digital twin is now getting recognition of being a part of industry 4.0 roadmap [5]. A manufacturing digital twin offers a great opportunity. It offers the opportunity to simulate and optimize the production system [8]. The growing adoption of cyber-physical system (CPS), internet of things (IoT), big data analytics, and cloud computing in manufacturing sector has paved the way for low cost and systematic implementation of digital twin [11].

There are different aspects driving the future of manufacturing and one of those is digital twin [19]. It is receiving a great deal of interest from manufacturers who make advanced products that have all the characteristics of complex systems. However, the success of the digital twin model will depend on a factor which is value, the value it creates for both the manufacturers and the users of their products [3]. A concept for the composition of a database and guidelines proposal for the implementation of the digital twin in production systems in small and medium-sized enterprises is presented by the authors in paper [17]. Digital twin can truly impact manufacturing greatly.

It can also play a major role in overall cost savings in the entire manufacturing budget of an object, product, system, etc. as the manufacturing budget mostly always has provision for some issues. When manufacturing budget is planned, at that time mostly always a provision is kept for remanufacturing of the some of the objects or products, etc. which might be required to be remanufactured due to certain issues as well there is provision in the budget in case of wastage occurring during manufacturing process due to some error. When errors and issues can be prevented prior to their arrival in reality, it will result in the overall cost saving in the entire manufacturing cost of an object, product or system, etc. which is being manufactured. Also, downtime can be prevented and predictive maintenance can be carried out using digital twin. Not just cost savings will happen due then to digital twin but also it will help in meeting deadlines fixed for manufacturing of objects or products.

Whenever due to any faults if remanufacturing is required then it will not only increase the overall cost involved in manufacturing but additional time will also be required in remanufacturing. If digital twin can prevent issues, errors, downtime and also predictive maintenance can be carried out digital twin then then manufacturing can be completed on time and it can thus meet its allotted deadline without requiring additional time.

One of the greatest plus points of this technology is that, it can present a replicate of the original product, system, etc. in a digital format. Such is the functionality of digital twin. Hence, digital twin which is created, be it of anything, like product, system, etc. will be in digital form and it can be viewed and from any remote location. Digital twin allows to monitor the original device, product, etc.

There is no compulsion or restriction of being present in person in front of the device or product to view or monitor it. This point about the digital twin makes it not only just advantageous or beneficial but also simplifies the work of the ones who will be working with this technology as and when required.

Nowadays many things have gone digital and are carried out online like work, study, etc. Any technology which allows remote monitoring of work is a plus point of that particular technology and it is highly beneficial for the users of that technology.

Along with various other important and key factors which paved way for development and introduction of digital twin technology, directly or indirectly the widespread and accessibility of digitalization has also been important for digital twin.

Had digitalization not been much developed, wide spread and accessible, it would affect the progress of digital twin technology during its attempt in reaching out to different sectors quickly. The widespread and accessibility of digitalization has also thus been indirectly important for digital twin technology.

To provide digital services in a product service system is it necessary to understand few things such as service ecosystem, service platform and value co-creation [15]. There is an increasing interest in adapting digital twin to get autonomous maintenance [9]. Digital twins are expected to enrich the existent asset information system [20]. Digital twin is now a salient and emerging trend in many applications which includes the construction sector as well. The construction sector hosts various applications for digital twin use [1, 18]. Seen as a basis of digital twin is linking of sensor data with city model [14]. A digital twin city can simulate designs based on the digital model similar to a real city [12].

The combination of the digital twins with trusted data sharing technologies (such as blockchain) could pave way to a new wave in supply chain studies [22]. Integrated digital twin and blockchain framework makes all data transactions traceable is what was found by authors in paper [10].

Digital twin can be helpful in different sector's various applications, for example, the digital twin can be helpful in manufacturing context. As per traditional definition, manufacturing is defined as a process which turns materials that are raw, into physical products [16]. Digital twin may be applied with great success in manufacturing contexts for gaining benefits in terms of optimization, maintenance and operations monitoring [6]. In different important sectors such as healthcare, digital twin can be of great help. The list of some different sectors where digital twin can be used is discussed later on in the chapter. While there has been a recent growth of interest in the digital twin, a variety of definitions employed across industry and academia remain [21].

Digital twin is a beneficial technology with great features. Its features are stated further on it the chapter. Overall, digital twin technology can be considered as a technology which will evolve and currently also it is evolving.

Digital twin is having great potential. With the help of its functionality, capabilities and advantages, it can ease out many difficulties of different sectors when applied for usage. Having briefly introduced digital twin, the basic definition and explanation of what is digital twin is stated below.

1.2   Basic Definition and Explanation of What is Digital Twin

Another basic definition of digital twin is as follows. Digital twin can be defined as a digital representation of any real world product, system or process. It replicates the original product, system or process in digital form. It lays out digital representation of any real world product, system or process.

Digital twin can showcase changes of the original product, system, etc. because it is linked or connected with it and receives real-time data. Such is the functionality and capability of digital twin. Digital twin accounts and includes the details as well of whatever it is replicating. Say for example a product's digital twin is being created. The digital twin will also have the different details that the original product consists of. It also replicates the different details of the original product. The behavior of the product is replicated by the digital twin as well.

In the year 2002, Dr. Michael Grieves had spoken about digital twin at a conference. In fact, he had given a presentation at this conference which was held at Michigan University and presented the digital twin concept but it was presented as "Conceptual Ideal for PLM". At that time, digital twin had not received its name as digital twin. However, the concept presented as "Conceptual Ideal for PLM" was consisting of all elements of digital. These elements are: real space, virtual space, the link for data flow from real space to virtual space, the link for information flow from virtual space to real space and virtual sub-spaces [23].

Back then in 2002, Dr. Michael Grieves was the one who had publicly introduced digital twin. When the history of digital twin is discussed, one will notice that this particular instance was a significant step towards the evolution of digital twin. This instance is well described further on in the chapter while discussing the history of digital twin.

There are two types of digital twin. They are Digital Twin Prototype (DTP) and Digital Twin Instance (DTI).

- **Digital Twin Prototype (DTP):** This type of Digital Twin describes the prototypical physical artifact.
- **Digital Twin Instance (DTI):** This type of Digital Twin describes a specific corresponding physical product that an individual Digital Twin remains linked to throughout the life of that physical product.

Digital Twins are operated on in a Digital Twin Environment (DTE). Below is the definition of DTE.

- Digital Twin Environment (DTE): This is an integrated, multi-domain physics application space for operating on Digital Twins for a variety of purposes that would include:
  - Predictive
  - Interrogative

Predictive: Here the digital twin would be used for predicting purpose. It will predict the future behavior as well as performance of the physical product [23].
Interrogative: This would apply to DTI's. Digital Twin Instances could be interrogated for the current and past histories [23].

DTPs should exist for all sophisticated manufactured products, while DTIs exist only for products where it is important to have information about that product throughout its life. Airplanes, rockets, manufacturing floor equipment, and even automobiles have or will have DTIs. Paper clips will not.

Digital Twin Aggregate (DTA) – this type of Digital Twin is the aggregation of all the DTIs [3].

Talking about the digital twin model throughout the lifecycle, the reference to PLM made in 2002 conference indicated that this particular conceptual model was intended and is still currently intended to be a non-static model which means the model was and is intended to be dynamic one such that it changes throughout the system's lifecycle. Initially at the beginning period of its lifecycle, the system emerges virtually, after that it in the production phase, it takes physical form, then it continues through its operational life and eventually is retired and disposed of [23].

Digital twin has a great capability that it can give an estimate or predict the hurdles and complications that could be encountered in the product or system prior to them turning up in reality. One can infer through this what measures need to be taken to avoid any problems and losses.

1.3   The History of Digital Twin

When it comes to the history of digital twin, the year 2002 and the name Michael Grieves are the ones which are quite talked about. Back then in 2002, Michael Grieves during Society of Manufacturing Engineers conference in Michigan University, introduced the digital twin model. This explains why the year 2002 and the name Michael Grieves are most talked about when it comes to the history of digital twin.

So in the year 2002, when the digital twin model got introduced by Dr. Michael Grieves, it got introduced as a concept for Product Lifecycle Management (PLM). A name was given to the model but later on, the name was changed. It was actually originally named the Mirrored Spaces Model (MSM) but later changed to the Information Mirroring Model. Then finally it was referred to as the Digital Twin, a name that John Vickers of National Aeronautics and Space Administration (NASA) had coined [3].

Prior to this, the concept of digital twins had been put forward by David Gelernter. This was also an important aspect in the journey of digital twin. David Gelernter had introduced the concept of digital twin through his book titled "Mirror Worlds" which was published in the year 1991. However, in actuality, NASA was the one who initially brought this concept in 1960's and put it to application during their Apollo 13 mission in 1970.

They had themselves physically developed a twin system of their space-craft. Through the spacecraft which was replicated at the ground level by NASA, they could work and try different approaches for the spacecraft which sent for a mission.

It indeed proved to be very helpful for NASA. In the year 2010, John Vickers from NASA in roadmap report coined the term Digital Twin and this is how this technology got its name. If one sees the journey of digital twin after getting its name, till the present time then it can be noted that during this period digital twin has evolved quickly and in fact is continuing to evolve.

It looks all set to rise further and looking at the way it is making its mark currently and going by its progress, it seems that in the same way it will continue making its mark in the future as well. The digital twin technology journey has been progressive. Its history has witnessed some key contributions and instances which led to its progress.

NASA has played a huge role in the journey of digital twin technology as they were the ones who had for the first time worked on it. So they contributed majorly towards this technology. Without their contribution towards this technology, its journey would have not reached till where it has reached in the present.

Digital twin technology's name was also coined by a person from NASA who is John Vickers. So, altogether, NASA has been a huge contributor towards this technology and John Vickers contribution towards this technology's journey has also been great and quite important.

David Gelernter's contribution towards the journey of digital twin has also been very important as he had introduced this technology's concept through his book "Mirror Worlds" which was published in the year 1991.

Introducing this technology and talking about it publicly for the first time was done by Dr. Michael Grieves which also contributed quite a lot towards the journey of digital twin. So the history of digital twin technology has rightly witnessed different key contributions and instances which led to its progress. Figure 1.1 below represents the journey of digital twin.

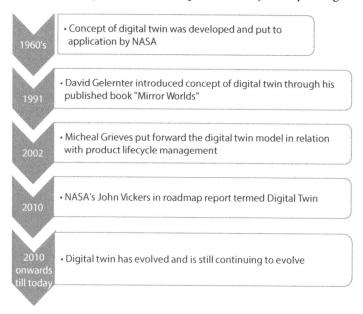

1960's • Concept of digital twin was developed and put to application by NASA

1991 • David Gelernter introduced concept of digital twin through his published book "Mirror Worlds"

2002 • Micheal Grieves put forward the digital twin model in relation with product lifecycle management

2010 • NASA's John Vickers in roadmap report termed Digital Twin

2010 onwards till today • Digital twin has evolved and is still continuing to evolve

Figure 1.1 Journey of digital twin technology.

1.4 Working

The working of digital twin is systematic. It is very easy to understand its basic working process which is explained as follows.

Whenever a digital twin of an existing product is created, it works and changes as per the input it receives from the real product. When there is change in the real product, it will be immediately and automatically conveyed to the digital twin which will change accordingly because the real product will be connected or linked with digital twin which ensures that there can be real-time data transmission.

Sensors are deployed on the real product to get real-time data. A replicate of the original product in virtual form is created i.e. a digital copy of the original product will be created.

The digital copy is linked with real product to enable real-time data transmission from real product to the digital copy. Linking them together is important. Data transmission in real-time will allow digital twin to update and change in accordance with the changes occurring in the real product. So whatever changes are occurring in the real product, those same changes will occur in the digital twin model also. Digital twin can be utilized to run different simulations. It can give information and important insights about the product. Digital twin has the ability to estimate or predict regarding the possible problems or issues that can be encountered in the real product which will help in preventing them. Certain fix can be found for the predicted problems or issues to help prevent them before they come in reality. This is the overall basic working of digital twin.

Thus using digital twin the possible problems or issues can be prevented or stopped before they come in reality in the real product which saves a lot of trouble.

If the above explained basic working of digital twin is observed then it can be noted that how systematically digital twin works. It is not at all complex and very easy to understand. Digital twin has its own share of advantages which it can offer its users and serve them better. It also enables them to gain benefits from this technology and make the most of this technology.

Based on the application purpose and the requirement, digital twin of parts, product, system and process can be made known as parts or component twins, product twins, system twins and process twins respectively. Let's understand them all one by one as follows:

- Parts twins
  Engineers can easily understand the mechanical, electrical and physical characteristics of a part using virtual representations of the individual components.
- Product twins
  Product twins are nothing but digital models of different components that ultimately forms a product being brought together at one place. The reason different components are brought together is to see how they are working with each other.

  Also, how environment can affect the components that when brought together ultimately forms a product, can be known using product twins. Product twins lets one know how these components will interact, thereby generating the performance data which one can analyze and utilize it for their future course of work.
- System twins
  A system comprises of various products. For making a system, wide range of products are required. System Twins are the ones which gives insight on how different products which come together to form a system work.

  On the basis of what system twins data suggests, if need be for improvement, then different solutions can be sought which can result in betterment of the system functionality and its efficiency overall.
- Process twins
  Process twins are the ones which can let you know and understand the process of manufacturing. At each juncture in which manner each and every particular system involved in the process of manufacturing, functions in presence of all other systems brought together can be known through process twins.

So basically, in other words, all the systems involved in the process of manufacturing are brought together and then process twins can tell how they all function at each juncture in the presence of all other systems.

Through data obtained and analyzed from process twins, any alterations required for smooth manufacturing can be done, thus allowing to prevent errors in future and thus increasing the efficiency.

1.5   Features

Digital twin is a technology which is opening doors to various possibilities in different sectors which will shall prove to be very fruitful. Below are some of the features of digital twin. Digital twin basically means a replicate digital model of any device or product.

1.5.1   Replication of Each and Every Aspect of the Original Device or Product

Digital twin actually replicates not just the looks but also each and every aspect of any device or product.

1.5.2   Helps in Product Lifecycle Management

Digital twin can be used throughout product lifecycle to provide entire information about it which makes product lifecycle management easier. Any issues in a product that could be encountered in any stage of the product lifecycle which will affect the product could be known prior to their occurrence which will help in taking necessary measures to avoid the errors and prevent major losses. With digital twin, the product can be then managed efficiently throughout its lifecycle. Thus it helps in product lifecycle management.

1.5.3   Digital Twin can Prevent Downtime

Digital twin can inform about issues prior to their arrival in real product and can thus prevent downtime.

1.6   Advantages of Digital Twin

Written and explained below are some advantages of digital twin.

1.6.1   Digital Twin is Helpful in Preventing Issues or Errors in the Actual Object, Product or Process

Digital twin has the ability to estimate or predict errors or issues that could be encountered in the actual object, product or process.

If any error or issue that could be encountered is known prior than it has happened or occurred in reality then it can be prevented. This is why and this is how digital twin is helpful in prevention of issues or errors.

1.6.2   Helps in Well Utilization of Resources

When a product's digital twin is created, it can predict any kind of complication, issue or error that could be encountered in the product which helps in avoiding it and allows for its better lifecycle management and thus ultimately resulting in well utilization of all resources involved in product development. When any kind of complication, issue or error is encountered in a product, object, etc. then it could even result in leaving the product unusable. The product and all resources involved in the development of it would be wasted in such a situation. However, digital twin can help in avoiding such a situation.

With digital twins ability to predict errors or issues which can be encountered in a product, object, etc. will help in avoiding them and will promote better lifecycle management of it and automatically avoid wastage of resources, thus encouraging proper and well utilization of resources.

1.6.3   Keeping Vigilance of the Actual Object, Product or Process Through Digital Twin is Possible

Through digital twin technology, keeping vigilance of the actual object, product or process being replicated is not only just possible but also quite easy as its vigilance can be kept from any location. Irrespective of the location, its vigilance can be done remotely through digital twin.

1.6.4   Helps in Efficient Handling and Managing of Objects, Device, Equipment, etc.

The digital twin technology will predict and inform any issues or hurdles in any object, device, equipment, etc. in advance that allows for carrying out predictive maintenance of it and also prevents any downtime. This leads to efficient handling and managing of object, device, equipment, etc. So, digital twin actually helps in efficient handling and managing of device, equipment, etc.

1.6.5   Reduction in Overall Cost of Manufacturing of Objects, Products, etc.

The cost involved in manufacturing of objects, products, etc. when due to any complication or issues they have to be remanufactured leads to increase in overall cost of manufacturing. However this increase in overall manufacturing cost can be reduced using digital twin technology.

Digital twin can estimate about the complication or issues which could be faced in manufacturing of objects, products, etc., thus helping in preventing it which means the requirement of remanufacturing might be completely erased. This will on its own result in reduction of overall cost of manufacturing of objects, products, etc.

1.7   Applications

Digital twin owing to its functioning, its capabilities and advantages, can be used in various different sectors. Some of them are as follows:

- Construction sector
- Automotive sector
- Oil and gas sector
- Healthcare sector
- Pharmaceutical sector, etc.

1.8   A Simple Example of Digital Twin Application

Consider the following example stating and discussing application of digital twin and what benefits it can provide.

If supposing for a product or object, digital twin technology is used then it can be useful in product lifecycle management and can be useful in other ways as well. For example, consider that for a product manufactured, there is a digital twin of it, then it can predict its performance and possible future errors which will allow for preventive measures to be undertaken in time to prevent those errors. It will enable the improvement of the product and help in development of it. Tesla, Inc. also uses digital twin. Every car it sells out, has its digital twin. So all data from sensors on the car is taken each day and analyzed. Useful insights are gained and accordingly to avoid errors and to improve performance, these insights are used to prepare software updates for their cars which are sent to their users. All the insights can be used for preparing the similar future products as well. Digital twin can thus proficiently help and provide different benefits as understood from the example.

1.9   Digital Twin Technology and the Metaverse

The term metaverse is gaining wide popularity lately. This comes naturally as Facebook is now officially renamed to Meta and its founder Mark Zuckerberg has announced that the company will be focusing on metaverse. Likewise, other large companies like Microsoft are also working on metaverse. Digital twin technology in context of the metaverse is also being talked about widely. Metaverse is a term coined by Neal Stephenson in his science-fiction novel entitled "Snow Crash". Metaverse means a virtual world or an online world. In other words, it can be even called as a simulated virtual environment. Here, users will have their own digital avatars through which they can have interaction with others, visit shopping mall, attend an office meeting, meet friends, etc. If the word metaverse is broken down then we get two different words that are meta and verse. "Meta" means beyond whereas "verse" is referring to the universe. Metaverse is also considered as the future of the Internet.

Digital twin is an essential block or element of the metaverse. Digital twin digitally represents the physical world. Digital twin is connected to the real-world object and receives real-time data. Digital twin can run simulations. It can predict possible problems that could occur in an object and can provide insight and information regarding the object. Likewise, as discussed in the chapter, there are various capabilities of digital twin, and due to its capabilities, it is an essential block or element of the metaverse. Digital twin can be used in different sectors. There might be various benefits digital twin could provide in metaverse which might be known better when it is more developed.

Metaverse could also bring various opportunities for different sectors but there are some concerns and challenges as well. For example, ensuring the privacy and security of data, the risk of people spending more time in virtual world leading to decrease in their real-world interaction with others, etc. However, as the metaverse is in its nascent stage, it is yet to be seen what will be the future of metaverse and how different companies will put it to utilization. Whatever the future is, digital twin will continue to remain an essential block or element of metaverse.

Digital twin technology currently faces certain challenges and some of them are discussed and explained below.

1.10 Challenges

There are different challenges for the digital twin technology. Some of them are as follows.

1.10.1 Careful Handling of Different Factors Involved in Digital Twin

The handling of different factors involved in digital twin can be challenging. First and foremost one of the most essential things for digital twin is data. The entire setup of sensors, the link for connecting the real space with virtual space and for the link for flow of information from virtual space to real space and virtual sub-spaces, are all very sensitive things to handle and take care of. Faulty sensor or breaking of the link with digital twin can be a serious hamper in the working of the digital twin.

Right from the start till the end everything has to be as per the requirement, then only the digital twin can be created and can work successfully. Thus handling everything efficiently is a challenge.

1.10.2 Expertise Required

Expertise will be required for working on creation of digital twin to taking care of whole functioning and managing everything related to it. Anyone who is not having the required expertise for working and looking after all the things related to digital twin if works on it then there are chances of things going wrong or not as per expectation due to any mistake in work caused by lack of expertise and knowledge. Hence when working on digital twin, anyone who has complete digital twin expertise and knowledge is required.

1.10.3 Data Security and Privacy

When a digital twin is created and used for any object, product or process, a lot is dependent on the digital twin. It is trusted and all the important decisions for the real object, product or process is based on the digital twin. In such a scenario, all the data security and data privacy concerns related to digital twin should be of the utmost priority and should be taken care of and looked after very well. Any particular technology, be it digital twin or any other technology, even though it might be considered to be completely secure when it comes to data security and privacy, no single loophole should exist that could risk the security and privacy of data. This needs to be underscored.

1.11   Conclusion

Viewing digital twin from the point of view of its capabilities, advantages and functioning, it can be said that digital twin is all set to rise further. In future with its evolvement, it could have a lot many applications and could be utilized in various new more sectors other than the ones mentioned in the book chapter. There can be numerous possibilities with digital twin and currently it is difficult to state them all as digital twin is still evolving but it will provide various benefits wherever it will be applied for usage.

Digital twin is a technology which is opening doors to various possibilities in different sectors which will shall prove to be very fruitful. Digital twin basically means a replicated digital model of any device or product. It has great abilities which can benefit various sectors when applied in those sectors.

This technology is growing with great pace. It has some really amazing and useful advantages. In this chapter all the basics of digital twin which includes understanding what it is, discussion regarding the beginning of this technology, its working, features, etc. were discussed. An entire overview of digital twin is presented in this book chapter.

References

1. Fuller, A., Fan, Z., Day, C., Barlow, C., Digital twin: Enabling technologies, challenges and open research. *IEEE Access*, 8, 108952–108971, 2020.
2. Barricelli, B.R., Casiraghi, E., Fogli, D., A survey on digital twin: Definitions, characteristics, applications, and design implications. *IEEE Access*, 7, 167653–167671, 2019.
3. Grieves, M.W., Virtually intelligent product systems: Digital and physical twins, in: *Complex systems engineering: Theory and practice*, S. Flumerfelt (Eds.), pp. 175–200, American Institute of Aeronautics and Astronautics, 2019.

4. Terkaj, W. and Urgo, M., A virtual factory data model as a support tool for the simulation of manufacturing systems. *Procedia CIRP*, 28, 137–142, 2015.

5. Mateev, M., Industry 4.0 and the digital twin for building industry. *Int. Sci. J. Ind. 4.0*, 5, 1, 29–32, 2020.

6. Cimino, C., Negri, E., Fumagalli, L., Review of digital twin applications in manufacturing. *Comput. Ind.*, 113, 103130, 2019.

7. Singh, M., Fuenmayor, E., Hinchy, E.P., Qiao, Y., Murray, N., Devine, D., Digital twin: Origin to future. *Appl. Syst. Innov.*, 4, 2, 36, 2021, https://doi.org/10.3390/asi4020036.

8. Kritzinger, W., Karner, M., Traar, G., Henjes, J., Sihn, W., Digital twin in manufacturing: A categorical literature review and classification. *IFAC-PapersOnLine*, 51, 11, 1016–1022, 2018.

9. Khan, S., Farnsworth, M., McWilliam, R., Erkoyuncu, J., On the requirements of digital twin-driven autonomous maintenance. *Annu. Rev. Control.*, 50, 13–28, 2020.

10. Lee, D., Lee, S.H., Masoud, N., Krishnan, M.S., Li, V.C., Integrated digital twin and blockchain framework to support accountable information sharing in construction projects. *Autom. Constr.*, 127, 103688, 2021.

11. Lee, J., Azamfar, M., Singh, J., Siahpour, S., Integration of digital twin and deep learning in cyber-physical systems: Towards smart manufacturing. *IET Collab. Intell. Manuf.*, 2, 1, 34–36, 2020.

12. Lee, A., Kim, J., Jang, I., Movable dynamic data detection and visualization for digital twin city. *2020 IEEE International Conference on Consumer Electronics—Asia (ICCE-Asia), IEEE Xplore*, pp. 1–2, 2020.

13. Brettel, M., Friederichsen, N., Keller, M., Rosenberg, M., How virtualization, decentralization and network building change the manufacturing landscape: An Industry 4.0 perspective. *Int. J. Mech. Aerospace Ind. Mechatron. Eng.*, 8, 37–44, 2014.

14. Ruohomaki, T., Airaksinen, E., Huuska, P., Kesaniemi, O., Martikka, M., Suomisto, J., Smart city platform enabling digital twin. *2018 International Conference on Intelligent Systems (IS), IEEE Xplore 2019*, pp. 155–161, 2018.

15. West, S., Gaiardelli, P., Rapaccini, M., Exploring technology-driven service innovation in manufacturing firms through the lens of service dominant logic, in: *IFAC-Papers online*, vol. 51, pp. 1317–1322, 2018.

16. Lohtander, M., Ahonen, N., Lanz, M., Ratava, J., Kaakkunen, J., Micro manufacturing unit and the corresponding 3d-model for the digital twin. *Procedia Manuf.*, 25, 55–61, 2018.

17. Uhlemann, T.H.-J., Lehmann, C., Steinhilper, R., The digital twin: Realizing the cyber-physical production system for industry 4.0. *Proc. CIRP*, 61, 335–340, 2017.

18. Rasheed, A., San, O., Kvamsdal, T., Digital twin: Values, challenges and enablers. *IEEE Access*, 8, 21980–22012, 2020.

19. Rosen, R., Wichert, G.V., Lo, G., Bettenhausen, K., About the importance of autonomy and digital twins for the future of manufacturing, in: *IFAC-Papers online*, vol. 48, pp. 567–572, 2015.

20. Macchi, M., Roda, I., Negri, E., Fumagalli, L., Exploring the role of digital twin for asset lifecycle management, in: *IFAC-Papers online*, vol. 51, pp. 790–795, 2018.

21. Jones, D., Snider, C., Nassehi, A., Yon, J., Hicks, B., Characterising the digital twin: A systematic literature review. *CIRP J. Manuf. Sci. Technol.*, 29, 36–52, 2020, https://doi.org/10.1016/j.cirpj.2020.02.002.

22. Longo, F., Nicoletti, L., Padovano, A., Ubiquitous knowledge empowers the smart factory: The impacts of a service-oriented digital twin on enterprises' performance. *Annu. Rev. Control*, 47, 221–236, 2019.

23. Grieves, M. and Vickers, J., Digital twin: Mitigating unpredictable, undesirable emergent behavior in complex systems, in: *Transdisciplinary Perspectives on Complex Systems*, F.J. Kahlen, S. Flumerfelt, A. Alves (Eds.), pp. 85–113, Springer, Cham, 2017, https://doi.org/10.1007/978-3-319-38756-7_4.

Introduction, History, and Concept of Digital Twin

N. Rajamurugu* and M. K. Karthik

Department of Aeronautical Engineering, Bharath Institute of Science and Technology, Chennai, India

Abstract

Digital twin has come into limelight in the recent past. It is a powerful technology, which got notability in the recent past. Even though it came into limelight recently, its existence is dated back to 1960s. It is making its place in different areas now. It can be used at many places in different sectors or areas. It is all set to achieve more notability and reach great heights. It can be truly beneficial in usage for many different sectors or areas. This is a great factor. In this chapter, digital twin is introduced. Along with introducing digital twin, its history and its concept is also explained.

Keywords: Digital twin, National Aeronautics and Space Administration (NASA), technology, virtual model

2.1 Introduction

The advent of advanced, innovative and complex engineered systems has established new technologies that are far more superior and perform well even in harsh environments [19]. In industry 4.0, specially, new technologies are seen to be emerging. Digital Twin technology is one such emerging technology concept that has become the centre of attention for industry and, in more recent years, academia [6].

The digital twin is considered as one of the key technology trends [8]. A digital twin is an intelligent and evolving model, which is the virtual

---

Corresponding author: rajamurugu.aero@bharathuniv.ac.in

Manisha Vohra (ed.) Digital Twin Technology: Fundamentals and Applications, (19–32) © 2023
Scrivener Publishing LLC

counterpart of a physical entity or process [5]. Digital twins are nowadays considered as collections of linked digital artefacts [22]. Digital twin provides virtual representations of systems along their lifecycle [10].

A Digital Twin is one of the enabling technologies of Industry 4.0 that couples actual physical systems with corresponding virtual representation [15]. A digital twin paradigm is able to continuously monitor complex engineering systems [17]. The notion "digital twin" is inspired by the developments known under terms like "Industry 4.0" or "Industrial Internet" [4]. The concept of using "twins" is rather old. It dates back to NASA's Apollo program [14].

Digital twin is a technology with great opportunities and advantages. It can provide great opportunities and advantages in various sectors. Digital twin means a virtual representation or a virtual model of a physical object or product where the virtual model resembles to and also acts or behaves like the original object or product.

Digital twin technology allows to run simulations. It can be used in various applications. Digital twin can receive real-time data from the original object whom it is replicating. This allows virtual model also to have the same changes in the virtual model itself in real time as happening in the physical object.

Digital twin application includes real-time monitoring, maintenance, etc. [1]. A manufacturing digital twin gives an opportunity to simulate and optimize the production system, [2]. Digital twin technology can help us understand better the maintenance needs and schedule it accordingly [9]. The industry 4.0 focuses on the establishment of intelligent products and the production processes [21].

The concept of the digital twin for a production process enables a coupling of the production system with its digital equivalent as a base for an optimization with a minimized delay between the time of data acquisition and the creation of the digital twin [11].

With the advent of Industrial Internet of things, even more data is being generated that further highlights the importance of Digital Twinning [7]. The information transfer from the physical to the digital twin is related to the observation and sensing of the physical twin [12]. With existing sensor data transmission (in real time), a digital twin can be created that monitors, controls and optimizes itself [16].

Digital Twins promise significant benefits for their different stakeholders when used to support the design, manufacturing management, monitoring and control as well as optimisation of manufactured products, and production equipment and systems in manufacturing [25]. A digital twin should be capable to guarantee well-defined services to support various activities such as monitoring, maintenance, management, optimization and safety [26].

A cyber-physical digital twin system plays a very important role in Industry 4.0 in manufacturing context [27]. Product and process designs are developed in the digital domain nowadays and digital twin can help here [18]. The digital twin can be even used in factories to map the entire factory floor and its existing levels [20].

Data acquired of the product or system in real-time provides a better understanding of the product or system. There can be many useful and innovative possibilities with digital twin technology. Digital twin technology has gained limelight and notability in the recent past few years. In 2017, it was named by Gartner in the top ten strategic technology trends. The advantages of digital twin will contribute to help digital twin achieve more notability and reach great heights.

Digital twin is a technology that can predict possible future problems, which could occur in an object, system, etc. Hence, the loss an individual or a company faces when problems are faced in their products or systems and they have to rework on their products or systems and find some solution, can be saved with digital twin. Necessary changes can be incorporated as and when required according to the prediction of problems, information and insight received from digital twin thereby preventing the problems in their products or systems.

This can be a game changer altogether. Whether it is an individual or a company, anyone would definitely want to use a technology, which can help to avoid problems in their product or system because if any major problem occurs in a company's product or system then it can cost them not just economically but it can lead to even failure of the product or system. All this can be prevented with digital twin efficiently. Digital twin is making its place and it can significantly contribute towards different sectors with its advantages.

Apart from predicting possible future problems, digital twin can also help in various other ways with its other advantages it can provide to its users. The different advantages of digital twin are explained later on in the chapter.

2.2   History of Digital Twin

Digital twin has an interesting history. This technology concept was used for the first time long ago in the year 1970 but it was only in the year 2010 that the name of this technology i.e. Digital Twin was coined. In the year, this technology concept was presented at a conference but it was presented as "Conceptual Ideal for PLM," and it all had the elements of digital twin.

PLM means project lifecycle management. Altogether, the history of digital twin is quite interesting. Let us know and understand the digital twin technology briefly.

The ideology of digital twin technology was introduced during 1991, courtesy to David Gelernter. Actually, David Gelernter in his book Mirror Worlds had written about the ideology of digital twin. Later, Dr. Michael Grieves, for the first time in 2002, had spoken about digital twins at a conference and had presented its concept there. The conference was held in Michigan University. Like mentioned above, it was this conference where the concept of digital twin technology was presented as "Conceptual Ideal for PLM," and all digital twin elements were present in it.

John Vickers from National Aeronautics and Space Administration (NASA) eventually coined the term "digital twin" in 2010. The name Digital Twin, which John Vickers coined, was written by him in a report. So finally, in 2010, this technology's name was coined. However, prior to all the evets mentioned about the history of digital twin till now, it was NASA had first worked on digital twin concept in 1960s. NASA had started working on this technology concept in 1960s. Later it was used when needed for their Apollo 13 program.

According to Glaessgen Stargel, "A digital twin is a comprehensive multi-physics, multi-scale, probabilistic simulation of a complex product that combines the best available physical models, sensor updates, etc., to mirror the life of its corresponding twin" [3].

It was in the year 1970 where the concept of digital twin was first used during the Apollo 13 mission of NASA. If the history of digital twin is seen carefully then it can be understood that from 1970, when it was used for the first time till the present time, its journey has been not just interesting but very progressive as well.

Earlier, digital twin had not got the exposure it needed to grow and progress but in the recent past, things changed, it came into limelight and it got all the exposure and support it needed for its growth. 2002 proved to be a turning point for digital as Dr. Michael Grieves had spoken about it at a conference and this marked as the first introduction of digital twin at a public event, though it was presented as "Conceptual Ideal for PLM" but it had all elements of digital twin. Hence, this sure was a turning point for digital twin technology.

However, despite this turning point in 2002 after this conference, digital twin was back then yet to receive the kind of exposure it needed. The needed exposure started to be received 2010 onwards when John Vickers from NASA coined the term "Digital Twin" for this technology. Till 2010, this name, i.e., Digital Twin was not given to this technology, and it was much needed for it to get a fixed name through it is addressed by everyone.

After John Vickers coining this name "Digital Twin" for this technology it was universally addressed as digital twin. From the time it got its name till the present time, in all these years slowly but steadily it came into limelight and progressed and is still progressing greatly.

Its usefulness is getting to be known by all. It can be used in various sectors and can play a crucial role in them.

2.3   Concept of Digital Twin

Digital twin concept is a very useful technology concept. Digital twin means creation of duplicate model, which is a virtual model of a physical product or object, where the virtual model resembles to the original product or object. Its behavior is also same as the original product or object. There are three different important parts of digital twin model. The first important part is comprising of physical products, to be precise, it is physical products in real space. The second important part is comprising virtual products, precisely it is virtual products in virtual space. The third important part is comprising of connections, it is the connection of information and data, which ties real products and virtual products together [23]. These connections can be also called as link. There is link is for flow of data and link for flow of information. The data flow takes place from real space to the virtual space and the information flow takes place from the virtual space to the real space and virtual sub-spaces [13].

[13] states there are types of digital twin. The first type is digital twin prototype, abbreviated as DTP and the second type is digital twin instance, abbreviated as DTI. Let us understand these types but before that it is important to know digital twin's operation is conducted is digital twin environment, which is abbreviated as DTE [13].

2.3.1   DTP

It is the one that gives description of prototypical physical artifact. DTP has great responsibility on itself. It has all bunch of information required for the description and production of a real-world version, which replicates or copies the digital version. Bunch of information consist of various things like what are the necessities, completely annotated 3D model, all different materials with listed specifications and their bill, different services bill with bill of disposal and processes and so on because it is not limited to only these mentioned things, there can be more things, which can be included here [13].

2.3.2   DTI

Here, this is the one in which an individual digital twin is connected to real world product throughout life cycle of real world product and it gives description of this product. On basis of usage, DTI digital twin could have different informational bunches like completely annotated 3D model with Geometric Dimensioning and Tolerancing (GD&T) which gives description of geometry of the physical instance and also all components of it and it also includes bill, which consists of a list of all past and present components. There is another bill also present, which is bill of process in which there is list of operations conducted while creation of this physical instance was going on. Even included are results of any tests and measurements on the physical instance, a record which is service record that gives description of previous services conducted in past and replacement components and operational states that were taken from real sensor data, present data, previous real data and the one which is predicted for future. Apart from all these mentioned things, more things can also be included here [13].

2.3.3   DTE

Now this is the one which is an integrated and multi-domain physics application space for operating on the digital twins for a various different reasons. These different reasons would include:

- Predictive
  Here, as the name suggests, digital twins utilization would be for prediction purposes. Prediction would be done for not just future behavior but also for future performance of the actual real product. In the prototype stage, prediction will be done for the behavior of the product, which is designed as well as for the components that differ between their low and high tolerances. During prototype stage, there would be prediction of behavior of the designed product along with components, which vary between its high and low tolerances, so as to make sure that the product, which was designed, actually met with the required or proposed requirements. In the instance stage, the prediction would be a specific instance of a specific physical product that included the actual components and component history [13].

- Interrogative
  This one would apply to DTIs where they could be interrogated for current, as well as past, histories. Different instances of products would provide data that would be correlated for predicting future states [13].
  Digital twin capability supports three of the most powerful tools in the human knowledge tool kit, which are conceptualization, comparison, and collaboration [23].

2.3.4 Conceptualization

By just looking at digital twin simulations, it allows people to view progress of the actual object or product, the way it is proceeding further and view information regarding characteristics of the actual product. This is much easier than having a look at performance report of a factory and trying to conceptualize regarding the product's movement through different stations [23].

2.3.5 Comparison

Using digital twin people can look at different characteristics, which are ideal and can also look at tolerance corridor close by or surrounding that ideal measurement, and also the actual trend line to find out for different kind of products if the work is where the ones working on it wants it to be. Basically, deviations, which include both negative and positive deviations that can be permitted prior to a result being considered impermissible are tolerance corridors. When this ability is present, it enables to conduct comparison and make adjustments for future operations [23].

2.3.6 Collaboration

The digital twin model permits sharing of conceptualization, which can be visualized in exact same way as it is by as many as number of people and these people need not be present at same location [23].

The NASA initially applied the digital twin concept during the Apollo 13 mission. According to NASA, the digital twin, is an imaginary component of the actual model that incorporates numerous computational models developed in a computer.

The crucial part of this technology is information flow, which happens between the actual and virtual systems. A number of authors have referred to digital twin in different terms and based on its applicability.

Hence when digital twin is being talked about or referred, it is done with different terms, such as digital model or digital model layout, digital counterpart, doppelganger, clone, digital footprint, software analog, etc.

Digital twin has a great advantage as compared to other digital simulation. Digital twin does not remain static. Digital twin has the ability to update in real time.

Engineers can use a simulation to execute tests and assessments on a virtual version of a physical object. However, the simulation is static. In other words, unless the engineer adds new parameters to the simulation, it will not keep up with the physical asset.

In contrast, a digital twin can obtain real-time activity update from the actual object, process, or system. As a result, any kind of evaluation and analysis work are done on the basis real-world scenarios.

The digital twin updates as it gets real-time data from the physical world, changing its state dynamically based on the changes taking place in the physical asset and delivering more accurate and valuable outputs.

2.4   Working Principle

To understand the working principle better, consider that a digital twin of an existing physical product has to be created. Creation of a digital twin of an already existing physical product means creation of a digital copy or duplicate version of that physical product in a virtual environment, where the digital copy or duplicate version resembles the original physical product.

The digital twin model receives input from the data given by sensors deployed on the real world product. The real world product can send data to the digital twin model, i.e., its digital counterpart in real time and the digital twin model can give information regarding the physical product.

So, the overall working principle involves real-time data of the product and to get this real-time data, sensors are deployed on the real world product. The digital copy of the real product is created and linked with the real product. Real-time data of the physical object is of prime importance and linking the real product with the digital copy allows real-time data transmission. The real world product can send data to its digital counterpart in real time. This enables the digital twin model to duplicate and recreate the actions or changes taking place in the original version in real time, allowing for giving information concerning performance of the product. The digital twin model will be actually able to change its state dynamically as per the changes in the physical product and give information, important particulars, and useful insights that could be applicable back to the physical product.

Whatever important information received from digital twin model, which will be essential for the physical product, different important particulars and insights can be applied to the physical product for its betterment. The digital twin can predict regarding the emergence of possible problems in the future. This allows to prevent them from emerging in reality in the product. This is its way of working and its working principle is clearly discussed and explained.

2.5 Characteristics of Digital Twin

Some of the characteristics of digital twin are explained as follows.

2.5.1 Homogenization

Digital twins enable data homogenization and are also the resultant of data homogenization. Be it any kind of information or any kind of material, it can be saved as well as sent in a same digital form. This allows it to be utilized for constructing a virtual form of a product. Due to this, the data is broken down from its real physical state. This break down of data from its real physical state and homogenization of data result into emergence of digital twins.

2.5.2 Digital Trail

Digital trail can cause digital trail to occur. This digital trail could be helpful to check and find out from the digital twin of a particular device that where things went wrong when it does not work as expected or it fails to work. This could be very helpful for the device manufacturer so that in future such things can be taken care of while working on device manufacturing.

2.5.3 Connectivity

Real-time data transmission from the original object or product to its digital twin gets enabled when the real object or product is linked or connected with the digital twin model. Without this linking or connectivity, the digital twin model cannot work. So connectivity is a very important characteristic when it comes to digital twin.

2.6   Advantages

Digital twin has a lot many advantages. Some of them are listed and explained below. They are as follows.

2.6.1   Companies Can Benefit From Digital Twin by Tracking Performance-Related Data

By continuously tracking performance-related data in real time, with the help of digital twin, companies can benefit from it. The different companies can then optimize their products through it and enable overall progress and gain.

2.6.2   Different Sector's Progress Can Be Accelerated

Different sector progress can also be accelerated by the use of digital twins because it can tell or predict the possible problems that can come.

Then, before the problem comes, some remedies for its prevention can be applied. This will be helpful. This will also save any loss, which could have happened due to the problems if they arise.

2.6.3   Digital Twins Can Be Used for Various Application

Digital twins can be used during product design and development. They can be used for any product's entire lifecycle management. They can be used for monitoring the manufacturing process of a product. Similarly digital twins can be used for various other applications.

2.6.4   Digital Twin Can Help Decide Future Course of Work

Based on the digital twin's prediction about the possible problems that can come in future, what is required to be done, can be decided so that possible future problems do not come. The information and insights digital twin provides could be applied back to the original object or product for it to improve and get better. This is yet another advantage of digital twin, which will help largely and this is how digital twin can help decide future course of work.

2.6.5   Manufacturing Work Can Be Monitored

All the activities of the manufacturing process are very important. They can be monitored through digital twin. Digital twin even makes remote monitoring possible. This is a great advantage of digital twin.

2.7   Limitations

Digital twin is a new technology that has a lot of potential. However, there are limitations as well, which impede digital twin's growth. Some of the limitations are as follows.

2.7.1   Data Transmission Could Have Delays and Distortions

As there is large amount of data generally generated by any physical product and collected by sensors, which needs to be communicated in real-time, delay and distortion could be caused while sending data to digital twin. This will then delay the changes that need to be updated in real-time in the digital twin.

2.7.2   Digital Twin Implementation Will Need Required Skills and Sound Knowledge About It

Digital twin cannot be implemented without having great sound knowledge about it. A person having great sound knowledge and required skills will only be able to correctly implement digital twin and look after it.

2.8   Example of Digital Twin Application

Explained below is one real application of digital twin.

2.8.1   Digital Twin Application in General Electric (GE) Renewable Energy

General Electric, abbreviated as GE has great presence in various different sectors like healthcare, renewable energy, aviation, etc. GE is very well utilizing digital twin for different purposes in its work across different sectors like healthcare, renewable energy, etc. Here, we are talking regarding digital twin application in GE renewable energy sector. GE has actually introduced a Digital Wind Farm. They have used digital twin technology, which helps to ensure that an optimum possible wind turbine is being built for the actual farm wherever it is situated [24].

From above example, it is clear that digital twin is not just useful but it also has a great positive impact when used in a particular application. It has a far-reaching effect, which can transform things quickly and provide great results.

2.9   Conclusion

Digital twin technology is receiving a lot of acclaim from different places. It is a technology, which is very highly useful. It can be used in different applications at various sectors. The concept of digital twin technology is very simple.

In digital twin technology, a virtual model of the original object is created, which looks the same as the original object. The digital twin also copies the original object's behavior and is not static and can update in real time by receiving real-time data from original object.

Digital twin name was coined by John Vickers from NASA in 2010. Originally, the digital twin technological concept was first applied in 1970 by NASA during their Apollo 13 Mission. Now digital twin technology is being applied in different applications successfully. Its advantages are great. Though there are some limitations in digital twin as discussed in the chapter, those limitations do not affect the advantages it can provide. However, attention needs to be paid at its limitations. With appropriate steps taken to overcome the limitations, they could be overcome.

The overall advantages of digital twin make it really very useful. It came into limelight in the recent past, and due to its great advantages, it will surely reach places. Various sectors will benefit from the digital twin technology. In this chapter, we saw a real example of application of digital twin in General Electric (GE) renewable energy. It truly helps them greatly. Likewise, there are at present various more applications of digital twin in different sectors, which are providing great results. Digital twin technology is indeed of great use.

References

1. Singh, M., Fuenmayor, E., Hinchy, E.P., Qiao, Y., Murray, N., Devine, D., Digital twin: Origin to future. *Appl. Syst. Innov.*, 4, 36, 2021, https://doi.org/10.3390/asi4020036.

2. Kritzinger, W., Karner, M., Traar, G., Henjes, J., Sihn, W., Digital Twin in manufacturing: A categorical literature review and classification, in: *IFAC-Papers online*, vol. 51, pp. 1016–1022, 2018.
3. Glaessgen, E. and Stargel, D., The digital twin paradigm for future NASA and U.S. Air Force vehicles. *53rd Structures, Structural Dynamics, and Materials Conference*, pp. 1–14, 2012.
4. Schluse, M. and Rossmann, J., From simulation to experimentable digital twins: Simulation-based development and operation of complex technical systems. *IEEE International Symposium on Systems Engineering (ISSE)*, IEEE, pp. 1–6, 2016.
5. Barricelli, B.R., Casiraghi, E., Fogli, D., A survey on digital twin: Definitions, characteristics, applications, and design implications. *IEEE Access*, 7, 167653–167671, 2019.
6. Fuller, A., Fan, Z., Day, C., Research. *IEEE Access*, 8, 108952–108971, 2020.
7. Banerjee, A., Dalal, R., Mittal, S., Joshi, K.P., Generating digital twin models using knowledge graphs for industrial production lines. *Proc. Workshop Ind. Knowl. Graphs (ACM Web Sci. Conf.)*, pp. 1–6, 2017.
8. Boschert, S., Heinrich, C., Rosen, R., Next generation digital twin. *Proc. TMCE*, 209–218, 2018.
9. Madni, A.M., Madni, C., Lucero, S.D., Leveraging digital twin technology in model-based systems engineering. *Systems*, 7, 1, 7, 2019.
10. Negri, E., Fumagalli, L., Macchi, M.A., Review of the roles of digital twin in CPS-based production systems. *Procedia Manuf*, vol. 11, pp. 939–948, 2017.
11. Uhlemann, T.H.-J., Lehmann, C., Steinhilper, R., The digital twin: Realizing the cyber-physical production system for industry 4.0. *Procedia CIRP*, vol. 61, pp. 335–340, 2017.
12. Schleich, B., Anwer, N., Mathieu, L., Wartzack, S., Shaping the digital twin for design and production engineering. *Annals*, 66, 1, 141–144, 2017.
13. Grieves, M. and Vickers, J., Digital twin: Mitigating unpredictable, undesirable emergent behavior in complex systems, in: *Transdisciplinary Perspectives on Complex Systems*, Kahlen FJ, S. Flumerfelt, A. Alves (Eds.), pp. 85–113, Springer, Cham, 2017, https://doi.org/10.1007/978-3-319-38756-7_4.
14. Rosen, R., Von Wichert, G., Lo, G., Bettenhausen, K.D., About the importance of autonomy and digital twins for the future of manufacturing, in: *IFAC-Papers onlne*, vol. 48, pp. 567–572, 2015.
15. Melesse, T.Y., Di Pasquale, V., Riemma, S., Digital twin models in industrial operations: A systematic literature review. *Proc. Manuf.*, 42, 267– 272, 2020.
16. Werner, A., Zimmermann, N., Lentes, J., Approach for a holistic predictive maintenance strategy by incorporating a digital twin. *Proc. Manuf.*, 39, 1743–1751, 2019.
17. D'Amico, D., Ekoyuncu, J., Addipalli, S., Smith, C., Keedwell, E., Sibson, J., Penver, S., Conceptual framework of a digital twin to evaluate the degradation status of complex engineering systems. *Procedia CIRP*, vol. 86, p. 61 7, 2020.

18. Maropoulos, P. and Ceglarek, D., Design verification and validation in product lifecycle. *CIRP Ann. – Manuf. Technol.*, 59, 2, 740–759, 2010.

19. Addepalli, S., Roy, R., Axinte, D., Mehnen, J., *In-situ'* inspection technologies: Trends in degradation assessment and associated technologies. *Procedia CIRP. 2017; 59(TESConf 2016)*, pp. 35–40.

20. David, J., Lobov, A., Lanz, M., Attaining learning Objectives by Ontological Reasoning using Digital Twins. *Procedia Manuf.*, 31, 349–355, 2019.

21. Brettel, M., Friederichsen, N., Keller, M., Rosenberg, M., How virtualization, decentralization and network building change the manufacturing landscape: An industry 4.0 perspective. *Int. J. Mech. Aerospace Ind. Mechatron. Eng.*, 8, 37–44, 2014.

22. Vrabič, R., Erkoyuncu, J.A., Butala, P., Roy, R., Digital twins: Understanding the added value of integrated models for throughlife engineering services. *Procedia Manufacturing*, pp. 139–146, 2018.

23. Grieves, M., Digital twin: Manufacturing excellence through virtual factory replication, in: *Digital Twin White Paper*, vol. 1, W. Michael (Ed.), pp. 1–7, Grieves LLC, 2014.

24. GE Renewable Energy, in: *Meet the Digital Wind Farm*, https://www.ge.com/renewableenergy/stories/meet-the-digital-wind-farm.

25. Romero, D., Wuest, T., Harik, R., Thoben, K.D., Towards a cyber-physical PLM environment: The role of digital product models, intelligent products, digital twins, product avatars and digital shadows, in: *IFAC-Papers Online*, vol. 53, pp. 10911–10916, 2020.

26. Cimino, C., Negri, E., Fumagalli, L., Review of digital twin applications in manufacturing. *Comput. Ind.*, 113, 103130, 2019.

27. Lin, W.D. and Low, M.Y.H., Concept design of a system architecture for a manufacturing cyber-physical digital twin system. *IEEE International Conference on Industrial Engineering and Engineering Management (IEEM)*, pp. 1320–1324, 2021.

3

An Insight to Digital Twin

Anant Kumar Patel[1]*, Ashish Patel[2] and Kanchan Mona Patel[1]

*[1]Department of Pharmacology, Swami Vivekanand College of Pharmacy, Indore,
Madhya Pradesh, India*
[2]Department of Medicine, M.G.M. Medical College, Indore, Madhya Pradesh, India

Abstract

In this modern world, technology is used everywhere almost in each sector. With many technologies already present and with many more to come in the future, there is a technology called digital twin, which is gaining popularity. Its popularity is greatly growing. Digital twin is replication of any object, any system, product, or process in virtual form. It provides great advantages and is a great technology. There are different types of digital twins present. In this chapter, an insight to digital twin technology is provided. This technology is explained in detail, and different aspects of it are also explained in detail, like the working of digital twin, its types, traits of digital twin, its advantages, etc. Some real examples of application of digital twin are also stated in the chapter.

Keywords: Digital twin, digitalization, technology, digital replica, National Aeronautics and Space Administration (NASA), digital model

3.1 Introduction

Digital twin is a technology with growing popularity. It has many advantages, which are truly helpful in different sectors, which is why digital twin popularity is growing. The concept of digital twin was introduced in the year 2002 by Dr. Michael Grieves in a conference.

This was the first time that the digital twin technology was mentioned and introduced in public at a conference. In 2010, John Vickers from

---

*Corresponding author: anantpatel08@gmail.com

Manisha Vohra (ed.) Digital Twin Technology: Fundamentals and Applications, (33–46) © 2023 Scrivener Publishing LLC

National Aeronautics and Space Administration (NASA) through the medium of their report coined the name Digital Twin.

If compared from then till now then, it can be noticed that digital twin has come a long way with respect to its growth, application areas, etc. At present digital twin can be used for applications in many sectors like healthcare, manufacturing, etc.

Initially when its name was coined, it was not much widespread as it is now. It has come a long way, it has grown. A lot of progress can be noticed but that's not all. Digital twin is currently also still evolving.

In the year 2017, Gartner listed digital twin technology in top ten strategic technology trends and listing in top ten is something which digital twin technology truly deserves. The potential this technology has can help different companies, individuals, in fact, it can help different sectors largely. Such is the potential of digital twin technology.

Digital twins concept has been around for decades and this technology, when combined with the other technologies such as AR/VR, mixed reality, 3D printing, etc., will open doors for new applications and potential [1, 11]. Digital twin is receiving interest from academic as well as industrial point of view [2]. A digital twin must be able to guarantee well-defined services to support various activities like monitoring, maintenance, safety, etc. [12]. Digital twin concepts aim to allow the observation of the behavior of the whole system and prediction of the system behavior during the utilization [13]. In a B2B context, digital twins of machine tools enable the customers of the products being produced to receive real-time insights in the manufacturing process [14]. Now recently, the need to formalize and utilize the full potential of digital twin concepts arises from a combination of technology push and market pull [3].

The digital twin lets virtual entities to exist simultaneously with physical entities [22]. With the help of communication, digital twins throughout their lifecycle change and evolve together with their physical counterparts [6]. To provide smart/digital services in a product service system is it clearly necessary to understand the three dimensions of technology-driven service innovation: service ecosystem, service platform and value co-creation [16]. Digital twin can be helpful here. Digital twin is a tool that can support joint decision making by translating technical considerations into a business context and helping to identify the consequences of different options [17]. Irrespective of the location of stakeholders, they can access and monitor the physical twin status, all thanks to digital twin [4].

For remaining competitive, manufacturers have to produce high-quality products at low cost, and at the same time retain sufficient flexibility and digital twin can definitely help manufacturers to achieve this objective

[15]. On the basis of system operation and maintenance history, digital twin is an important enabler for improving system maintenance over time [8]. Digital twin seems to be the best suitable source of knowledge within the Smart Factory [18]. Digital twins are expected to enrich the existent asset information system, thus enhancing the informed decision-making in asset management [23]. A digital twin framework is also offered as a commercial solution [24].

In industry 4.0, digital twin application is highly being encouraged. Apart from digital twin, cyber-physical digital twin is something that is gaining attention and is being talked about a lot regarding its application in Industry 4.0. It only took off in recent years with the advancement of ICT technologies [9]. Other sectors like construction, automotive are also experiencing the increasing growth of digital twin application. For example, in automotive sector, digital twins are used to simulate cars driving in close-to-reality environments [5]. In healthcare sector as well, digital twin application is growing. However, the digital twin architectures need to make sure that accurate system health management predictions are made to help avoid excessive runtime costs [19].

3.2   Understanding Digital Twin

Digital twin is a technology, which works in a virtual environment. It can transform things greatly in a particular sector where it is applied. It can provide many advantages.

Digital twin is replication of any object, system, product or process in virtual form. Digital twin can also be called a digital replica of any object, system, product or process. When a digital twin of an existing object or system is made, it remains linked or connected with its original real world counterpart throughout the lifecycle of that particular object or system. This connectivity is a great characteristic of digital twin. With the help of this connectivity, all real-time data of the real world object or system can be transmitted to the digital twin. This enables digital to update in real-time.

Digital twin will also go through the same changes that the real world object or system is going through. The digital twin model works in a virtual environment as mentioned earlier. This both things are advantageous as these both things allows and makes monitoring the real world object or system using digital twin effective and easier as remote monitoring then becomes possible and can be done. The behavior of the real object or system will also be copied by digital twin, i.e. digital twin will also behave like the original real world object or system. Digital twin can predict any issue or problem before it occurs in real world object or system and can inform regarding it. This is like a damage or loss prevention advantage of digital twin as through this advantage, any issue or problem which could occur in the real world object or system can be prevented from occurring which will prevent the damage or loss it could have caused.

When discussing and talking about digital twin technology, there are different terms which come into light like Digital Model, Digital Shadow, Digital Twin. There are some misconceptions regarding these terms in literature. Below all three terms are defined which will help to clear the misconceptions [25].

The first term is Digital Model, the second term which will be defined is Digital Shadow and the third term that will be defined is Digital Twin.

Digital Model: In a digital model there is no exchange of data happening automatically between real object and digital model. The Digital model can be understood as digital version of an already existing real object or a digital version of a real object which is planned. The fact that there is no automatic exchange of data taking place between digital model and the real object or system is a vital defining feature. So after creating a digital model, any changes if made to the real object will not at all have any kind of impact on the created digital model either way [25].

Digital Shadow: Digital shadow is basically a digital representation of a real object. In Digital Shadow, there is one way data flow taking place between real object and digital version of the object.

Digital Twin: It is the one where there is flow of data between an already existing real object and a digital object and they are fully integrated in both directions [25].

In 2002, digital twin technology concept was presented at a conference by Dr. Michael Grieves. He presented it as an "Ideal Concept for Project Lifecycle Management (PLM)" as back then in 2002, digital twin technology was not recognized by its same name. Its name was coined later on in 2010. Digital twin is useful in project lifecycle management and in the presentation given by Dr. Michael Grieves at the conference in 2002, his Ideal Concept for PLM" had all elements of digital twin. The elements were virtual space, real space, link for flow of data from real to virtual space and link for flow of information from virtual to real space and virtual subspaces [10]. This conference presentation has always been an important part in the history of digital twin.

3.3   Digital Twin History

Digital twins history can be understood from some digital twin related important developments that have taken place from the time of its origin till now. National Aeronautics and Space Administration (NASA) had utilized digital twin concept in 1970 during the Apollo 13 program. Thus, digital twin concept is dated back to Apollo program of NASA [7]. So this is marked as the maiden instance where digital twin technology was used. Though before 1970, NASA was working on digital twin concept, in 1960s but its use during the Apollo 13 program was marked as the first instance of its use.

Thereafter, in the book Mirror Worlds David Gelernter had written about digital twins. It was published in 1991. Michael Grieves was the first person who presented or introduced the digital twin topic in public in 2002 in one conference. This concept was named the "digital twin" by NASA's John Vickers in a 2010 in a report. After that till today, digital twin has gained a lot of popularity and is being applied in different sectors.

3.4   Essential Aspects From Working Perspectives of Digital Twin

There are some essential aspects of digital twin from its working perspective. Before understanding the working of digital twin in detail, let us go through and understand some of the essential aspects.

A digital twinning model of the original object is one of the most essential aspects from working perspectives which is required to be create. Original object data are also another most essential aspect. For getting data, sensors would be needed. The sensors will give data and hence even they are one of the essential aspects from working perspectives. The linking of the object in real world with digital twin in virtual world which can be viewed and considered as the linking of the real world with virtual world is yet another essential aspect from the working perspective.

Thus, from working perspectives of digital twin, the digital twinning model of the original object, object data, sensors, etc. are some of the essential aspects as discussed above.

3.5   How Does a Digital Twin Work?

The digital twin model created an object or system that already exists in real world will have the same looks or appearance as that of the original physical object or system. So if there is an object or system, which is already produced, and its digital twin is created, then how it will work is explained below.

Sensors are deployed to obtain real-time data from the original object, which includes different aspects related to the performance of the object, its functionality, etc. Hence, sensors play a very important role here. A digital copy of the original object is created. It is the replicated version of the original object in a virtual environment.

For sending real-time data to its digital copy, a connectivity between them is required, and hence, they are connected or linked together. By this linking, real-time data can be transmitted easily and whenever there are changes in the real object, in accordance to it, there will be those same changes in the digital twin model as well.

Linking is very important. It allows transmission of data and keeps the digital twin in sync with the original object in real time. Digital twin model can run simulations. It can predict possible problems which could be faced in the object. It can give information and insights, which are very useful. This is how its work is carried out. Monitoring of the object using digital twin model can also be done.

So according to the elements of digital twin as rightly stated by [19] which are explained above, it can be seen its working also involves and relies on it, the real object in real space, the virtual or twin model created in virtual space, and the link between the two.

3.6   Insights to Digital Twin Technology Concept

Digital twin working is easy to understand as seen above. Now let us gain some insights to digital twin technology concept.

In digital twin technology, depending upon the type of application, we can have:

- Parts twins or components twins
- Product twins,
- System twins and
- Process twins.

3.6.1   Parts Twins

There is always a need for durable parts. It lies at the heart of digital twinning. Engineers can now grasp the different characteristics like the mechanical, electrical, etc. of a part through virtual representations of the individual components.

3.6.2   Product Twins

Individual parts when they work together will form a product. Product twins will allow to understand the manner in which these individual parts interact and will give important performance related informational data which can be processed and insights can be gained and given to the manufacturers.

3.6.3   System Twins

System twins allows to view how disparate products come together and work to achieve a system-level goal of obtaining a functional system. Basically, system twins allow to view how different products come together for forming a system, which is functional. System twins provides insight about products interaction and can give suggestions to improve performance.

3.6.4   Process Twins

Process twins are the ones which actually tell how different systems work with each other for creating a manufacturing facility. Whether the different systems that are working with each other are in sync to operate at peak efficiency or if there is a delay in supposing any one particular system then will the other systems working together be affected as well are things that need to be known. Process twins can help here. It can find out the exact timing schemes which will eventually have an impact on overall efficiency.

3.7   Types of Digital Twin

During defining digital twins in paper [10], authors Dr. Michael Grieves and John Vickers have discussed and described types of digital twin. They are:

- Digital Twin Prototype (DTP) and
- Digital Twin Instance (DTI).

Digital twins (DTs) are operated on in a Digital Twin Environment (DTE) [10].

Let us understand these types in detail.

3.7.1   Digital Twin Prototype (DTP)

It is digital twin type, which tells about prototypical physical artifact. DTP has information sets that are much needed to tell and produce a real physical version which replicates or twins the virtual version [10].

3.7.2   Digital Twin Instance (DTI)

An individual digital twin is kept linked to a particular corresponding physical product throughout the life of this particular product and particular product is described by DTI digital twin [10].

3.7.3   Digital Twin Environment (DTE)

This is an integrated, multidomain physics application space for operating on digital twins for a variety of purposes. These purposes include:

- Predictive
- Interrogative

Predictive: Here, the digital twin would be used for making prediction of future behavior and performance of the physical product.
Interrogative: This would apply to DTIs. The DTIs could be interrogated for the current and past histories [10].

3.8   Traits of Digital Twin

There are different traits of digital twin. Some of them are listed and explained below.

3.8.1   Look Same as the Original Object

Digital twin have the same look as that of the original object. Since digital twin replicates the original object, it has the same look that the original object has. This eases the work of the ones using digital twin for their work. For example, if suppose a company for one of their product is using digital twin. They do not have to visualize changes taking place in their product. They can view it and that too from remote location, thanks to digital twin. Having same look as the original object is a great trait of digital twin.

3.8.2 Consists Different Details of the Original Object

The digital twin just does not looks same as the original object, it even includes and consists of different minor details of the original object. Different details of the original object is included in the original object. This trait adds to the efficiency of the digital twin technology and thanks to this trait of digital twin, monitoring of the original object from any remote location can be not just done but it can be done very effectively. If digital twin would look the same as the original object but would not consist of different details of the object then it would not be an effective replicate. Hence, this trait of digital twin is also a great trait of digital twin.

3.8.3 Behaves Same as the Original Object

The digital twin behaves the same as the original object. When digital twin replicates the look and all the minor details of the original real world object, it even replicates how the original object behaves. Digital twin model very well copies the behavior of the original object and behaves same as the original object.

3.8.4 Can Predict and Inform in Advance About Problems That Could Occur

Digital twin can predict and tell in advance about different problems that could occur. Digital twin has this wonderful trait that it can actually predict the possible future problems that can occur which is a great advantage of using digital twin. When the problems that could possibly occur in an object, product, process, etc. is known in advance with the help of digital twin, then it can be avoided from occurring in reality. This will be so useful. Hence, this trait of digital twin is a phenomenal trait.

3.9 Value of Digital Twin

The thought or argument for digital twin is that information is substitute for waste gone resources, namely, energy, time, and material. All these are important physical resources. When information is used, it can, to a great extent, reduce all this wastage of resources which are energy, time and material i.e. physical resources. When digital twin is viewed through its lifecycle, it can be viewed clearly that in creation phase or create phase, all the physical resources which are energy, time, and material that get wasted along with time occupying expensive production of actual real prototypes can be saved, and they are actually allowed to be saved by modeling and simulating the behavior, as well as the form through digital twin prototype. Then in create or creation phase and downstream, resources can be saved and are in fact saved by discovering unpredicted undesirable (UU) behavior and finding out predicted undesirable (PU) behavior with simulations. Thereafter, talking about production phase, here trial and error manufacturing can be decreased by simulating manufacture prior to it actually occurs and this is how trial and error manufacturing can be decreased. To comprehend which components with which specifications are in each system that is produced, the as-built information needs to be collected. Collecting this information will only allow to comprehend about the components and its specifications in each system which is produced. With digital twin, we can comprehend how to maintain the system more effectively and efficiently in support/sustainment or operations phase as digital twin is the one which can allow us to do so. Additionally, the cost of unforeseen "normal accidents" can be well saved if unpredicted, as well as predicted undesirable behaviors can be prevented. It is claimed that life of a human is precious, it is priceless but by limiting the tests for a cost is put on life. This means we only test for a subset of states the systems can take. However, by using digital twin the cost that is incurred in preventing loss of life by testing more states can be dramatically lowered. If we are having the information regarding the system, to be specific, information regarding how the design of the system was done to be safely retired and/or decommissioned in the disposal phase then this will be very helpful. It will, to a great extent, decrease the impact which is cost on the environment [10]. Thus, it can be seen clearly that digital twin has great value and is helpful to a great extent. It is so useful. It is having potential to largely reduce resource wastage occurring in different system lifecycle [10].

3.10   Advantages of Digital Twin

Below are some of the advantages of digital twin.

- Anticipation or prediction of problems is possible using digital twin. The problems which could possibly turn up in future in a product, object, etc. can be predicted using digital twin.

- It can be used in monitoring the real object, product or process. Digital twin can receive real-time data and update in accordance with the changes occurring in real object, product or process. It will also go through the same changes as the real object, product or process goes through and that too in real-time.
- Predictive maintenance work of objects, products, etc. can be carried out using digital twin.
- It can be used in getting insights and information regarding the real object or product's working performance. The insights can be applied to the real object or product.

3.11   Real-World Examples of Use of Digital Twin

Digital twin is already being used in real-world application in different places. Below are some real world examples of use of digital twin technology.

Digital twin is being used by Tesla, Inc. for their cars. Tesla, Inc. is a well-renowned company. This company very well uses the digital twin technology for their cars. All Tesla cars that are sold have a digital twin for it. A digital twin is specially created for every car that Tesla is selling. On an everyday basis then, all the data collected by the sensors from each car is taken into account and then used for updating its software accordingly and then software update is sent. This means the software updates are very efficiently prepared taking into account all the data given by sensors from each car. This ensures all the bugs, existing loopholes, and all other issues and shortcomings are dealt with in the required manner and overcome with the correct solution or response needed via the software update. Tesla then sends this efficiently prepared updates for the cars. Tesla thus very well uses the digital twin technology for their cars. Similarly, just like this example of Tesla, there are other real world examples of use of digital twin at different places. General electric (GE) is using digital twin technology for their wind turbines. They are creating digital twin of their turbines [20]. Digital twin technology is proving to be useful for them. Bridgestone Corporation is using digital twin technology for their tyre development [21]. Similarly companies make use of digital twin technology for different application. Digital twin has surely made its place in different sectors, for various applications but to become a commonly used technology at different places, it has a long way to go. It is still evolving.

3.12   Conclusion

Digital twin is an effective technology. It has great advantages which are discussed, seen, and explained in this chapter. Also, the essential aspects from working perspectives of digital twin are discussed in this chapter. The work of digital twin is also explained in the chapter. Its work is easy to understand. Digital twin is an efficient technology. On receiving real-time data of an existing original object, the digital twin will also update according to it and present the changes happening in the original object. The existing original object remains linked and connected with the digital twin throughout the period of its lifecycle. Such is the connectivity in digital twin which helps in keeping the original object and the digital twin of it in sync together.

There are different types of digital twins present as explained in the chapter. Digital twin technology concept was first used in 1970 and it proved to be useful. At that time, it was used in one particular application but now, this technology is being used in different applications. Digital twin is very helpful in product development, anticipation or prediction of problems, cost saving, etc. and can be used in different sectors to optimize existing operations and services, and can even help to bring transformation and innovation. Its presence in whichever particular application it is being used is helpful and it does make a great difference. Altogether, with different advantages that digital twin provides, it is a supportive and helpful technology.

Some real world application examples of digital twin are also stated in this chapter. Tesla uses digital twin technology for their cars. Tesla are great example of real world application of digital twin which is stated in this chapter. Similarly, GE and Bridgestone also use digital twin technology for their wind turbines and tyre development respectively. Thus, digital twin when used in a particular application, it provides different benefits. It is clear that digital twin technology is highly helpful in different applications and is an useful technology.

References

1. Singh, M., Fuenmayor, E., Hinchy, E.P., Qiao, Y., Murray, N., Devine, D., Digital twin: Origin to future. *Appl. Syst. Innov.*, 4, 36, 2021.
2. Jones, D., Snider, C., Nassehi, A., Yon, J., Hicks, B., Characterising the digital twin: A systematic literature review. *CIRP J. Manuf. Sci. Technol.*, 29, 36–52, 2020.
3. Rasheed, A., San, O., Kvamsdal, T., Digital twin: Values, challenges and enablers. *IEEE Access*, 8, 21980–22012, 2020.
4. Barricelli, B.R., Casiraghi, E., Fogli, D., A survey on digital twin: Definitions, characteristics, applications, and design implications. *IEEE Access*, 7, 167653–167671, 2019.
5. Schluse, M. and Rossmann, J., From simulation to experimentable digital twins: Simulation-based development and operation of complex technical systems, in: *IEEE International Symposium on Systems Engineering (ISSE)*, IEEE, pp. 1–6, 2016.
6. Vrabic, R., Erkoyuncu, J.A., Butala, P., Roy, R., Digital twins: Understanding the added value of integrated models for through-life engineering services. *Proc. Manuf.*, 16, 139–146, 2018.
7. Rosen, R., Wichert, G.V., Lo, G., Bettenhausen, K.D., About the importance of autonomy and digital twins for the future of manufacturing, in: *IFAC-Paper online*, vol. 48, pp. 567–572, 2015.
8. Madni, A., Madni, C., Lucero, S., Leveraging digital twin technology in model-based systems engineering. *Systems*, 7, 7, 2019.
9. Lin, W.D. and Low, M.Y.H., Concept design of a system architecture for a manufacturing cyber-physical digital twin system, in: *IEEE International Conference on Industrial Engineering and Engineering Management (IEEM)*, pp. 1320–1324, 2021.
10. Grieves, M. and Vickers, J., Digital twin: Mitigating unpredictable, undesirable emergent behavior in complex systems, in: *Transdisciplinary Perspectives on Complex Systems*, Kahlen FJ, S. Flumerfelt, A. Alves (Eds.), pp. 85–113, Springer, Cham, 2017, https://doi.org/10.1007/978-3-319-38756-7_4.
11. David, J., Lobov, A., Lanz, M., Leveraging digital twins for assisted learning of flexible manufacturing systems, in: *2018 IEEE 16th International Conference on Industrial Informatics (INDIN)*, IEEE, Porto, pp. 529–535, July 2018.
12. Cimino, C., Negri, E., Fumagalli, L., Review of digital twin applications in manufacturing. *Comput. Ind.*, 113, 103130, 2019.
13. Lohtander, M., Ahonen, N., Lanz, M., Ratava, J., Kaakkunen, J., Micro manufacturing unit and the corresponding 3d-model for the digital twin. *Proc. Manuf.*, 25, 55–61, 2018.

14. Romero, D., Wuest, T., Harik, R., Thoben, K.D., Towards a cyber-physical PLM environment: The role of digital product models, intelligent products, digital twins, product avatars and digital shadows, in: *IFAC-Papers online*, vol. 53, pp. 10911–10916, 2020.
15. Jeon, S.M. and Kim, G., A survey of simulation modeling techniques in production planning and control (PPC). *Prod. Plan. Control*, 27, 360–377, 2016.
16. West, S., Gaiardelli, P., Rapaccini, M., Exploring technology-driven service innovation in manufacturing firms through the lens of service dominant logic, in: *IFAC-Papers online*, vol. 51, pp. 1317–1322, 2018.
17. West, S., Stoll, O., Meierhofer, J., Züst, S., Digital twin providing new opportunities for value co-creation through supporting decision-making. *Appl. Sci.*, 11, 3750, 2021.
18. Longo, F., Nicoletti, L., Padovano, A., Ubiquitous knowledge empowers the smart factory: The impacts of a service-oriented digital twin on enterprises' performance. *Annu. Rev. Control*, 47, 221–236, 2019.
19. Khan, S., Farnsworth, M., McWilliam, R., Erkoyuncu, J., On the requirements of digital twin-driven autonomous maintenance. *Annu. Rev. Control*, 50, 13–28, 2020.
20. GE Renewable Energy, Meet the Digital Twin Wind Turbines, Building a Digital Twin, Bolstering the Power of a Wind Turbine. https://www.ge.com/renewableenergy/stories/improving-wind-power-with-digital-twin-turbines.
21. Bridgestone, How Bridgestone's Virtual Tyre Modelling Revolutionalising Tyre Development. https://www.bridgestone.co.uk/story/mobility/how-bridgestones-virtual-tyre-modelling-is-revolutionising-tyre-development.
22. Kaarlela, T., Pieskä, S., Pitkäaho, T., Digital twin and virtual reality for safety training. *Proceedings of the 2020 11th IEEE International Conference on Cognitive Infocommunications (CogInfoCom)*, pp. 115–120, 2020.
23. Macchi, M., Roda, I., Negri, E., Fumagalli, L., Exploring the role of digital twin for asset lifecycle management, in: *IFAC-Papers online*, pp. 790–795, 2018.
24. Josifovska, K., Yigitbas, E., Engels, G., Reference framework for digital twins within cyber-physical systems, in: *Proceedings of the 5th International Workshop on Software Engineering for Smart Cyber Physical Systems (SEsCPS'19)*, IEEE Press, pp. 25–31, 2019, https://doi.org/10.1109/SEsCPS.2019.00012.
25. Fuller, A., Fan, Z., Day, C., Barlow, C., Digital twin: Enabling technologies, challenges and open research. *IEEE Access*, 8, 108952–108971, 2020.

4

Digital Twin Solution Architecture

Suhas D. Joshi

Olyphaunt Solutions, Pvt. Ltd., Pune, India

Abstract

A digital twin simulates the state and the behavior of a physical object in real time. This work focuses on primarily the digital twin solution architecture. The emphasis is on how the digital twin can be designed to deliver common use cases. From an architecture standpoint, a digital twin is a collection of several different software services, applications and data stores. In this chapter, we will first review how the physical object can be connected to the digital twin through the Internet of Things (IoT) and then see a layered view of the digital twin solution architecture. A description of the layered view and components in each layer will follow. An explanation of the data flow across digital twin components will show how various components work together. The digital twin solution architecture is explained through various viewpoints including data stores, user experience, integration with external applications, application programming interface (API), and cyber security. The solution architecture is presented at a conceptual level and is not tied to a framework, platform, or solution from a particular vendor. Concepts in the digital twin solution architecture are illustrated through examples from the world of discrete manufacturing.

Keywords: Digital twin use cases, digital twin solution architecture, digital twin services, digital twin applications, digital twin development considerations, digital twin definition, digital twin integration with other applications

4.1 Introduction

As the speed of digital transformation increases globally, more and more physical objects are being represented as digital twins in the cyber-world.

Email: Suhas.Joshi@Olyphaunt.com

Manisha Vohra (ed.) Digital Twin Technology: Fundamentals and Applications, (47–76) © 2023 Scrivener Publishing LLC

A digital twin simulates the state and the behavior of a physical object in real-time. The physical object could be a sensor, a machine, a building or an airport. The benefits of a real-time digital twin solution are better actionable insight in the working of the object, significant reduction in waste and improvement productivity without compromising quality.

In this chapter, we will review how to design the digital twin software solution to:

- Model a physical object and the eco-system in which it operates
- Connect to the physical object in the real-world and process data from the object
- Simulate in real-time the operation of the physical object to determine any potential issues and risks
- Track the present performance and predict the future performance of the object.

After reviewing "what" the digital twin has to deliver to the various user persona, this work presents "how" the digital twin will deliver the expected requirements. The digital twin conceptual solution architecture is presented through several viewpoints such as a functional model, logical model, data stores, interfaces, user experience and cyber security.

The focus of this chapter is on presenting a conceptual solution architecture for a digital twin. Our discussion will not include proprietary or commercial off-the-shelf solutions, services, frameworks or a platform provided by a specific vendor. Also, we will not describe physical infrastructure, such as servers, storage, network, firewalls, and load-balancers, required for implementing a digital twin solution because that depends upon specific functional and non-functional requirements.

In order to give a practical example after describing the conceptual solution architecture, we will review an example from the world of discrete manufacturing to illustrate how a digital twin can be designed.

4.2   Previous Work

Many researchers and practitioners have published about digital twins. A review of 87 implementations of digital twin and a proposal for a generalized architecture instead of domain specific architecture is found in [26]. The digital twin concept is reviewed in 6 dimensions including industrial sector, purpose, physical reference object, completeness, creation time, and connection. A review of the state of the art concerning the key components of digital twins, development of digital twin, and the major digital applications in industry are described in [27].

An explanation of how digital twin can be used in manufacturing for production planning and control, process control and condition based maintenance is given in [28]. A description of the role a digital twin plays in the context of Industry 4.0 is presented in [29]. [30] focuses on creating a digital twin for an aircraft. Topics discussed include product identification, life cycle, configuration, models and software applications in the aircraft digital twin.

There are several works related to the architecture of digital twins. [31] describes the digital twin concept and how it applies across the product life cycle in understanding and testing system behavior. [32] lists the development tools that may be used for developing a digital twin with a focus on Big Data and Artificial Intelligence. Six possible digital twin architectures are proposed in [33] including IIoT, big data, mixed reality, simulation, complex systems and cloud computing. [34] focuses on using UML and OCL models for a high level digital twin design. [35] models the interactions between cyber-cyber and physical-cyber systems. [35] also shows how a Bayesian network and fuzzy logic can be used to select models for inter-system interactions. [36] lists several new use cases that a digital twin will have to support for smart connected product systems (SCPS).

The adoption of blockchain technology is increasing for tracking assets and transactions in a network. Use of blockchain will increase in the digital twin also. Also, data related to transactions, logs, and history are not secure or tamper-proof. Systems and technologies leveraged for the creation of digital twins are mostly centralized and fall short of providing trusted data provenance, audit, and traceability, according to [37]. A blockchain-based creation process of digital twins is suggested to guarantee secure and trusted traceability, accessibility, and immutability of transactions, logs, and data provenance.

4.2.1   How This Work Differs

This work is somewhat different compared to the other works mentioned earlier in that it explains step-by-step, how to design a digital twin for a physical object. This work demystifies the design of a digital twin and shows how to structure the digital twin solution in a clear, comprehensive and pragmatic way. The architecture approach presented in this work covers all the possible viewpoints such as functionality, scalability, security, openness, agility, integration with other applications, ease of use and user experience. An incremental approach is presented so that the architect can first focus on the foundation and then build additional functionality as needed. Throughout this work, the solution architecture concepts are illustrated with an example of a digital twin for a grinding machine.

4.3   Use Cases

Persona, such as users or operators, managers, and maintenance technicians, generally work with different types of physical objects, whether the object is a machine, a plant, or a building. Depending on the physical object the digital twin represents, the specific use cases may be different, but the following table is an example of what various persona would require from a digital twin.

	Persona	Sample use cases
1	User	1. Remotely monitor the status of the object, i.e., whether it is in service or running in degraded mode or out of service. 2. Receive alerts if the object has failed or is going to fail 3. View any active errors and warnings 4. Need object performance metrics along with a comparison between planned and actual performance 5. View Work Instructions regarding how to complete a specific operation with the object 6. Need automatically generated recommendations based on the current performance of the physical object
2	Manager	7. Know "Remaining Useful Life (RUL)" for the object 8. Need to see digital data such as object status, along with any alerts and the possible financial impact of the alert, superimposed over the physical view of the object 9. Determine the status, alerts and values of critical parameters by running queries across a set of digital twins in the enterprise.

(*Continued*)

(*Continued*)

3	Maintenance Technician	10. View Work Instructions regarding how to complete a repair task super-imposed over the physical view of the object. 11. Receive an alert from the digital twin about replacing a part before the part fails 12. Receive recommendations about how to recover from an error, malfunction or a condition that is causing the object to under-perform
4	User in training	13. Receive work instructions regarding how to complete a specific operation. Work instructions should be super-imposed over the physical view of the object.
5	Design Engineer	14. See estimated critical property values when property values are not physically available from the object. 15. View calculated parameters for a range of objects while the objects are in use
6	Analyst	16. Would like to write ad-hoc reporting applications based on the data generated by the digital twin
7	Spare part management application	17. Digital twin should be able to send an order to the spare part management application.
8	Production planning application	18. Digital twin should be able to receive the production planning schedule from the planning application.

4.4   Architecture Considerations

Users of a digital twin will focus primarily on digital twin functional requirements. But solution architects, need to keep in mind the following important considerations.

- **Ability to work for different physical objects**: The digital twin solution will be able to work for multiple objects and not just one object.

- **Scalability**: Digital twin should be only constrained by resources, such as memory and storage. The design and should not limit the number of instances to a fixed value.
- **Data Sharing**: Digital twin should be able to share the output data so that developers or citizen users can write ad-hoc applications to use the output data.
- **Open architecture**: The digital twin should integrate with other applications in the eco-system. It should receive and send data to other applications through well-defined application programming interfaces (APIs).
- **Event driven**: Digital twin solution architecture should be designed to process events in real time. For example, as data are generated, it should get processed.
- **Cyber-Security**: The solution architecture should implement security of data at rest and data in motion and role-based access control (RBAC).
- **User Experience**: The digital twin solution should be designed to support local, as well as remote users. Secondly, user experience should support the ability to view the physical object and super-impose digital data on the physical view.

4.5   Understanding the Physical Object

Before working on the digital twin solution architecture, it is important to understand how the physical object operates. The following is a sample list of sample questions that the solution architect will have to ask.

- **Object Properties**: What are the properties, e.g., unique identifier, location, etc. associated with the physical object? Example: Suppose that a digital twin needs to be developed for a grinding machine in a manufacturing plant. There are several grinding machines in the plant. Each machine should have a unique identifier, e.g., "GR001."
- **Calculated data**: What is the data available from the physical object? Is the data generated in real-time or produced in bulk? If certain data are not available directly from the physical object, but is of interest, how can it be derived? What is the model that will help derive the required data?

Example: In case of a grinding machine, the speed (in revolutions per minute) at which the grinding wheel is spinning is available through a sensor and is available in real-time every second. The temperature of the grinding wheel is of interest but is not available from a sensor. The temperature increases in a nonlinear way with grinding wheel speed. Grinding wheel wear is based on the highest temperature and the duration. In this case, the digital twin will be able to calculate the temperature and wear based on other available data.

- **Process Model**: What is the function of the physical object? What is the input, process and output implemented when the object operates? Can the operation of the physical object be modeled as a state machine? How long will the physical object be in a certain state? What is the speed at which work is done when the physical object is in a particular state?

  Example: There are multiple states that describe the operation of the grinding machine: idle, working and "out of service." Working state has three substates, i.e., ramp-up, grinding, and ramp-down. When the grinding wheel is not spinning, it is in idle state. If it is spinning with a speed greater than 0 but less than 500 RPM, it is in ramp-up state. If the grinding wheel spins at a rate of 500 RPM or higher, it is in grinding state. If the grinding wheel speed drops below 500 RPM, it is considered in ramp-down state provided it was previously in grinding state. At any time, there is an issue with the grinding machine, the user will push a button on the grinding machine and signal the "out of service" state.

- **Context**: What is the overall eco-system, which the physical object belongs to? Are there relationships (e.g., a parent-child relationship) with other objects and potentially other digital twins? Are there components within the physical object that need to be modeled as digital twins also?

  Example: A specific grinding machine has a relationship with other entities in the context such as the manufacturing line in which the machine is located. Also, the grinding machine has other components such as the electrical motor and coolant delivery system which can be separately modeled. A sample context diagram for machines in a manufacturing plant is shown in Figure 4.1 as follows.

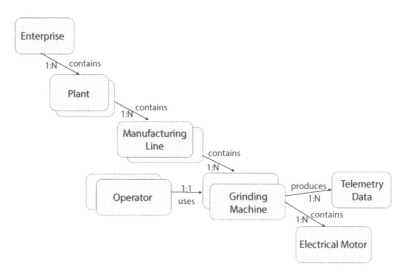

Figure 4.1 Example context diagram.

When a suitable point and click user interface is implemented to support the context, a user will be able to navigate through the context and display the desired content. Similarly, the user will be able to formulate queries, such as show the status of all grinding machines in all plants in a specific geographic region.

- **Physical Details**
  Is there a 3-D drawing that can be used for knowing more details about the physical object? Does a bill of materials exist that shows all the components that make up the physical object?
  Example: There is a 3-D drawing available for the grinding machine. The 3-D model will help in visualizing the physical object in various applications.
- **Components**
  What are the components contained within the physical object?
  Example: The grinding machine contains two electrical motors. Each has a different capacity and speed of operation.
- **Telemetry Data**
  What is the data generated by the physical object? Is the data sent as an event e.g., periodically? How frequently is the data sent?

Example: When the grinding operation is in progress, the grinding machine sends the speed (RPM) at which the grinding wheel is running, every 5 seconds. The grinding machine sends the state when the state value changes. For example, initially the state is idle, then it changes to running or out of service.

- **External applications and systems**
  What are the external applications or systems that the physical object will work with? How will the digital twin make data available to other applications? How will the digital twin have to consume data from other applications?
  Example: Grinding machine maintenance is tracked in an ERP system and maintenance activity records are tracked there. Grinding wheel replacement can be ordered from the Spare Part management system through an API.

4.5.1   Modeling Considerations

As noted above in "Architecture Considerations," the digital twin architecture should be able to simulate multiple physical objects. Also, as discussed in the previous section, each physical object has properties, relationships and components. Digital twin definition (DTD) is the construct for modeling each physical object completely. Thus, a DTD captures the physical object properties, relationships, telemetry data, and component information and any other data that is needed for simulating the physical object. A DTD expressed in a machine-processable language can be analyzed for correctness with the help of tools.

In order to model the properties of a physical object, a good starting point would be to see if an ontology exists for the physical object. Properties of various common physical objects (e.g., room, automobile, thing, etc.) have been defined through ontologies [1]. The ontology will provide various properties for the object. For instance, for modeling a machine, a starting point can be the product ontology. The product ontology has various attributes, such as manufacturer, model number, etc. along with their data types defined already. Additional data attributes may be added to show telemetry data, components, etc.

For modeling the digital twin definition (DTD) for a physical object, various tools are available including lexical data modeling languages, such as digital twin definition language (DTDL) [2], GraphQL [3], JSON-LD [4], and OWL [5]. Additionally, graphical languages, such as unified model language (UML) or entity relationship diagram (ERD), may be used for modeling the DTD.

4.6   Digital Twin and IoT

Internet of Things (IoT) technology uses Internet to connect physical objects to applications such as digital twin that process the data from physical objects. The following figure shows the end-to-end solution architecture, including the physical object and the digital twin.

A brief explanation of the data flow in Figure 4.2 is as follows.

1. The IoT gateway registers itself with the device management service, which allows the IoT gateway to send and receive data.
2. The IoT Gateway connects to physical objects using a "Field Bus Protocol" such as OPC/UA [6], ModBus [7], ProfiNet [8], ProfiBus [9], WiFi [10], BlueTooth [11], Ethernet IP [12] etc. and receives the data from the physical object.
3. The IoT gateway then transmits the data received in step 2 through a secure network communication protocol such as AMQP [13] or MQTT [14].
4. The data ingestion component receives the data from multiple IoT Gateways. Data ingestion is responsible for ensuring the quality of the data. For example, any duplicate data is discarded, and then data are stored in the data lake.
5. The digital twin subscribes to an event that signals the availability of data. So, when new data arrives in the data lake, digital twin receives notification and can start processing the data. A more detailed explanation of various functions in the digital twin is presented later in this chapter.

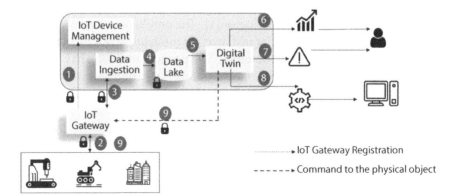

Figure 4.2 Internet of Things and digital twin.

6. Digital twin processes the input data, simulates the physical object's operation, and provides the status.
7. Digital twin provides the alerts about the physical object.
8. Digital twin exchanges data with an external application as required.
9. Digital twin sends an advisory warning to the user of the physical object recommending that a certain action be taken. Alternatively, depending on the use case, the digital twin sends a command to the physical object to change the object's operation because it may not be possible for a human operator to act quickly. Thus, data communication between the physical object and the digital twin is a two-way street and technology allows digital twin to communicate with the physical object all the time.

4.7   Digital Twin Solution Architecture

Throughout this chapter, we will describe the solution architecture by showing various components, inter-connections between components and explain how data flows across the components.

4.7.1   Conceptual Digital Twin Solution Architecture

Figure 4.3 below shows a conceptual solution architecture for the digital twin. There are multiple layers in the digital twin architecture and an explanation for each layer is given below.

4.7.2   Infrastructure Platform and IoT Services

At the very bottom of the figure, there is the infrastructure layer, which provides the compute, network and storage capabilities. Above that are capabilities such as cyber-security and high availability. Above that layer is the IoT layer which supports registering and managing physical devices/gateways, and data ingestion to ensure data quality before storing the data in the Data Lake. Data Lake provides various ways to store data including relational database, time-series database, flat files, non-SQL document style database.

4.7.3   Digital Twin Data and Process Model

Above the IoT layer is the digital twin data and process model layer. Components in this layer are described as follows.

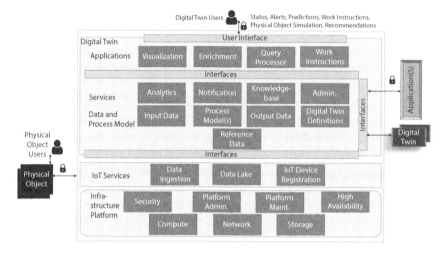

Figure 4.3   Digital twin solution architecture.

1. **Input Data**: Data received from the physical object through the IoT stack is the input data for the process model. Physically, data received through IoT resides in the data lake and should be accessible to digital twin components. The box called "Input Data" is just a logical representation of this data. Users of this data include the process model, as well as digital twin services, such as analytics.

2. **Process Model**: The process model represents what the physical object does. The virtual object implemented in software will "simulate" the physical object operations. It will process the input data and produce output that represents the output of the physical object. Output data will be stored in the data store, where it will be available to services such as visualization, analytics, etc. The digital twin should be able to support multiple physical objects, e.g., each component in a machine can each have a different process model. See Figure 4.4 below for an example of a process model in which the states of a grinding machine are modeled. Each state is shown within the circle and input data is used to determine what the next state should be. In this example, the criterion for determining the state is the grinding wheel speed in RPM. In the example below, the sensor in the grinding machine sends the grinding wheel speed as 510.

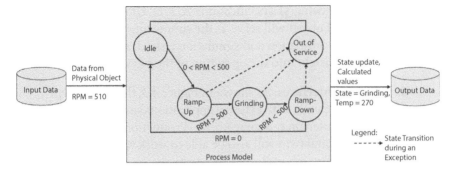

Figure 4.4 Process model example.

Process Model may also include "Virtual Sensor" capability. As mentioned earlier in the section entitled "Calculated data", in the Process Model for the grinding machine, the temperature of the grinding wheel can be calculated based on the grinding wheel speed. So even though there is no temperature sensor, the "Virtual Temperature Sensor" will calculate the temperature value and will make it available for consumption. In the above figure, based on the speed of 510 RPM, the virtual sensor calculates the temperature as 270°C.

3. **Output Data**: Various types of data will be generated by the digital twin, such as:

   1. Object Status updates
   2. Virtual Sensor outputs as explained earlier
   3. Outputs from Machine Learning (ML) models
   4. Alert data containing the reason for the alert and a timestamp.

4. **Digital Twin Definition Data**: The digital twin definition schema describes a specific instance of the digital twin. The schema will contain a set of properties, operations performed and relationships to other digital twins.

5. **Reference Data**: Reference data will not be updated very often. It is stored for use by several services and applications.

   1. Context model: A model showing the relationship of the object to other objects.
   2. Rules data: A set of rules that will help in determining the next set of actions in the event certain conditions regarding the physical object.

3. 3-D Drawing(s) specification: A 3-D Drawing for the physical object will serve as the supporting model, as the base for animation and simulation tasks. It will give additional insight into the operation of the physical object.

6. **External Interfaces**: As shown in Figure 4.3, the digital twin will inter-operate with external applications such as ERP systems, Maintenance Management, Production Scheduling, etc. The digital twin will also be able to work with other digital twins through well-defined interfaces.

4.7.4   Digital Twin Services

Regardless of the type of object that is being modeled, there is a set of services that will be commonly required by digital twin applications. These services are briefly described as follows.

1. Analytics: This service includes running pre-determined Machine Learning (ML) models such as forecasting or anomaly detection on the data received.
2. Notifications: If the outcome of analytics needs attention, the notification service sends an alert to a pre-determined distribution list through mechanisms such as e-mail, SMS text message, etc.
3. Knowledgebase: Through a set of rules, Knowledgebase determines the steps required to take when a specific event happens. For example, based on the forecasting ML model output, it is predicted that the diameter of the grinding wheel will dip below the threshold in 24 hours. The Knowledgebase will recommend the next steps to take in this situation. The Knowledgebase may also execute a step in which a command is sent to the physical object. For example, if temperature of the grinding wheel exceeds a threshold, the speed at which the grinding wheel is spinning is dropped until the temperature is within the operating range.

   Knowledgebase is an evolving service because as new operational situations are discovered, new rules will be added, or existing rules will be updated.
4. Administration: The administration service allows for creating new digital twin instances based on the digital twin definition (DTD), starting, stopping and deleting the operation of each newly created digital twin.

4.7.5   Digital Twin Applications

Digital twin applications use underlying services and databases. Applications interface with the digital twin users through a user interface. Applications may also interface with other systems through APIs. Examples of possible applications are described as follows.

1. **Visualization**: Visualization will enable the user gain insight into the current status as well as any pending alerts. The virtualization application will query from the input data, output data, and reference data stores and make it available to the user through the user interface.
2. **Enrichment**: An Enrichment application is like Visualization in terms of retrieving data from underlying services and databases with the addition of fetching data or sending data to external systems. For example, if the status of the grinding machine is Out of Service, the Enrichment application will query the external system used by Maintenance engineers. Through the query, any open maintenance tickets will be shown.
3. **Query Processor**: A Query Processor application will allow a citizen user to build a query through a user interface and then it will direct the query to an appropriate data source such as the Generated data to obtain the results and display them. For example, the user will be able to build a query such as "What is the average Remaining Useful Life (RUL) for the grinding wheel on all the grinding machines in the plant?"
4. **Work Instructions**: A Work Instruction application can be constructed based on the 3-D drawing as the reference information. Augmented Reality (AR) technology is ideal for such applications because digital data such as work instructions are super-imposed over the image of the physical object. Work Instruction applications will typically be used on a mobile device or a hands-free device such as smart glasses.

4.7.6   Sample Basic Data Flow through Digital Twin

Figure 4.5 below shows a sample data flow through digital twin components.

1. When an administrator user wants to create a digital twin instance physical object, they use the application called

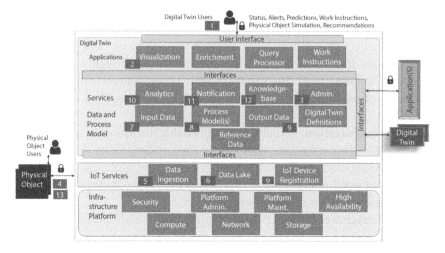

Figure 4.5 Basic data flow through the digital twin.

Visualization. User will enter required properties, such as digital twin unique Identifier, location, etc. through a user interface.

2. Visualization will then invoke the administration service API to create a digital twin definition.

3. Administration service will create a digital twin definition. As mentioned earlier, the definition tracks the properties such as identifier, location, etc. as well as the relationships.

4. Data generated by the physical object is sent by the IoT Gateway and is received in the Data Ingestion layer.

5. Data Ingestion checks data quality. Erroneous, duplicate data is discarded.

6. All valid Data is then stored in the Data Lake. Data is stored in appropriate stores, i.e., relational, flat files, time-series or non-SQL database.

7. When data is available in the Data Lake, an event is generated to signal that Input data is available for the Process Model.

8. Process Model for the object runs and simulates the operation of the physical object. Based on the value of the input data received, the state of the object is updated. If a Virtual Sensor is available, it will calculate values based on input data. All calculated values, status, etc. are stored as "Output Data".

9. When data is stored in the Output data, an event will be created to start the analysis of incoming data. Output Data may also be used for analytics.

10. The Analytics service contains various ML models such as forecasting or anomaly detection. ML models will retrieve datasets from both Input data and Output data. The ML models will store results of analytics in Output data.

4.7.7   Sample Data Flow for Exception Handling

The steps outlined may run only in the event of an exceptional situation and may not represent the normal data flow.

11. If the ML model detects an outcome that needs further action, an event will be generated for the notification service to act on. For example, in case of a grinding machine scenario, the ML model detects that the thickness of the grinding wheel will fall below a threshold in the next 24 hours and the machine will come to a complete stop unless the grinding wheel is replaced. In this case, the notification service will send an alert to the user.

12. Based on the event generated based by the ML model, the Knowledgebase service can programmatically suggest the next set of steps. The Knowledgebase service will retrieve the rules which are part of the reference database. Any recommendation will be entered in the Output data. For instance, in case of the grinding machine, if the ML model predicts that in the next 24 hours the grinding wheel thickness will fall below the threshold, the rule may be to order another wheel from the Spare Part management system, after confirming that the grinding wheel has already gone through the required number of dressing cycles.

13. On a case-by-case basis, the Knowledgebase will send a command to the physical object through the IoT Gateway, to change the configuration and hence the operation of the physical object.

4.7.8   Sample Data Flow through Digital Twin Applications

For understanding the data flows through digital twin applications, please refer to Figure 4.6 below.

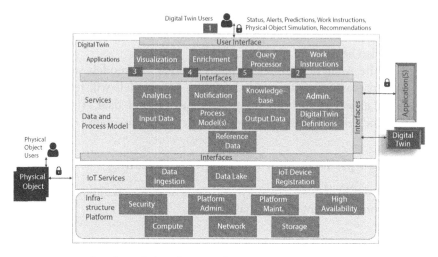

Figure 4.6 Data flow through digital twin applications.

1. User has the Work Instruction App installed on a mobile phone they are carrying. The user starts the App and looks at a marker posted on an object such as a machine.
2. Based on the marker the App knows that the user wants to see the instructions for how to replace a specific part in the object.

   The App shows a 3-D view of the object and asks the user to follow step 1 in the Work Instruction. After the user provides a confirmation that step 1 is complete, the App shows what to do for the next step. In this way, the entire part replacement is completed.
3. Visualization: From the Visualization user interface, the user selects a menu to display the status.

   The Visualization applications queries the Output data table and determines the current status as well as any actual values and calculated values.

   Example: In case of the grinding machine, the Visualization application queries the Output data and finds out that the latest grinding wheel speed value is 510 RPM and temperature is 270°C. Visualization passes on the above-mentioned values to the User Interface which in turn shows the above-mentioned values in a visual form.
4. Enrichment: The basic flow will be very similar to the above-mentioned data flow for Visualization. The only

difference will be that the Enrichment application will use the API for an external system to get additional data.

Example: Enrichment application will retrieve latest status value from the output data store. But additionally, it will use an API to get data about open maintenance tickets from the maintenance management system.

5. Query Processor: The Query Processor shows the list of active digital twins from the digital twin definitions table. The user selects a specific digital twin or all the available digital twins. The query processor then guides the user to make a query, e.g., "List all grinding machines which are currently in out-of-service state."

The query processor then queries the output data store and responds to the user with the response.

4.7.9   Development Considerations

The following table is not a recommendation, but it will give an idea about the possible choices.

	Components	Development choices
1	Applications: Visualization, Enrichment, Query Processor	Java, Python, C# or C++
2	Work Instruction Application	Augmented Reality [15] will be ideal for this use case. Augmented Reality Application Studio.
3	Services: Notifications, Administration	Java, Python, C#, C++
4	Service: Analytics (ML Models)	Python ML libraries for time-series analysis e.g., NumPy [16], TensorFlow [17]
5	Service: Knowledgebase	Rule base, developed with a Rules Engine
6	Process Model	A state machine may be a good design model, implemented in Java, Python, C# or C++.

4.8   Database Considerations

The following data stores will be designed and used by the digital twin. Obviously, the exact schema for the items will depend upon the object for which the digital twin will be implemented.

	Data store	Data content	Example	Data store type
1	Input data	Object state changes, i.e., events	Grinding operation starts	Relational database
		Data with object properties and values sent periodically	Grinding wheel diameter and torque are sent after each cycle	Relational database
		Streaming data, i.e., object property values sent continuously	Electrical current and voltage values	Time-series database
		Bulk data	Vibration signal	Sequential file
2	Output data	Alerts	Grinding wheel diameter below threshold	Relational database
		Calculated object property values	Grinding wheel temperature	Relational database
		Predicted or calculated object property values	Remaining useful life	Relational database
		Recommendations	Actionable recommendation for user	Relational database
3	Digital Twin Definitions (DTDs)	Digital Twin Definitions (DTDs)	DTD instances as created by administration	Non-SQL database

(Continued)

(*Continued*)

4	Reference data	Context diagram showing entities and relationships	Grinding machine in the enterprise	Relational database
		Rules	If predicted grinding machine diameter is < 25 mm then recommend user to order a spare grinding wheel	Relational database
		3-D Drawing	Grinding machine and grinding wheel drawing	File(s) in a format readable by augmented reality studio.
		Bill of Materials	All the parts of the grinding machine	Relational database
		Production planning schedule	Production plan that will be used by the grinding machine	Relational database

4.9 Messaging

In the solution architecture we have described components such as services, applications, data stores and process model. The following table describes in detail how each digital twin component interacts with other components. Both synchronous and asynchronous interactions should be supported. Synchronous interactions will be through calling well-defined APIs. Asynchronous interactions will be supported through messaging over a message bus. Messaging could be point-to-point or publish-subscribe. The following table shows a set of possible publish-subscribe interactions.

	Component	User interface	Component type	Subscribes to	Publishes
1	Process Model	Not required	Multi-threaded server with one thread for each instance of Digital Twin Definition (DTD)	Input Data Available event	Object State Changes, Alerts
2	Analytics (ML Models)	Not required	Service modeled as an Event Handler	Input Data Available event	Alerts
3	Knolwedge-base	Not required	Service modeled as an Event Handler	Alerts	Recommen-dations
4	Notification service	Not required	Continuously running service	Alerts	Sends alerts by email
5	Adminis-tration	Yes	Continuously running service	Not required	Not required
6	Visualization	Yes	Application	Notification	Displays alerts
7	Enrichment	Yes	Application	Not required	Not required
8	Query Processor	Yes	Application	Not required	Not required

Numerous choices possible for a message bus include JMS [18], Kafka [19] and ZeroMQ [20].

4.10   Interfaces

The following table lists the main APIs that the digital twin will support. APIs for data stores allow separation between the logical and physical representations of data. The API users see only the logical representation. Database implementers are free to decide the physical modeling of the data and will be able to change it, as needed, without requiring the API users, i.e., application and service developers to change their code. APIs can be used to integrate a digital twin with an external enterprise application or another digital twin.

	API	Explanation	Supported by	Used by
1	Input Data API	Select and read data from the Input Data Store	Data Lake	Process Model, Visualization, Query Processor
2	Output Data API	Select and read data from the Output Data store	Digital Twin Output Data Store	Visualization, Enrichment applications
3	Reference Data API	Retrieve from the Reference Data store	Reference Data Store	Administration, Process Model
4	External Application API	Get data from an application	External Applications	Enrichment, Other applications (as required)
5	External Application API	Set data in Digital Twin from another application	Digital Twin	Setting data into the Digital Twin, e.g., Production Planning Schedule

REST style APIs with get and set operations are preferred. For modeling and documenting, various tools are available, such as Swagger [21] and PostMan [22].

4.11   User Experience

The digital twin user experience functionality will consist of both client and server-side components. The user facing client-side logic will execute in a Web Browser or on a mobile application. Client-side functionality will include user authentication, user authorization, as well as providing a menu of various possible features, such as administration, visualization of status, simulation, alerts, etc.

On the server-side, the functionality will include using the API for the appropriate service or application. For example, if the administrator user wants to create a new digital twin, the user interface function on the server side will use the administration service API to create a new digital twin definition.

Applications, such as visualization and enhancement, will have server-side components that will respond to user inputs.

For client-side browser-based implementation, use of Angular-JS [23] may be worth considering. For client-side applications running on mobile applications, consider using the software development kit (SDK) recommended for the mobile device operating system. Applications using augmented reality (AR) technology should run on mobile devices including smart glasses. Typically, smart glasses run the same operating system that mobile devices do. Using the AR application development studio, it should be possible to generate an application that runs on both mobile devices and smart glasses.

4.12   Cyber Security

As shown in the digital twin solution architecture diagram, data security must be provided for data in motion as well as data at rest. Access to the digital twin should be made available only to registered users and applications. Various security considerations are as follows.

- Securing data coming from physical objects is handled by the IoT gateway. Communication with the physical object should meet cyber security standards through public and private key encryption.

- IoT device registration service will ensure that only authenticated physical objects will be sending data.
- Digital twin users should be authenticated against the enterprise level directory of usernames and passwords.
- Role-based access control (RBAC) must be implemented, i.e., some users may have only read-access, some may have read-write and some will have administrator level access. Only administrators should be allowed to create or delete new digital twin instances.
- External applications, which want to get data from the digital twin or send data to the digital twin, must be registered in the enterprise level directory and should be given credentials.
- Data exchanged with the external application should comply with cyber-security standards through public and private key encryption.

4.13   Use Case Coverage

In the table below, we verify that the use cases we reviewed earlier are fulfilled by the digital twin services and applications.

	Use case functionality	Use cases	Digital twin component	Explanation
1	Visualization of object status including alerts	1, 2, 3, 9, 15	Query processor, user interface	User interface will send a query. Query processor will send queries to the appropriate data stores, collect the response and return to user interface.
2	Show calculated (not actual) values of specified properties	14	Virtual sensor	Virtual sensor will calculate values based on a model of how the physical object operates.

(Continued)

(*Continued*)

3	Enriched data, i.e., show all maintenance issues resolved, related to the current issue/status.	8	User interface, query processor, special application	User interface and query processor are described earlier. Special application will be written to get maintenance ticket data.
4	Predict remaining useful life	7	ML model for forecasting, user interface	Predict values of certain variables based on model
5	Automatic recommendation and notification generation	6, 11, 12	ML model for anomaly detection, generate recommendations, rule base, generate notifications, orchestrator	ML model will be used to detect anomalies. Generate recommendations, which is a custom application, will be used decide what recommendation to make based on a Rule Base. Recommendations will be sent as notifications. Through the orchestrator service, multiple services will be invoked as required.
6	Work instructions for operating and for repairing a component	5, 10, 13	Custom augmented reality (AR) application	A custom AR application will be created using AR studio tool.

(*Continued*)

(*Continued*)

7	Comparison of actual against planned performance	4	Custom application	Custom application will compare actual performance of the object against expected performance.
8	Write ad-hoc applications	16	Custom application	Custom application will access data produced by the digital twin.
9	Order Spare part	17	Custom application	Custom application will use the spare part management system API to place an order for the spare part.
10	Receive production planning schedule	18	API to receive planning schedule data.	Production planning application will use the digital twin API to set the planning schedule.

4.14   Future Direction and Trends

The digital twin value proposition is quite strong across many industry verticals such as manufacturing, healthcare services and real-estate management to name a few.

After building a digital twin, it will be possible to integrate it with other digital twins, thus forming a digital twin eco-system. When digital twins from different organizations are integrated, the digital thread will be formed. For example, in manufacturing, the digital twin that virtualizes product design can integrate with the digital twin for a machine that produces the product, which can further integrate with the digital twin that simulates the quality process and the shipping process. An end-to-end digital thread built by linking digital twins will provide actionable insight into the operation of the entire supply chain.

In the future, as the digital thread gets implemented between various organizations, blockchain technology may be used to implement a distributed ledger. Depending on the business requirements, the digital twin will be integrated with a blockchain. As an example, suppose the grinding machine digital twin detects that the grinding wheel needs to be ordered from a 3rd party supplier. In that case, the digital twin will place an order with the supplier through a blockchain API.

Digital twin consortium [24] will accelerate the formation of standards and will thereby promote interoperability between digital twins. Glossary of digital twin [25] will be helpful in better understanding of the digital twin terminology and will help in increasing the speed of development.

4.15   Conclusion

Since there are many technology disciplines at work in the digital twin, including IoT, artificial intelligence and machine learning, simulation, augmented reality, messaging and cyber-security, architecting a digital twin could be a daunting task. Many papers have been written to describe the components of a digital twin. This work shows a systematic, comprehensive and step-by-step approach to design the digital twin solution architecture for a physical object.

The foundational digital twin components are process model, analytics, visualization, and notification. Depending on the business case, it may be useful to create work instruction applications. Knowledge base and the capability to send commands to the physical object through the IoT gateway can be added in a later phase.

After implementing the digital twin, it will be essential to continuously refine it so that it tracks the physical object well. For example, if there is a difference between the value calculated by the digital twin and the actual value, that difference will have to be minimized by tweaking the model implementing within the digital twin.

References

1. Ontologies for various objects, https://schema.org/docs/documents.html.
2. Digital Twin Definition Language, https://github.com/Azure/opendigitaltwins-dtdl/blob/master/DTDL/v2/dtdlv2.md#digital-twins-definition-language, 2020.

3. GraphQL, https://graphql.org/learn/schema/, 2015.
4. JSON for Linking Data (JSON-LD), https://json-ld.org/, 2010.
5. Web Ontology Language (OWL), https://en.wikipedia.org/wiki/Web_Ontology_Language, 2009.
6. OPC/UA, https://opcfoundation.org/about/opc-technologies/opc-ua/, 2006.
7. ModBus protocol, https://modbus.org/, 2005.
8. ProfiNet protocol, https://us.profinet.com/technology/profinet/, 2003.
9. ProfiBus protocol, https://www.profibus.com/, 2003.
10. WiFi protocol, https://www.wi-fi.org, 2000.
11. BlueTooth protocol, https://www.bluetooth.com, 1998.
12. Ethernet IP protocol, https://www.odva.org/technology-standards/key-technologies/ethernet-ip/, 2001.
13. AMQP protocol, https://www.amqp.org/resources/specifications, 2011.
14. MQTT protocol, https://mqtt.org/mqtt-specification/, 1999.
15. Azuma, R., Overview of Augmented Reality. *ACM SIGGRAPH 2004 Course Notes*, https://dl.acm.org/doi/abs/10.1145/1103900.1103926, 2005.
16. NumPy Library. https://numpy.org/doc/stable/reference/, 2015.
17. TensorFlow Library, https://www.tensorflow.org/learn, 2015.
18. Java Messaging Library, https://docs.oracle.com/javaee/6/tutorial/doc/bncdq.html, 2013.
19. Kafka, https://kafka.apache.org/intro, 2011.
20. ZeroMQ, https://zeromq.org/languages/python/, 2011.
21. Swagger, https://swagger.io/, 2011.
22. PostMan, https://www.postman.com/, 2014.
23. AngularJS. https://angularjs.org/, 2010.
24. Digital Twin Consortium, https://www.digitaltwinconsortium.org/, 2021.
25. Glossary of Digital Twins, https://www.digitaltwinconsortium.org/glossary/index.htm#digital-twin-applications, 2021.
26. Enders, M.R. and Hoßbach, N., Dimensions of Digital Twin Applications-A Literature Review Completed Research, in: *Technical report*, 2019.
27. Tao, F., Zhang, H., Liu, A., Nee, A.Y., Digital twin in industry: State-of-the-art. *IEEE Trans. Ind. Inf.*, 15, 2405–2415, 2019.
28. Kritzinger, W., Karner, M., Traar, G., Henjes, J., Sihn, W., Digital twin in manufacturing: A categorical literature review and classification, in: *IFAC-Papers online*, vol. 51, pp. 1016–1022, 2018.
29. Negri, E., Fumagalli, L., Macchi, M., A review of the roles of digital twin in CPS-based production systems. *Proc. Manuf.*, 11, 939–948, 2017.
30. Ríos, J., Hernández, J.C., Oliva, M., Mas, F., Product avatar as digital counterpart of a physical individual product: Literature review and implications in an aircraft. *Adv. Transdiscipl. Eng.*, 2, 657–666, 2015.
31. Grieves, M. and Vickers, J., Digital twin: Mitigating unpredictable, undesirable emergent behavior in complex systems, in: *Trans-Disciplinary Perspectives on System Complexity*, F.-J. Kahlen, S. Flumerfelt, and A. Alves, (eds.), p. 85–114, Springer, Switzerland, 2016.

32. Rathore, M., Shah, S., Shukla, D., Bentafat, E., Bakiras, S., The role of AI, machine learning, and big data in digital twinning: A systematic literature review, challenges, and opportunities, in: *IEEE Access*, vol. 9, pp. 32030–32052, 2021.

33. Ghita, M. and Siham, B., Digital twin development architectures and deployment technologies: Moroccan use case. *(IJACSA) Int. J. Adv. Comput. Sci. Appl.*, 11, 2, p. 468–478, 2020.

34. Munoz, P., Troya J., Vallecillo, A., Using UML and OCL models to realize high-level digital twins, in: *2021 ACM/IEEE International Conference on Model Driven Engineering Languages and Systems Companion (MODELS-C)*, pp. 212–220, Fukuoka, Japan, 2021.

35. Alam, K.M. and El Saddik, A., C2PS: A digital twin architecture reference model for the cloud-based cyber-physical systems, in: *IEEE Access*, vol. 5, pp. 2050–2062, 2017.

36. Grieves, M., Virtually intelligent product systems: Digital and physical twins, in complex systems engineering: Theory and practice, S. Flumerfelt, *et al.* (eds.), American Institute of Aeronautics and Astronautics. p. 175-200, 2019.

37. Hasan, H.R., Salah, K., Jayraman, R., Omar, M., Yaqoob, I., Pesic, S., Taylor, T., Boscovic, D., A blockchain-based approach for the creation of digital twins, in: *IEEE Access*, vol. 8, pp. 34113–34126, 2020.

Role of Digital Twin Technology in Medical Sector—Toward Ensuring Safe Healthcare

S.N. Kumar[1]*, A. Lenin Fred[2], L.R. Jonisha Miriam[3], Christina Jane I.[3], H. Ajay Kumar[3], Parasuraman Padmanabhan[4] and Balazs Gulyas[4]

[1]Department of EEE, Amal Jyothi College of Engineering, Kanjirapally, Kerala, India
[2]Department of CSE, Mar Ephraem College of Engineering and Technology, Marthandam, Tamil Nadu, India
[3]Department of ECE, Mar Ephraem College of Engineering and Technology, Marthandam, Tamil Nadu, India
[4]Lee Kong Chian School of Medicine, Nanyang Technological University, Singapore, Singapore

Abstract

In today's scenario, digital technology is gaining prominence in different sectors like business, healthcare, education, security, aerospace, construction, automotive, etc. Digital twin technology is a novel technology. It represents virtually physical objects or process. The basic building block of a digital twin is internet of things (IoT) and the goal of digital twin technology is to create, test, and validate in the virtual environment. In the perspective of the healthcare sector, the digital twin virtually represents physical entity or process. The chapter organization is as follows: introduction to digital twin technology, generic applications of the digital twin, the role of digital twin technology in healthcare, and finally, the conclusion.

Keywords: Digital twin, IoT, big data, telemedicine, COVID 19, healthcare

Corresponding author: appu123kumar@gmail.com

Manisha Vohra (ed.) Digital Twin Technology: Fundamentals and Applications, (77–96) © 2023 Scrivener Publishing LLC

5.1   Introduction to Digital Twin

Digital Twin technology is an emerging concept [28]. A digital twin means virtual representation of a real thing or item. The digital twin's mechanism incorporates sensors connected to the physical object that capture data, such as physical, manufacturing, and operating data. Internet of Things (IoT), Big Data Analytics, artificial intelligence (AI), and automation solutions play a prominent role in Industry 4.0 and are deployed in the formulation of digital twin [1]. Digital twin provides virtual representations of systems along their lifecycle [53]. Digital twin application includes real-time monitoring, maintenance, etc. [52].

Healthcare, construction, automotive IoT, retail, and smart cities are among the sectors impacted by digital twins. The digital twin primary idea entails collecting information from the various networks and platforms that are related. Following data collection, data are redirected to the digital environment through sensors for further study. Analytics techniques are used to generate observations, which are made possible by algorithms. The primary aim of the digital twin is to recognize any opportunities for improving quality and performance, lowering costs, and alerting the physical twin to any unexpected changes [2]. This digital twin has a big influence in all fields [3], and the engineering phases of the digital twin are comprised three phases:

  (a) design phase,
  (b) build phase, and
  (c) operational phase.

Design phase: In this phase, the actual parts are brought together and converted into a virtual component using a specific software. Separate elements or components are correlated with one another and brought into production compatible with the operation.

Build phase: This phase focuses on yield and demonstrates how the product has been changed or adjusted to meet the requirements. It is all about keeping the product within the design parameters. It also requires fine manufacturing techniques to get the components within the necessary tolerances. As a result, the product or final assembly produces sufficient operating and functional performance.

Operational phase: Using a digital twin, the whole system's output can be accurately predicted. This often reveals the system's real age or the length of time the device has been used under various terrestrial environments. They also have necessary details about how they respond to changes in weather and climate. It also provides accurate information on changes in tolerance effects during the operating and work phases. It is done to enhance the operation process, and recalibration happens in conjunction with feedback.

5.2   Generic Applications of Digital Twin

The digital twin is a new intelligent manufacturing technology that can understand the status of industrial automation systems in real-time and forecast device failures. In He and Kai-Jian [4], the related material of industrial automation is first examined and includes industrial automation devices, processes, and facilities.

The long-term viability of intelligent production is often addressed. Following that, a digital twin and its implementation, as well as the advancement of industrial automation based on digital twin technology, are discussed. Finally, the potential growth path of intelligent production is discussed in conjunction with the existing state. Two main characteristics of digital twin technology are as follows:

(a) each description stresses the relationship between the physical model and its simulated equivalent; and

(b) second, sensors are used to produce real-time data, which is used to create the relation. The computer modeling model of a digital twin is used to create a solid model, which is then extended to product packaging and assembly to gain accurate quality control. The manufacturing process simulation, automated production line, and equipment status tracking are all included [4].

A digital twin paradigm is able to continuously monitor complex engineering systems [5]. For making the maintenance of a system better throughout the entire lifecycle of a system, digital twin are very useful and efficient. Till now digital twin has not yet realized its complete potential but still it many advantages in different sectors including healthcare. The characteristics of the digital twin are represented in Figure 5.1. Artificial intelligence gains much prominence in the digital twin since it can be called the heart of the digital twin, and each digital twin has a unique identifier. The sensors are deployed to sense the input parameters, the security and trust aspect is vital for any digital twin model. Communication and representation are other notable features that help the users interact with the digital world.

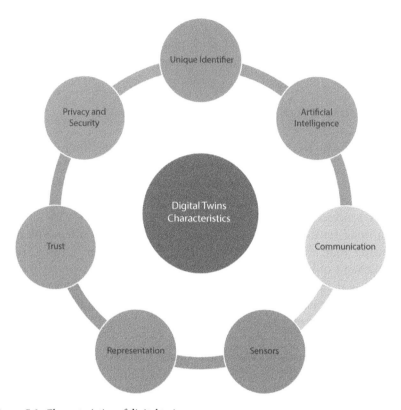

Figure 5.1 Characteristics of digital twin.

In Wei *et al.* [6], a model continuity preservation approach for the computer numerical control machine tool (CNCMT) machine tool (MT) digital twin is detailed. To begin, the architecture for the digital twin model's quality preservation approach is structured to include both digital and physical space. In digital space, the concepts of data processing and output attenuation upgrades are discussed. The CNCMT digital twin model is then investigated in terms of performance parameters and a case study for the development and deployment of a high-fidelity test bench digital twin model is conducted to demonstrate the proposed method's implementation flow and effectiveness. Data management is concerned about data that have been derived from the physical environment. Following data preprocessing, modeling information is stored as standard working conditions for later use, which requires CNCMT digital twin model status changes and system updates. The three aspects of the performance attenuation update theory are

- model performance attenuation update,
- updated CNCMT digital twin model design,
- model validation.

The goal of the work of Agnusdei *et al.* [8] is to examine the various domains in which digital twins can be used to ensure system safety. To assess the actual state of knowledge VOSviewer was used to do a bibliometric analysis to assess studies and implementations of digital twins in engineering and computer science, as well as to classify academic groups and potential trends. The results show that digital twin systems have been validated and built in recent years to assist operators in routine and emergencies, as well as to improve their ability to monitor safety levels [8].

Using a digital twin and minimal field telemetry, the Particle Swarm Optimization solution was able to decide the optimum PF in RT, demonstrating that digital twins of feeders can solve field measurement limitations to generate state estimations and create centrally optimized distributed energy resource (DER) set points. The results also show that using power hardware-in-the-loop (PHIL) will aid in identifying any coordination issues that could exist before deploying any DER control in the sector [9].

The digital twin with a paradigm shift, described in Glaessgen and Stargel [10], integrates ultrahigh precision simulation with the vehicle's onboard advanced vehicle health management system. The approach employed in Tuegel *et al.* [11] uses an ultrahigh precision model of individual aircraft by tail number, known as a digital twin, to calculate structural deflections and temperatures in response to flight conditions, as well as resulting local disruption and material state evolution.

The Digital Twin model requires massive amounts of information and computing capability. Its progression will rely on advances in computer and communications technology. The Digital Twin is about information. While much has been written about information, it still is a relatively fuzzy concept. Many focus on the "inform" part of information and deal with it as a transmission issue. However, the core premise for the Digital Twin model is that information is a replacement for wasted physical resources, i.e., time, energy, and material [12]. The vehicular digital twin captures real-time data from sensors and compares it to data collected previously from the same vehicle. Based on these results, the digital twin will decide whether or not to issue a warning in the event of a dangerous condition. The framework concept introduced in this paper would aid in addressing the safety and security issues. The suggested model aims to detect, analyze, and quantify risks, as well as provide the consumer with the ability to take a proactive response to ensure protection and security in self-driving cars using digital twins [13]. An aircraft health monitoring system based on digital twin using dynamic Bayesian network was proposed in Li *et al.* [14].

The comparative analysis of big data and digital twin was proposed in Qi and Tao [15], and it highlights the usage of the digital twin in a cyber-physical system. The challenges in cyber-physical production systems (CPPS) are highlighted in the study of Park *et al.* [16]. Implementation of the cyber-physical system in industrial manufacturing is called CPPS. A digital twin is a key factor in CPPS, It is used to improve performance. The key role of the Internet of Things and digital twin in the healthcare sector is described in the study of Patrone *et al.* [17].

The real-time data monitoring and aiding the physicians and patients are also highlighted in this work. A model-based definition for digital twin was proposed in the study of Miller *et al.* [18]. To create a path for the required digital twin using model-based definition was difficult and unclear. To overcome this problem, the behavioral information was integrated with the shape. The model-based definition framework was implemented using 3D CAD software. It achieves high efficiency [18].

A digital twin technique and the genetic algorithm were proposed for structural health management of aircraft. The undetected structural damage in the aircraft leads to loss of control of the craft. To avoid this load level of aircraft must be below the load-carrying capacity. To find the load-carrying capacity, the wave propagation response and genetic algorithm are used. Thus, it yields high accuracy [19].

The optimized sensor locations based on a digital twin fiber-optic-based sensing net of unmanned aerial vehicle (UAV) was proposed in [20]. By estimating the boom reaction to both the static and dynamic loading during a ground test fiber Bragg grating (FBG) point sensors are used. As received by a fiber-optic sensing net, to be subsequently utilized as a digital twin stage for optimizing sensor areas is used for precise contamination identification. Moreover, for the second phase, a similar FBG sensing net was utilized to take the loading spectra and dynamic behavior of boom during flight. For optimizing, an structural health monitoring (SHM) damage detecting framework, the digital twin is utilized for damage detection ought to be a cost-effective technique. The remaining useful life prediction for offshore wind turbine power converter with digital twin framework was proposed in Sivalingam *et al.* [21].

The digital twin (digital twin) has given a promising chance to carry out smart assembling by incorporating the digital and actual universe in manufacturing. The assistance adapted architecture may grow the elements of digital twin. Through maintenance, digital twin can have high expected applications in architecture, manufacturing, and prognostic and health management (PHM). Therefore, it needs significantly more attempts to improve the techniques for digital twin designing and service [22].

5.3   Digital Twin Applications in Medical Field

The different modules of a typical digital twin in medical field application are depicted in Figure 5.2. The first module is data acquisition and in the medical field, data are acquired from smart health devices.

The second module deals with data storage and cloud computing are widely used. The third module deals with data analysis and AI, machine

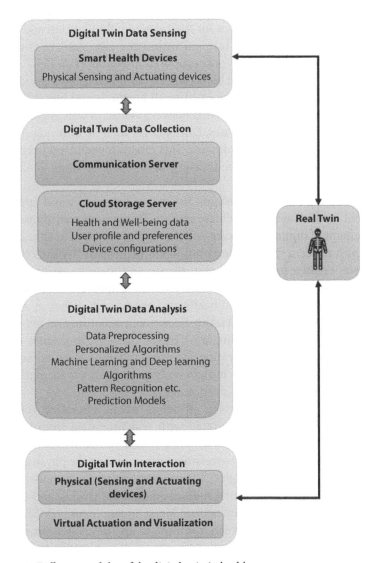

Figure 5.2 Different modules of the digital twin in healthcare.

learning algorithms are mainly used. The fourth module is termed digital twin interaction and deals with the interpretation of analyzed results and taking corrective measures.

5.3.1   Biosignal and Physiological Parameters Analysis for Body Area Network

An architecture prototype for a countywide blood management system that uses the Internet of Things and digital twin to allow any hospital or blood bank in the area to search for their desired blood group and donate to the nearest blood bank or hospital within the city, state, or country if there is an excess blood supply was proposed in Shaikh *et al.* [25].

Data on hospitals and blood banks will be compiled using a cloud-based software application that will be open to all hospitals and blood banks in the world. These records will provide delivery status, as well as global positioning system (GPS) coordinates. Donors may include information, such as their address and GPS coordinates. This research would aid in reducing blood waste and improving the transportation of blood units to all places of need [25].

Using the digital twin paradigm, this paper introduces and applies an intelligent context-aware healthcare system. This system contributes to the advancement of digital healthcare and the improvement of healthcare processes. As a result, a machine learning-based ECG heart rhythms classifier model was created to identify heart disease and identify cardiac attacks. Combining digital twin and healthcare will improve healthcare processes by bringing patients and healthcare providers together in an intelligent, inclusive, and flexible Health-Ecosystem, according to the results. Implementing an electrocardiogram (ECG) classifier to predict cardiac problems also serves as inspiration for using machine learning and artificial intelligence with various human body measurements for statistically controlling and abnormality detection [26].

The digital twin improves the efficiency of the operating rooms in healthcare, which was demonstrated with real-time data from hospitals through ANOVA analysis, which avoids artificial variability [27].

Digital twins is used for gait assessment in simulating the physical mechanism of lower body joint angles. The memory polynomial model is used to reduce the number of inertial measurement units (IMU), and the performance is evaluated with Normalized Mean Square Error (NMSE) [29].

Five-dimensional digital twin techniques are developed from three dimensions but they won't produce accurate results for healthcare. To overcome this problem, a five-dimensional digital twin technique is developed for prognostic health management. The objective is to obtain high accuracy and efficiency in prognostic health management. It combines both virtual and physical interaction to obtain accurate data. Results show that the digital twin technique was efficient and useful for high-value data monitoring [30].

A digital twin (digital twin) based hospital services for discrete event simulation incorporating with healthcare and IoT information framework was proposed in Karakra et al. [31]. This method empowers surveying the productivity of existing medical services and assessing the effect of changes in services without disrupting the everyday movement of hospitals. The developed digital twin method vitalized several key clinic health delivery services, based on the applicable information recovered progressively. Even though the model reacts to four administrations, at first as proof of the idea, however, it develops an overall system, which can be extended to incorporate different services. This method should consider evaluation strategies for surveying how the dependability of the method at producing solid outcomes. The digital twin gains importance in gait analysis and rehabilitation. The memory polynomial model was found to be efficient in the design of digital twins with a low normalized mean square error value of -20dB [32].

For Singapore's Greenfield hospital, the authors in [33] have showcased that a digital twin of its future operations with robotic process automation (RPA) solutions can actually help for productivity improvement.

The importance of the digital twin in the biologic manufacturing industry is highlighted in [34]. The human virtual model by digital twin finds its application in cyber-physical systems for continuous monitoring of physiological parameters [35].

5.3.2   Medicinal Drug Delivery

In cancer treatment and rehabilitation, the digital twin is gaining prominence. Researchers use Ansys and computational fluid dynamics in traditional drug delivery, where healthy cells are often killed due to chemotherapeutic drugs distributed by aerosol because of misinterpretation of healthy tissues. The Computational Bio fluidics and Biomechanics Laboratory (CBBL) at Oklahoma State University discovered that 20% of the inhaled substance meets the target. The stimulation of aerosol particles was studied using a digital twin model of the respiratory system, CT/MR imaging is used to build patient-specific digital twins.

The digital twin technology was found to be proficient in the drug delivery using dendrite, a novel nanomaterial, the precision of drug delivery was improved through the usage of digital twin [41]. The statistical and mechanistic techniques when coupled with digital twin enable precision cardiology healthcare. The data analyzed are used for the treatment and prediction of disease [42].

The virtual liver, an application of digital twin enables the physicians to model the anatomy of the liver, disease analysis, and effect of treatment and impact of drug [43]. The digital twin with artificial intelligence was employed for the analysis of people with multiple sclerosis for analyzing the clinical parameters [43].

The importance of digital twins in the biopharmaceutical industry is highlighted in [44], the role of the digital twin in personalized medicine and the pharmaceutical industry was also highlighted in Portela *et al.* [45].

5.3.3   Surgical Preplanning

The concept of a surgical digital twin is the concept that a patient model is developed, and the procedure can be prepared in a multidisciplinary team group, practiced beforehand in a simulator, and referred to throughout the procedure to check anatomy and prevent inadvertent structural harm [47]. This real-time patient model could also lead to clinical trials in which experimental tools, procedures, or treatments are tested first on the digital twin, reducing patient risk. Visual reality systems, in combination with digital twins, will improve surgical preparation for residents by allowing the simulated experience in the sense of and patient's unique anatomical and physiological difference, as well as offering a practical account of success with the potential to calculate intraoperative parameters. Aneurysms are a form of neurodegenerative disease affected by the enlargement of blood vessels. They affect about 2% of the population. Clots form, strokes occur, and death occurs. In surgical preplanning of neuro disorders, the digital twin gains importance [48].

In Chakshu *et al.* [49], inverse research is used to suggest a framework for enabling cardiovascular digital twins for inverse analysis of nonlinear processes, such as blood flow in the coronary system (systemic circulation) using a recurrent neural network and a virtual patient database. With the aid of long short-term memory (LSTM) cells, blood pressure waveforms in various vessels of the body are inversely measured by inputting pressure waveforms from three noninvasively open blood vessels (carotid, femoral, and brachial arteries). Using neural networks, the inverse analysis method created in this way is used to diagnose abdominal aortic aneurysm (AAA) and its magnitude. A digital twin, or simulated simulation of a person, can aid in patient-oriented diagnosis by providing a constant stream of data, improving precision. The digital twin is of three types they are active digital twin, which monitors and updates for every circulation, a passive digital twin, which is used as offline mode, and a semiactive digital twin, which uses the data from offline mode and do the processing online. A database containing computationally generated, reliable blood pressure waveforms are initially developed using a reduced-order model and machine learning. The neural network is then programmed and configured to model uncertain blood pressure waveforms using open waveforms as input data. At last, to diagnose and determine the extent of abdominal aortic aneurysms, an additional neural network is designed to evaluate the waveforms predicted from the inverse model (AAA) [49].

In the surgical process, data mining is applied to a huge amount of real medical data for probability distribution calculation using plant simulation software. The digital twins are based on simulation for surgical process using discrete event approach and optimize accordingly [50]. The carotid stenosis severity in patients was sensed by the digital twin based on head vibrations. The computer vision algorithm was developed to sense the *in vivo* head vibrations [51].

5.3.4   COVID 19 Screening and Diagnosis

Personal digital twins (Pdigital twins) can synchronize all sources of information, including:

- electronic health reports (EHRs),
- healthcare data,
- patient portals,
- public records,
- laptops,
- wearable devices,
- IoT gadgets,
- social networks, and more.

This synchronization is to provide a comprehensive picture of one's health. Pdigital twins can be used in combination with machine learning (ML) algorithms to anticipate various user conditions, identify early symptoms for preventive steps, predict the transformation from normal states, and allow the estimation of optimal care and also therapeutics.

A new structure for the human-robot collaborative (HRC) alliance is introduced in [54], which is based on the digital twin (digital twin). The proposed framework's data processing structure incorporates all types of data from digital twin environments. The double deep deterministic policy gradient (D-DDPG) is used as an optimization procedure in digital twin to obtain the HRC strategy and action sequence in a complex setting. The consistency model was used to analyze the consistency of durability configuration during installation.

Finally, an alternator configuration case is used to test the suggested framework, demonstrating that digital twin-based HRC integration improves module performance and protection significantly. The concept proposed by Michael Grieves consisted of all the elements of digital twin:

- real space,
- virtual space,
- the link for data flow from real space to virtual space,
- the link for information flow from virtual space to real space and virtual sub-spaces [24].

It uses a digital model to map all of the components of the physical environment into the virtual environment. Physical sensors capture environmental data in real-time, and the assembly technique is optimized synchronously. The assembly task and the state of the assembly mechanism are predicted using the prediction module. Here, reinforcement learning (RL) is used as the optimal model for the digital twin.

The proposed digital twin architecture for HRC assembly consists of four parts:

(a) physical assembly space,
(b) virtual assembly space,
(c) data management system, and
(d) digital twin data.

The digital twin-based HRC assembly system's virtual assembly space is mapped to the actual assembly space. The compilation of real-time data is used to track HRC assembly using physical sensors. The digital equipment increases real-time data storage and enhances mutual strategy simulation. The RL model used in assembly offers the best action sequence and increases the assembly system's learning ability. Based on the recognition of human assembly actions, the robot can make auxiliary preparations ahead of time. Data interface among digital twin layers improves assembly system interoperability [54].

An IoT monitoring system called Health@Hand real-time monitors vital and administrative data in the digital twin of intensive care unit (ICU) for assisting the medical experts with a visual interface for management and medical data [55]. In the COVID 19 scenario, the telemedicine role is inevitable in ensuring efficient healthcare and minimizing the interaction with others, and saves time [57].

The digital twin ensures the efficient design of ventilators and the robotic workers are utilized in factories for the manufacturing of ventilators [7]. The digital twin of the patient's lungs helps to battle COVID 19, the patient-specific digital twin helps to ensure efficient pulmonary healthcare [23].

5.4   Ongoing and Future Applications of Digital Twin in Healthcare Sector

The issues in the modern healthcare sector are analyzed in Volkov *et al.* [36] and the role of the digital twin in solving the challenges is highlighted through IoT and artificial intelligence termed smart healthcare. A detailed study on applications of the digital twin in the industry, smart city, and healthcare sector is discussed [37].

The formulation of a digital twin for multiple sclerosis is highlighted in Voigt *et al.* [38] for clinical decision making; however, before using it for decision making in disease prediction, the model has to be studied in detail and verified by the experts. The proficiency of the digital twin would make it suitable for personalized medicine and public healthcare [39].

The digital twin has its role in virology too, the AI aids the digital twin technology in disease prediction and current state by fetching medical data from patients subjected to viral infection (COVID 19) [40].

A detailed review on the importance of digital twins in tissue culture was carried out in paper [46]. Digital twin is analyzed and presented with respect to COVID-19 in paper [56], digital twin role in personalized healthcare was stated in Wickramasinghe *et al.* [56], three models of a digital twin for healthcare highlighted;

(a) gray box digital twin,
(b) surrogate digital twin, and
(c) black box digital twin.

The black box digital twin was found to be satisfactory for uterine cancer care.

5.5   Conclusion

This chapter pays attention on the concept of the digital twin and its importance. The characteristics and engineering phases of digital with generic applications are also highlighted in this work. The applications of the digital twin in the medical field are mainly highlighted in this work.

In the medical field, the digital twin of patients and medical devices are gaining prominence. The digital twin of patients deals with the transfer of patients' data into the digital world. The digital twin technology is closely related to telemedicine in the data storage and transfer for precise disease diagnosis, as well as for surgical preplanning and guidance.

IoT-based devices are widely used in the healthcare sector for monitoring the physiological parameters and Body Area Network employs wearable sensor devices for data acquisition and transfer. The digital twin highly relies on machine learning and big data and in the future, digital twin technology is going to be dominant in all fields providing optimum solutions, especially in the healthcare industry.

Acknowledgments

The authors would like to acknowledge the support provided by DST under the IDP scheme (no. IDP/MED/03/2015). Parasuraman Padmanabhan and BalazsGulyas also acknowledge the support from Lee Kong Chian School of Medicine and Data Science and AI Research (DSAIR) center of NTU (Project Number ADH-11/2017-DSAIR and the support from the Cognitive NeuroImaging Centre (CONIC) at NTU. Author S.N Kumar would also like to acknowledge the support provided by the Schmitt Centre for Biomedical Instrumentation (SCBMI) of Amal Jyothi College of Engineering.

References

1. Minerva, R., Lee, G.M., Crespi, N., Digital twin in the IoT context: A survey on technical features, scenarios, and architectural models. *Proceedings of the IEEE*, vol. 108, pp. 1785–824, 2020 Jun 18.
2. Madni, A.M., Madni, C.C., Lucero, S.D., Leveraging digital twin technology in model-based systems engineering. *Systems.*, 7, 1, 7, 2019 Mar.
3. Shahat, E., Hyun, C.T., Yeom, C., City digital twin potentials: A review and research agenda. *Sustainability*, 13, 6, 3386, 2021 Jan.
4. He, B. and Bai, K.J., Digital twin-based sustainable intelligent manufacturing: A review. *Adv. Manuf.*, 9, 1, 1–21, 2021.

5. D'Amico, D., Ekoyuncu, J., Addipalli, S., Smith, C., Keedwell, E., Sibson, J., Penver, S., Conceptual framework of a digital twin to evaluate the degradation status of complex engineering systems. *Procedia CIRP*, 86, 617, 2020

6. Wei, Y., Hu, T., Zhou, T., Ye, Y., Luo, W., Consistency retention method for CNC machine tool digital twin model. *J. Manuf. Syst.*, 58, 313–322, 2021.

7. Malik, A. A., Masood, T., Kousar, R., Repurposing factories with robotics in the face of COVID-19. *Sci. Robot.*, 5, 43, 2020.

8. Agnusdei, G.P., Elia, V., Gnoni, M.G., Is digital twin technology supporting safety management? A bibliometric and systematic review. *Appl. Sci.*, 11, 6, 2767, 2021.

9. Darbari-Zamora, R., Johnson, J., Summers, A., Jones, C. B., Hansen, C., Showalter, C., State estimation-based distributed energy resource optimization for distribution voltage regulation in telemetry-sparse environments using a real-time digital twin. *Energies*, 14, 774, 2021.

10. Glaessgen, E. and Stargel, D., The digital twin paradigm for future NASA and US Air Force vehicles. *53rd AIAA/ASME/ASCE/AHS/ASC structures, structural dynamics and materials conference 20th AIAA/ASME/AHS adaptive structures conference 14th AIAA*, 2012.

11. Tuegel, E.J., Ingraffea, A.R., Eason, T.G., Spottswood, S.M., Reengineering aircraft structural life prediction using a digital twin. *Int. J. Aerospc. Eng.*, 2011, 1–14, 2011.

12. Grieves, M. and Vickers, J., Digital twin: Mitigating unpredictable, undesirable emergent behavior in complex systems, in: *Transdisciplinary Perspectives on Complex Systems*, Kahlen FJ, S. Flumerfelt, A. Alves (Eds.), pp. 85–113, Springer, Cham, 2017, doi: https://doi.org/10.1007/978-3-319-38756-7_4.

13. Almeaibed, S. *et al.*, Digital twin analysis to promote safety and security in autonomous vehicles. *IEEE Commun. Standard Mag.*, 5, 1, 40–46, 2021.

14. Li, C., Mahadevan, S., Ling, Y., Choze, S., Wang, L., Dynamic Bayesian network for aircraft wing health monitoring digital twin. *AIAA J.*, 55, 3, 930–941, 2017 Mar.

15. Qi, Q. and Tao, F., Digital twin and big data towards smart manufacturing and industry 4.0: 360 degree comparison. *IEEE Access*, 6, 3585–93, 2018 Jan 15.

16. Park, H., Easwaran, A., Andalam, S., Challenges in digital twin development for cyber-physical production systems. *Cyber Phys. Syst. Model-Based Design*, 4, 28–48, 2018.

17. Patrone, C., Lattuada, M., Galli, G., Revetria, R., The role of internet of things and digital twin in healthcare digitalization process, in: *In The World Congress on Engineering and Computer Science*, Springer, Singapore, pp. 30–37, 2018 Oct 23.

18. Miller, A.M., Alvarez, R., Hartman, N., Towards an extended model-based definition for the digital twin. *Comput.-Aided Design Appl.*, 15, 6, 880–991, 2018 Nov 2.

19. Seshadri, B.R. and Krishnamurthy, T., Structural health management of damaged aircraft structures using digital twin concept, in: *25th AIAA/AHS Adaptive Structures Conference*, p. 1675, 2017

20. Kressel, I., Ben-Simon, U., Shoham, S., Don-Yehiya, G., Sheinkman, S., Davidi, R., Tur, M., Optimal location of a fiber-optic-based sensing net for SHM applications using a digital twin, in: *9th European Workshop on Structural Health Monitoring, Manchester*, UK, pp. 10–13, 2018 Jul.

21. Sivalingam, K., Sepulveda, M., Spring, M., Davies, P., A review and methodology development for remaining useful life prediction of offshore fixed and floating wind turbine power converter with digital twin technology perspective, in: *2018 2nd International Conference on Green Energy and Applications (ICGEA)*, IEEE, pp. 197–204, 2018 Mar 24.

22. Qi, Q., Tao, F., Zuo, Y., Zhao, D., Digital twin service towards smart manufacturing. *Proc. Cirp.*, 72, 237–242, 2018 Jan 1.

23. Feng, Y., Chen, X., Zhao, J., Create the individualized digital twin for non-invasive precise pulmonary healthcare. *Signif. Bioeng. Biosci.*, 1, 2, 2018. SBE.000507.

24. Grieves, M. and Vickers, J., Digital twin: Mitigating unpredictable, undesirable emergent behavior in complex systems, in: *Transdisciplinary Perspectives on Complex Systems*, Kahlen F.J., S. Flumerfelt, A. Alves (Eds.), pp. 85–113, Springer, Cham, 2017, https://doi.org/10.1007/978-3-319-38756-7_4.

25. Shaikh, F. and Karwande, V., Analysis on nation's blood management system and wastage using internet of things and digital twin. *Open Access Int. J. of Sci. & Eng.*, 6, 1–4, 2021.

26. Elayan, H., Aloqaily, M., Guizani, M., Digital twin for intelligent context-aware IoT healthcare systems. *IEEE Internet Things J.*, 8, 23, 16749–16757, 2021.

27. Patrone, C., Lattuada, M., Galli, G., Revetria, R., The role of internet of things and digital twin in healthcare digitalization process, in: *The World Congress on Engineering and Computer Science*, Springer, Singapore, pp. 30–37, 2018 Oct 23.

28. Fuller, A., Fan, Z., Day, C., Barlow, C., Digital twin: Enabling technologies, issues and open research. *IEEE Access*, 8, 108952–108971, 2020.

29. Alcaraz, J.C., Moghaddamnia, S., Fuhrwerk, M., Peissig, J., Efficiency of the Memory Polynomial Model in Realizing Digital Twins for Gait Assessment, in: *2019 27th European Signal Processing Conference (EUSIPCO)*, IEEE, pp. 1–5, 2019 Sep 2.

30. Tao, F., Zhang, M., Liu, Y., Nee, A.Y., Digital twin driven prognostics and health management for complex equipment. *Cirp Annals.*, 67, 1, 169–72, 2018 Jan 1.

31. Karakra, A., Fontanili, F., Lamine, E., Lamothe, J., Taweel, A., Pervasive computing integrated discrete event simulation for a hospital digital twin, in: *2018 IEEE/ACS 15th International Conference on Computer Systems and Applications (AICCSA)*, IEEE, pp. 1–6, 2018 Oct 1.

32. Alcaraz, J.C., Moghaddamnia, S., Fuhrwerk, M., Peissig, J., Efficiency of the memory polynomial model in realizing digital twins for gait assessment, in: *2019 27th European Signal Processing Conference (EUSIPCO)*, IEEE, pp. 1–5, 2019 Sep 2.

33. Liu, W., Zhang, W., Dutta, B., Wu, Z., Goh, M., Digital twinning for productivity improvement opportunities with robotic process automation: Case of greenfield hospital. *Int. J. Mech. Eng. Robot. Res.*, 9, 2, 258–63, 2020 Feb.

34. Zobel-Roos, S., Schmidt, A., Mestmäcker, F., Mouellef, M., Huter, M., Uhlenbrock, L., Kornecki, M., Lohmann, L., Ditz, R., Strube, J., Accelerating biologics manufacturing by modeling or: Is approval under the QbD and PAT approaches demanded by authorities acceptable without a digital-twin? *Processes*, 7, 2, 94, 2019 Feb.

35. Buldakova, T.I. and Suyatinov, S.I., Hierarchy of human operator models for digital twin, in: *2019 International Russian Automation Conference (RusAutoCon)*, IEEE, pp. 1–5, 2019 Sep 8.

36. Volkov, I., Radchenko, G., Tchernykh, A., Digital twins, Internet of Things and mobile medicine: A review of current platforms to support smart healthcare. *Program Comput. Soft.*, 47, 578–590, 2021.

37. Yang, D., Karimi, H.R., Kaynak, O., Yin, S., Developments of digital twin technologies in industrial, smart city and healthcare sectors: A survey. *Complex Eng. Syst.*, 1, 3, 1–21, 2021.

38. Voigt, I., Inojosa, H., Dillenseger, A., Haase, R., Akgün, K., Ziemssen, T., Digital twins for multiple sclerosis. *Front. Immunol.*, 12, 1556, 2021.

39. Kamel Boulos, M.N. and Zhang, P., Digital twins: From personalized medicine to precision public health. *J. Pers. Med.*, 11, 8, 745, 2021.

40. Laubenbacher, R., Sluka, J.P., Glazier, J.A., Using digital twins in viral infection. *Science (New York, N. Y.)*, 371, 6534, 1105–1106, 2021.

41. Zhu, Y., Liu, C., Pang, Z., Dendrimer-based drug delivery systems for brain targeting. *Biomolecules*, 9, 12, 790, 2019 Dec.

42. Corral-Acero, J., Margara, F., Marciniak, M., Rodero, C., Loncaric, F., Feng, Y., Gilbert, A., Fernandes, J.F., Bukhari, H.A., Wajdan, A., Martinez, M.V., The 'Digital Twin' to enable the vision of precision cardiology. *Eur. Heart J.*, 41, 48, 4556–64, 2020 Dec 21.

43. Subramanian, K., Digital Twin for Drug Discovery and Development—The Virtual Liver, in: *Journal of the Indian Institute of Science*, vol. 1, pp. 1–0, 2020 Oct.

44. Voigt, I., Inojosa, H., Dillenseger, A., Haase, R., Akgün, K., Ziemssen, T., Digital twins for multiple sclerosis. *Front. Immunol.*, 12, 1556, 2021 May 3.

45. Portela, R.M., Varsakelis, C., Richelle, A., Giannelos, N., Pence, J., Dessoy, S., von Stosch, M., When is an in silico representation a digital twin? A biopharmaceutical industry approach to the digital twin concept. *Adv. Biochem. Eng. Biotechnol.*, 176, 35–55, 2021.

46. Möller, J. and Pörtner, R., Digital twins for tissue culture techniques—Concepts, expectations, and state of the art. *Processes*, 9, 3, 447, 2021.

47. Ahmed, H. and Devoto, L., The potential of a digital twin in surgery. *Surg. Innov.*, 3, 1553350620975896, 2020 Dec.

48. Groth, C., Porziani, S., Biancolini, M., Costa, E., Celi, S., Capellini, K., Rochette, M., Morgenthaler, V., The medical digital twin assisted by Reduced Order Models and Mesh Morphing, in: *International CAE Conference*, 2018.

49. Chakshu, N.K., Sazonov, I., Nithiarasu, P., Towards enabling a cardiovascular digital twin for human systemic circulation using inverse analysis. *Biomech. Model. Mechanobiol.*, 20, 449–465, 2021.

50. Galli, G., Patrone, C., Bellam, A.C., Annapareddy, N.R., Revetria, R., Improving process using digital twin: A methodology for the automatic creation of models, in: *Lecture notes in engineering and computer science: Proceedings of the world congress on engineering and computer science*, pp. 22–24, 2019.

51. Chakshu, N.K., Carson, J., Sazonov, I., Nithiarasu, P., A semi-active human digital twin model for detecting severity of carotid stenoses from head vibration—A coupled computational mechanics and computer vision method. *Int. J. Numer. Methods Biomed. Eng.*, 35, 5, e3180, 2019 May.

52. Singh, M., Fuenmayor, E., Hinchy, E.P., Qiao, Y., Murray, N., Devine, D., Digital twin: Origin to future. *Appl. Syst. Innov.*, 4, 36, 2021, https://doi.org/10.3390/asi4020036.

53. Negri, E., Fumagalli, L., Macchi, M.A., Review of the roles of digital twin in CPS-based production systems. *Procedia Manuf.*, 11, 939–948, 2017.

54. Lv, Q., Zhang, R., Sun, X., Lu, Y., Bao, J., A digital twin-driven human-robot collaborative assembly approach in the wake of COVID-19. *J. Manuf. Syst.*, 60, 837–851, 2021.

55. Nonnemann, L., Haescher, M., Aehnelt, M., Bieber, G., Diener, H., Urban, B., Health@ Hand A Visual Interface for eHealth Monitoring, in: *2019 IEEE Symposium on Computers and Communications (ISCC)*, IEEE, pp. 1093–1096, 2019 Jun 29.

56. Wickramasinghe, N., Jayaraman, P.P., Zelcer, J., Forkan, A.R., Ulapane, N., Kaul, R., Vaughan, S., A vision for leveraging the concept of digital twins to support the provision of personalised cancer care. *IEEE Internet Computing*, 2021.

57. Akmal, J.S., Salmi, M., Mäkitie, A., Björkstrand, R., Partanen, J., Implementation of industrial additive manufacturing: Intelligent implants and drug delivery systems. *J. Funct. Biomater.*, 9, 3, 41, 2018 Sep.

6

Digital Twin as a Revamping Tool for Construction Industry

Greeshma A. S.[1*] and Philbin M. Philip[2]

¹Construction Management Department, Purdue University, Indiana, U.S.A.
²Philbin M. Philip, Production and Quantitative Methods (P&QM) Area,
Indian Institute of Management, Ahmedabad, India

Abstract

Construction is a broad phrase that refers to the formation or creating structures. The construction industry looks after the installation, preservation, renovation of buildings and other immovable structures, as well as the construction of roadways, amenities, etc. that form fundamental components of structures and are necessary for the structure's complete development and usage. In construction industry, digital twin can provide a dynamic, up-to-date copy of a structure, a site, a rail line, etc. Simulations can be run which can give predictions and judgments. In construction industry during implementation of planned structure, various problems arise which can be overcome with digital twins. This chapter discusses and tries to explain the role of digital twin technology in construction industry. In the context of construction related work, this chapter tries to find out how the use of digital twin technology could transform the construction industry and come across as a game-changing technology. The chapter also analyzes the different perspectives of the role of digital twin in this industry.

Keywords: Digital twin, construction industry, project management, structure, building, construction site

6.1 Introduction

Construction industry is an industry with great value. Different structures like houses, roads, offices, public bridges, etc. are all essential structures which are utilized and very much required in day to day life of people. The

*Corresponding author: greeshmaas28@gmail.com

Manisha Vohra (ed.) Digital Twin Technology: Fundamentals and Applications, (97–110) © 2023 Scrivener Publishing LLC

construction industry undertakes the work of building these different kind of structures which are needed and are part of day to day life of people. Therefore construction industry along with great value has great responsibility also.

Construction of any structure involves a systematic process and different stages which include for example the design stage, construction stage, etc. Let us discuss some of basic aspects of the process and some stages in simple words to get some clarity and a fair understanding of the construction related work of a structure. Before beginning to work on any structure, there is a lot of pre-construction work like site survey, its information gathering, etc. There are a number of things taken into consideration and a lot of pre-construction work done before starting to actually build a structure on any given site. Any structure to be built requires to be designed first. The design work is needed to be done. So the design work stage which can be also called as part of the pre-construction work of the structure where the structure which is going to be built is designed. It is an important stage as on the basis of the finalized design, the structure will be built. Apart from this, there is other pre-construction work as well. This is also very important work. Everything required for the construction work to commence is made available and ready to use. All the arrangements for the construction work is done. Evaluation of materials, components, etc. to be involved in construction is carried out. Once everything is sorted and finalized, then the construction work is started. So these are some of the basic aspects of the process and some stages involved in construction related work of any structure which help us to get some better understanding about the construction related work.

As the construction industry scrambles to meet the desire for innovative facilities amid Covid-19, digital twins offer to be a significant facilitator. Digital twin is a digital depiction or digital representation of real-world object or system. The digital representation is the accurately identical replication of the real-world object or system. For various reasons, companies use digital twins, including evaluating new assets or procedures before introducing them in the real world. In practice, such technology in construction industry can contribute to ensure that the buildings fulfill the demands of sustainability, efficiency, and regulation. Moreover, a digital twin can allow you to foresee certain failures before they happen or some possible future problems before they come so that solutions can be sought to prevent them.

Each and every structure, whether it is our house or public bridge, roads, etc. should be well built and secure and these are main objectives of the construction industry and also this is the main requirement people have during construction of any structure. In this world of technology, when there is option of digital twin technology which can help the construction industry that too in different ways then definitely its application in construction industry will rise.

6.2   Introduction to Digital Twin

Digital twin is at the forefront of the Industry 4.0 revolution facilitated through advanced data analytics and the Internet of Things (IoT) connectivity [7]. For Industry 4.0 initiatives, the digital twin is a significant enabler [4]. Digital twin is a digitally represented version of real-world object or system or it can be called as digital depiction of real-world object or system. In the digital representation, the digitally represented version looks same like the real-world object or system. Typically described as consisting of a physical entity, a virtual counterpart, and data connections in between, digital twin is increasingly being explored as a means of improving the performance of physical entities through leveraging computational techniques, themselves enabled through virtual counterpart [9]. Conceptually, a digital twin mimics the state of its physical twin in real time and vice versa [8]. Digital twin is a useful technology which is progressing quickly. Dr. Michael Grieves' "Conceptual Idea for PLM" which he presented in conference held at Michigan University had all the elements of the Digital Twin: real space, virtual space, the link for data flow from real space to virtual space, the link for information flow from virtual space to real space and virtual sub-spaces [12].

When a digital twin of an object or process is made, it can know and give prediction about the future failures that can occur or the future possible problems that can come in the physical object or process. When this is known, the possible problems or failures can be prevented. This adds to the reasons why digital twin technology is useful. It is actually one big reason of digital twin being useful.

Other than this it can do vigilance work of the real-world object or system whom it is digitally representing which is yet another reason of it being useful. The digital representation of the real-world object or system do not remain still. The digital representation is done by creating digital model of that object or system. The digital model replicates that object or system and is connected to them. This created digital model which is connected to the real world object or system is the digital twin model.

The constant connection of the real world object or system with the digital twin allows real-time data to be transmitted by the connected objected or system to the digital twin. This constant connection is the reason behind the digital representation of the object or system not remaining still because it is receiving all live data i.e. real-time data. So with any difference caused in the object or system, it will be represented digitally by the digital twin model.

Hence the digital representation seen in the form of the digital model does not remains still. In other words, there is a seamless connection between digital twin and its physical twin. Thanks to the seamless connection, the digital twin continuously receives dynamic physical twin data, which describe the physical twin status and change with time along its lifecycle, and dynamic environment data describing the surrounding environment status [6]. This is also another reason why digital twin is useful. This technology is clearly different from other technologies. The fact that it can predict the future possible problems or failures in objects and systems makes it not just useful but it is also a factor which is the highlight advantage of digital twin technology.

Digital twin technology helps and encourages development and progress. It certainly makes path for different innovations as well. Digital twins are not just limited to application in one particular industry. It can be used in construction industry as well as other industries like automobile industry, healthcare industry, etc. The concept of digital twin offers many new perspectives to our rapidly digitalized society [5]. Digital twin is seeming to be the choice of different industries as it is evolving and showing potential advantages of using it.

6.3   Overview of Digital Twin in Construction

When digital twin of any object is made, it not replicates its looks but it also takes into account its characteristics, behavior, all specifics about it. When a digital twin of a structure will be made, it will also not just be its replicate in its looks but it take into account its characteristics, all specifics like materials involved, reaction at different instances, environmental factors impacting it, behavior, etc. Hence digital twin in construction industry can be very revolutionary for the construction industry.

Building designs always need to be carefully developed as per the security requirements. They are first approved before beginning to work on implementation of the design to ensure that everything is as per the security requirements. Developers also follow the approved design carefully for working on different structures. The reason for this is the developers want to ensure the security requirements are met. With digital twin, developers can, however, test effects of changes in the designs.

For digital twin, the existing data and data gathered by sensors which includes all relevant real world variables for example, such as gravity, weather, etc. is used. Digital twin can help to know regarding the safety, practicality, and sustainability of the work as well. From all this there are great benefits that can be achieved. Many resources could be saved with digital twin that would go waste while building a structure.

Digital twin can help in saving energy resources and also help in meeting the security requirements, thus avoiding any risk and also saving time and cost. Proactive, data-driven energy management in construction could have a huge positive impact on the environment as well and all this is feasible with the digital twin.

A digital twin is an asset for the architecture, engineering and construction (AEC) business. Take the example of an office building and its digital twin, for instance, the precise digital representation of the entire structure from the roof to the heating, ventilation and air conditioning (HVAC) system and mechanical, electrical and plumbing (MEP) can be made using digital twin. The present the physical building can be replicated in a digital, dynamic version as a digital twin. A digital twin is not static, as is the case with a digital model or a simulation. Digital twin can receive real-time data. The real-time data helps indicate and inform what new developments or changes are taking place in the original structure. Digital twin on receiving the real-time data modifies in accordance with the original structure. This functionality of the digital twin makes it very helpful for different applications which includes different areas such as healthcare industry, manufacturing, construction industry, etc. Specifically talking about construction industry, digital twin application in it can be very useful. Digital twin technology has the potential to transform the construction industry [2]. Informed decisions based on real world construction circumstances can also be simulated and predicted by digital twin.

6.4 The Perks of Digital Twin

According to the experts, digital twin technology can provide organizations with several benefits. Real-time connectivity or linking the actual system or object and digital twin allows digital twin to update from the data and information being received and provide real-time updated virtual representation of system or object which helps in keeping vigilance on the real-world system or object.

Digital twin can also help in testing of actual system or object design. In addition, virtual representation of physical things helps in avoiding errors. Efficient virtual simulation by digital twin allows to go through the entire development process and gain information regarding the potential expected outcome or the end product. The heart of the digital twin is linking of virtual and real items with data, which help companies with decisions. Effective connectivity of virtual and physical system or object enables companies to identify irregularities and analyze data obtained.

Not just companies but different organizations and any person using digital twin can identify different irregularities and analyze different aspects. Real-time virtual depiction of physical systems provides an opportunity to anticipate the what-if situations of complicated physical systems, so that organizations can be prepare for the likely results of the automation and control system. The adoption of digital twins makes it possible for companies to be more competitive in terms of data and can give customers more information by analyzing the data. Conversations and cooperation with the owners help prioritize the use of the asset and the performance expectations and determine the data types needed to achieve the goals that save a lot of time.

Prediction of possible errors and outcome is possible with digital twin and can be helpful. Decision-making on the basis of digital twin can extend asset value and life cycle and can result in total costs being reduced. Operators can also optimize energy usage with the help of performance data and analysis.

6.5   The Evolution of Digital Twin

Digital twin applications and prospective research have been to some extent at least pushed by the need to monitor and regulate infrastructure throughout their lifespan and technical developments have gone forward. A book by David Gelernter of the title 'Mirror Worlds' was published in 1991. In this book David Gelernter had written about digital twin technology's concept. For the first time in 2002, Dr. Michael Grieves who was the faculty at the University of Michigan publicly spoke about the digital twin concept at a conference and introduced it there. Some years later John Vickers from National Aeronautics and Space Administration (NASA) coined the name "digital twin" in 2010 in one of his reports.

However, the concept of digital twin can be noticed quite earlier from all the events stated above. NASA in 1960's had started working on digital twin concept. They had even utilized this concept for one of their mission.

For Apollo 13 mission in the year 1970 they utilized the digital twin technology concept.

In 2002, when Dr. Michael Grieves spoke about digital twin, it was with regards to product lifecycle management, the notion of digital twin came into light - the concept later grew in neighboring disciplines as well with the emergence of modern technologies.

6.6 Application of Digital Twin Technology in Construction Industry

In the construction related work of any structure digital twin can help in various application in different ways. So these applications are discussed below.

Digital twin can aid in the construction industry at design stage, at construction stage, for management and operation and maintenance of structural sites, buildings, etc. ensuring that scope for errors is reduced. If errors are reduced then this will decrease the possibility of extra costs.

The authors in paper [11] conducted various literature review and study which included semi-structured interview and on the basis of all this found and stated in one of the statements in their paper that data-centric technologies under the digital twin concept can provide opportunities to extend the capabilities of the current building information and modeling (BIM) to capture behaviors and relationships and develop a new breed of data-centric decision-making process. Therefore, a digital twin is intended to offer improved data-driven decision making during asset operation and management. The applications of digital twins can benefit different processes within built-environment projects across the design, construction, and operation [11].

As compared to BIM, the concept of a Digital Twin conveys a more holistic socio-technical and process-oriented characterisation of the complex artefacts involved by leveraging the synchronicity of the cyber physical bi-directional data flows [1].

Digital twin can be important and helpful for the design stage. Design changes effects can be tested with the help of digital twins. Architectural designers can make informed judgments by using digital twins. They can receive great information about their design using digital twin. On the basis of it, the design can modified as required. All the important information can be stored in the database and can be also useful for future projects for reference of architectural designers. A digital twin can be used by the architects to improve the performance of future buildings [3].

Apart from this, digital twin can also help in making early choices concerning the different aspect of projects, energy analysis, sustainability issues and function as pre-construction guidelines. The construction project's key participants communicate their goals but to achieve their goals requires great planning and proper execution of their plans. Digital twins can help in construction right from the design stage, truly comprehend the project and help with it throughout the project's life cycle. The efficient capabilities of digital twin can help organizations and construction project's key participants in their work.

Digital twin technology is useful not just for design process but also for constructing a structure or a building. This modern technology could be very valuable during the construction phase. The usage and creation of digital twin models can provide great insights and help the people assigned the construction work to be able to efficiently plan out the construction activities from beginning to end to maximize process efficiency, achieve and ensure smooth conductance of work. The information digital twin can provide will benefit the construction industry.

Digital twin can also help in work monitoring and management, error prediction, etc. Based on the observance and analysis of the monitoring of the work being carried out and possible future error prediction given by digital twin, scheduling of the work can be done on-site of construction accordingly. Different solutions implantation to avoid predicted errors can be also scheduled. Digital twin can help in monitoring and identifying the discrepancies, risk areas in construction. Digital twin is an effective tool for discrepancy monitoring and safety hazard identification during the construction process.

Falling behind a timeline due to errors is one of the common reasons for a construction site to go beyond budget but with digital twin technology when utilizing it in construction work, it can help in reducing the chances of this by monitoring and guiding throughout the process, predicting possible future errors to avoid them and thus stay on schedule. With the digital twin's capability being so vast that it can indicate regarding the possible future problems and security hazards so that all workers on site are informed and know where and when to be most careful, it saves distress. Stakeholders can also be kept informed regarding all the information received.

A general digital model of any structure which is either completely constructed or partially constructed i.e. under construction can be a precise depiction of the structure but it will not be able to update itself with real-time inputs from the constructed structure. For updating itself with real-time inputs from the actual structure irrespective of the fact that which is constructed completely or partially, digital twin model is needed and not a general digital model.

In ongoing construction work of any structure, construction work management is very important. And for construction work management, its monitoring is required. Digital twin technology can be utilized in the management of construction work by providing help in monitoring it. Since digital twin updates itself with real-time inputs from structure that is being constructed, all the live updates of the happenings that the under construction structure is going through at the construction site will be updated at the digital twin side which supports and provides help in monitoring of construction work.

Digital twin's possible future problem prediction ability and monitoring ability are two key abilities which are very useful. The information received from these two abilities of digital twin can change many things in the construction industry which will help it progress. Huge key decisions can be taken on the basis of the information received and can prove to be a game changer. Just for example, consider the construction work supervisors are aware about a problem which can occur in construction work later on then in order to avoid this kind of thing, some key decisions need to be taken by the supervisors. Also, consider another example that during the construction work something is not going as per the planning done which is found during monitoring the work then in order to avoid any unwanted situation or loss again some key decision need to be taken by the supervisors. In both these examples digital twin abilities are the ones which can truly prove to be a game changer.

Also, digital twin can provide information about building performance that can help in energy usage optimization, etc. Avoidance of possible future problems can also lead to decrease in construction costs, increase in work efficiency and promote effective construction work management. So digital twin when used in construction, can help in the work management as well.

Digital twin can also help in modular construction. It can help in finding out regarding the feasibility of materials to be used in construction. The different process involved in construction work can be also better understood with the help of digital twin. Lendlease Group had off lately made a digital twin model for the sole purpose of testing and finding out the feasibility of building a multistory complex at a river location using from sustainable timber (exhibit). Actually this particular timber had been used previously but since the multistory complex was going to be a 28 and 29 story complex and for such heighted buildings, it had not been tested. Hence digital twin was decided to be used which helped them greatly [10].

Several stakeholders are generally involved in a building project. They all also require the updated information regarding the building under construction from time to time. Digital twin can help by providing different important information about the ongoing work, information about building performance, etc. which is stated and explained above. All this flow of information can be shared with people related to the building being constructed like the stakeholders, supervisors, architect, civil engineer, etc. Digital twin can help in improving the construction project's efficiency by allowing for condition monitoring and intelligent data driven decisions.

For operation and maintenance work in construction industry, digital twin technology can work wonders. Digital twin can help in monitoring the ongoing work of construction of any particular structure as well as can help in monitoring an already constructed structure. Through this the structural health of the constructed structure can be known at any given point of time. If there is need for some maintenance related work, it can be known well in advance with the help of digital twin. In fact, digital twin can help in carrying out predictive maintenance which will be very helpful. So in construction industry, altogether, digital twin has various application as explained and discussed above. It can truly aid in different applications of construction industry in various ways.

6.7   Digital Twins Application for Construction Working Personnel Safety

One of the issue in the construction environment safety category is that important safety information is mixed up with other construction work information in complicated construction settings, making it difficult for both construction managers and on-site personnel to discern. This also hampers the effective execution of building safety standards. Also, many times, the risk factors and risk areas for the working personnel safety are sometimes difficult to be identified and known.

For these issues in building projects the solutions can be found with the digital twin technology. The construction site can be monitored using digital twin. If during monitoring, any building environment safety issues are found, they can be immediately looked after. All real-time data of construction site can be monitored to ensure all the workforce at the site is working in a secure environment, thus ensuring their safety. The risk factors and risk areas can be identified with the help of digital twin which will be helpful for the safety of working personnel safety.

6.8   Digital Twin Applications in Smart City Construction

In smart city, digital twin can play great role. It can be very helpful. Right from the planning work of the smart city, digital twin can be used. This technology can in fact turn out to be a game changer when it comes to smart city.

Digital twin can be a very useful technology in planning and development work of smart cities. The city planners with digital twin can get to test different scenarios which will support them to try and work on innovative ideas and also be ready with solutions for different situations.

Stakeholders twin in a virtual environment, with the help of digital twin may participate in the work process. this will help in sharing the information of the work and will also bring in more transparency for the stakeholders.

Digital twin technology for smart cities can also help to share important information which is received using this technology with various departments of the smart city. However, there are some obstacles as well. For example, the need of very high speed computing, guarantee requirement of data security and data privacy, etc.

6.9   Discussion

Digital twins provide the chance to fix problems before they appear in the real scenario. The impact on building projects can be useful. Right from the design stage to the maintenance related work of the building projects in the construction industry, digital twins can smooth out different work for this industry efficiently. The use of digital twins can assist in determining which aspects of a particular object or work process need to be worked upon and requires re-engineering.

Future activities should be examined further during the development and planning of a building project using a digital twin. Throughout the building period, a large amount of information is obtained. To aid in the project's management and maintenance, all the information obtained from the digital twin would prove to be very useful.

During the construction phase, the digital twin can help to effectively cut construction costs while simultaneously improving quality that the prior technique could not achieve by trying to fix problems before they occur in real scenario.

Throughout the project's building phase, more research in governance, process improvement, financial planning, and benefits analysis is always required. Using digital twins, major research attempts may be done to extend the spectrum of analysis and measurements in infrastructure projects. Digital twin technology can be greatly beneficial for the construction industry with all the advantages it can provide as discussed and explained in the chapter. In fact, construction industry has already started to use digital twin technology as seen in the real world example of application of digital twin done by LendLease Group. Digital twin application in industry can provide various opportunities and bring in innovation. Digital twin can be really effective in construction industry.

6.10   Conclusion

The usage of digital twins is growing in different industries and if largely used in construction industry, it can revolutionize the construction industry to a great extent. However, for this, the construction industry has to be flexible and make use of the possibilities of digital twin applications and other smart technologies. This chapter provides a thorough panorama of digital twins in the construction or building industry and discusses the different aspects of it.

While digital twin is anticipated to gain a lot of advantages in the design and building environment in the following years, there are many challenges to its success. Adopting Digital twin calls for a spectrum of software and technology that is not straightforward.

For the digital twin to be created it needs time and money investment. In addition to this, there is a need to extend our perspectives and anticipate possible issues that may be encountered or generated while implementing and using digital twin technology. With digital twin, its features, its benefits, how it may be applied, its obstacles and all the other aspects are crucial if we are to realize the technology's full potential and implement it successfully on a large scale in construction industry.

References

1. Boje, C., Guerriero, A., Kubicki, S., Rezgui, Y., Towards a semantic construction digital twin: Directions for future research, in: *Automation in Construction*, vol. 114, p. 103179, Elsevier, 2020.
2. Opoku, D.G.J., Perera, S., Osei-Kyei, R., Rashidi, M., Digital twin application in the construction industry: A literature review, in: *Journal of Building Engineering*, vol. 40, p. 102726, Elsevier Ltd, 2021.
3. Khajavi, S.H., Motlagh, N.H., Jaribion, A., Werner, L.C., Holmstrom, J., Digital twin: Vision, benefits, boundaries, and creation for buildings. *IEEE Access*, 7, 147406–147419, 2019.
4. Mateev, M., Industry 4.0 and the digital twin for building industry. *Int. Sci. J. Ind. 4.0*, 5, 1, 29–32, 2020.
5. Rasheed, A., San, O., Kvamsdal, T., Digital twin: Values, challenges and enablers. *IEEE Access*, 8, 21980–22012, 2020.
6. Barricelli, B.R., Casiraghi, E., Fogli, D., A survey on digital twin: Definitions, characteristics, applications, and design implications. *IEEE Access*, 7, 167653–167671, 2019.
7. Fuller, A., Fan, Z., Day, C., Barlow, C., Digital twin: Enabling technologies, challenges and open research. *IEEE Access*, 8, 108952–108971, 2020.
8. Singh, M., Fuenmayor, E., Hinchy, E.P., Qiao, Y., Murray, N., Devine, D., Digital twin: Origin to future. *Appl. Syst. Innov.*, 4, 36, 2021. doi: https://doi.org/10.3390/asi4020036.
9. Jones, D., Snider, C., Nassehi, A., Yon, J., Hicks, B., Characterising the digital twin: A systematic literature review. *CIRP J. Manuf. Sci. Technol. CIRP*, 29, 36–52, 2020.
10. McKinsey & Company, Global Infrastructure Initiative, Voices on Infrastructure, Scaling Modular Construction, Voices. 1–45, September 2019. https://www.mckinsey.com/~/media/mckinsey/business%20functions/operations/our%20insights/voices%20on%20infrastructure%20scaling%20modular%20construction/gii-voices-sept-2019.pdf.
11. Shahzad, M., Shafiq, M.T., Dean, D., Kassem, M., Digital twins in built environments: An investigation of the characteristics, applications, and challenges. *Buildings*, 12, 120, 1–19, 2022.
12. Grieves, M. and Vickers, J., Digital twin: Mitigating unpredictable, undesirable emergent behavior in complex systems, in: *Transdisciplinary Perspectives on Complex Systems*, F.J. Kahlen, S. Flumerfelt, A. Alves (Eds.), pp. 85–113, Springer, Cham, 2017, https://doi.org/10.1007/978-3-319-38756-7_4.

Digital Twin Applications and Challenges in Healthcare

Pavithra S.*, Pavithra D., Vanithamani R. and Judith Justin

*Department of Biomedical Instrumentation Engineering,
Avinashilingam Institute for Home Science and Higher Education for Women,
Coimbatore, India*

Abstract

Digital twin is an efficient technology. With digital twin evolving, various sectors can gain advantages from it. The advancement of the Internet of Things (IoT), has helped digital twin to evolve. A digital twin is identical in all aspects with its original counterpart and can be used in running simulation, predicting errors of objects, products, etc. In connection to the healthcare sector, digital twin can help in it in different ways. Just like how it can provide advantages to various sectors, namely manufacturing sector, aviation sector, etc., similarly it can provide advantages to the healthcare sector as well. Using this technology, the healthcare sector can benefit largely. In this chapter, a literature based survey is presented on the application of Digital Twin and its challenges in healthcare. It is found that there are different applications of digital twin in healthcare sector. A real life example of the use of digital twin in healthcare application is also discussed and explained briefly in this chapter. The challenges digital twin face in the healthcare are also not just briefly discussed but also explained in this chapter.

Keywords: Digital twin, healthcare, IoT, data security, medical devices, data privacy

7.1 Introduction

Healthcare sector is a very essential sector. Healthcare is of great importance. This sector has been evolving with many technologies being brought

---

*Corresponding author: pavithrasusi@gmail.com

Manisha Vohra (ed.) Digital Twin Technology: Fundamentals and Applications, (111–124) © 2023
Scrivener Publishing LLC

and introduced for application in this sector. This has led to the path of advancements in healthcare sector. For example, the introduction and inclusion of telemedicine in healthcare has made healthcare services like diagnosis, consultation, monitoring all this possible remotely.

Various more advancements are seen in healthcare like the introduction of precision medicine, inclusion of robotics for surgery related applications as well as some other applications in healthcare, wearable devices for heart-rate monitoring, etc.

With many technologies being introduced and leading towards the path of advancements in healthcare sector, there is yet another technology which can lead towards the path of advancements in healthcare sector. It is the digital twin technology. It is having great potential to be useful and beneficial in the healthcare sector.

7.2   Digital Twin

The digital twin is receiving an increase in interest from the academic perspective and the industrial perspective as well [11]. The digital twin, means a system's digital counterpart along its lifecycle [15].

Conceptually, a DT mimics the state of its physical twin in real time and vice versa [1]. A digital twin, just similarly like a virtual prototype, is a dynamic digital representation of a physical system [8]. The digital twin in its original form is described as a digital informational construct about a physical system, created as an entity on its own and linked with the physical system in question [13].

Digital twin concept aims to enable the observation of the behavior of the whole system and also along with it, the digital twin concept aims to enable the prediction of the system behavior during its utilization [6]. Digital twin lets the virtual entities to exist simultaneously with the physical entities [10].

The digital twin was first spoken about in a public event in the year 2002. National Aeronautical Space Administration (NASA) first used digital twin in Apollo 13 Program in 1970. NASA has also released a paper titled "The Digital Twin Paradigm for Future NASA and U.S. Air Force Vehicles" [27] which is a very helpful documented work on Digital Twin. It has set a milestone for the development and research on Digital Twin. The definition of digital twin given in [27] is as follows:

"A Digital Twin is an integrated multi-physics, multiscale, probabilistic simulation of built-in vehicle or system that uses the best available physical models, sensor updates, fleet history, etc., to mirror the life of its corresponding flying twin" [27].

With recent developments, many researchers have presented their views on digital twin technology. There are also various definitions given by different researchers defining digital twin technology.

Digital Twin technology connects digital and the physical world. Digital twin is a digital copy of an original object in the physical world. In digital twin technology, virtual models are formed which are the copy of the original object in the physical world. These virtual models have the task of mimicking the original object.

To make digital twin there is integration of the original object with virtual models or virtual twin which are made same as the original object whom they are mimicking. After integration live data is sent from original object to virtual twin. As a result, the digital twin is created of the original model. The behavior of the original object can be studied with digital twin.

It can predict failure or breakdown or problem in advance only, before it happens, which helps in preventing the failure, breakdown or problem. With this technology, problems, breakdown can be prevented so there will be overall cost savings and avoidance of downtime as well.

Digital twin model needs very large amounts of information as well as computing capability [4]. Digital twin technology can help to understand maintenance needs and schedule maintenance as per requirement [8].

The digital twin gives real-time information for more informed decision making and the digital twin can even make predictions about how the asset will evolve or how the asset will behave in the future [14].

There has been tremendous growth in Digital Twin technology. Digital twin has many applications. Some applications will be discussed in this chapter. There are different possible applications of Digital Twin technology in various fields like manufacturing industries, smart cities, intelligent healthcare, etc. [2, 3].

The application of digital twins provides value creation within the fields of operations and service management [23]. The increasing utilization of information and communication technology allows digital engineering of products and production processes [16].

In the very recent years, the digital twin in industry has attained a relevant attention not just from researchers but also from practitioners as well [25].

Digital twin is also attaining very large interest from manufacturers that make products that are advanced and have complex systems all characteristics [26].

Digital twins promise great benefits for their different stakeholders when they are used to support the design, to support the manufacturing management, to support monitoring and control as well as optimisation of manufactured products, and the production equipment and systems in manufacturing [24].

Digital twin for a production process can be useful. The digital twin for a production process enables a coupling of the production system with its digital equivalent as a base for an optimization with a minimized delay between the time of the data acquisition and the creation of the digital twin [12].

The information provided by a digital twin can offer various optimization possibilities for a cyber-physical system [7]. A concept for the realization of the digital twin contribution to the development of a cyber-physical production system (CPPS) in small and medium-sized enterprises (SME) is presented [12].

From a simulation point of view the digital twin approach is the next wave in modeling, simulation and optimization technology [9]. The digital twin appears to be the most suitable source of knowledge within the smart factory from literature stated as per authors in paper [5]. Below discussed are different applications of Digital Twin.

7.3   Applications of Digital Twin

The digital twin technology is gaining importance due to its potential. Some of the applications areas of digital twin are smart cities, manufacturing sectors, healthcare, etc.

7.3.1   Smart Cities

The concept of smart cities is gaining importance. Smart cities are beneficial in different ways, hence they are gaining importance. Using digital twin for smart cities can be really very helpful. Employment of digital twin for smart cities application can help in different ways. It can help in planning related work of smart cities. Along with it, digital twin can help in development work of smart cities. Digital twin can also help the different departments of the city with its advantages, it can also help in monitoring the environmental parameters and changes, etc. So application of digital twin can be beneficial for smart cities.

7.3.2   Manufacturing Sector

By introducing digital twin in manufacturing sector, problems can be predicted before they come. If any problems are going to come in a product which is being made then corrections required in the product can be done before the final production of the product.

7.3.3   Healthcare

With digital twin, hospital management, patient healthcare, medical equipment manufacturing, etc. can be benefitted in the healthcare sector. Digital twin helps in avoiding problems, it also helps in smarter decision making, etc. which is useful in healthcare sector. Detailed discussion on the application of digital twin in healthcare is discussed in section 7.5.

7.3.4   Aviation

In the aviation field, digital twin can help with predictive maintenance. It can predict the requirement for structural maintenance and repair works. The structural life of the aircraft can be also predicted using digital twin.

7.3.5   The Disney Park

In 2019, Hitachi formed an alliance with Disney Parks, to work on data-driven solutions to increase operation efficiency and create great experiences for their guests who will visit Disney Parks. Their data-driven solutions include digital twin.

7.4   Challenges with Digital Twin

In each and every technology there are always some challenges faced. In digital twin technology also, there are some challenges. For example, some common challenges with digital twin are training requirement for working on digital twin technology and expenses of creating digital twin. Training and expertise would be needed to work properly and correctly. Digital twin cannot be just simply created and worked on without appropriate training and without having the much needed expertise. Also, there will be expenses involved in creating digital twin. From the software to the hardware requirements of digital twin will include its expenses. So these are some of the common challenges faced with digital twin.

7.5   Digital Twin in Healthcare

Healthcare sector is very vital. In healthcare sector, technology plays a very great role. Digital twin technology is having great importance in this sector. There are existing significant applications of digital twin in healthcare sector. Besides with the existing applications, there can be several more applications of digital twin in healthcare. On the basis of the literature survey carried out, discussed below are some applications of digital twin in healthcare which include existing real-world applications as well.

- Digital Twin for Hospital Workflow Management
- Digital Twin for a Healthcare Facility
- Digital Twin for Different Medical Product Manufacturing
- Cardiovascular Digital Twin
- Digital Twin Utilization for Supporting Personalized Treatment
- Digital Twin for Multiple Sclerosis (MS)

7.5.1   Digital Twin for Hospital Workflow Management

The workflow management of a hospital is very necessary. If there is no proper workflow management in a hospital then things will turn out to be very messed up. In each and every hospital there needs to be a proper work discipline which should be followed so that the workflow can be managed well. Hospital being a very highly important place, there are certain rules that every hospital has along their own particular schedule and work discipline which they follow strictly and especially when there are large number of patients visiting hospital, a proper disciplined workflow management becomes even more essential. Imagine the workload of hospitals during pandemic. The workload of hospitals during pandemic is skyrocketing. Even during regular non-pandemic times, hospitals always look forward for having a smooth and efficient workflow management. Despite the best efforts hospitals always put, sometimes the hospital workflow management work gets messed up in complex situations. Digital twin technology is best in such cases. It can very well help in smooth hospital workflow management. Consider the following example of usage of digital twin technology in Mater Private Hospital (MPH) in Dublin where this technology is employed for hospital workflow management. This is one of the real world application of digital twin in healthcare sector.

Mater Private Hospital (MPH) in Dublin, has included digital twin technology in their hospital. MPH engaged Siemens Healthineers Value Partners for Healthcare Consulting to optimize care delivery and create more value using a Digital Twin for Workflow Excellence. Hospital management of Mater Private Hospital felt an urge for having a change in their department of radiology. MPH were facing problems such as patient demand were growing, the infrastructure was becoming old, etc. All the problems were making it most difficult to provide productive patient care. Hence, they engaged Siemens Healthineers Value Partners for Healthcare Consulting. Digital twin for workflow excellence was used and the result was amazing. The hospital noticed the wait times were shorter for the patients thereafter for computed tomography (CT) scans and magnetic resonance imaging (MRI) and the turnaround time for patient for both CT scans as well as MRI was faster. The equipment utilization was more and there was yearly cost savings as well [20]. From this example, one can clearly notice that how well digital twin can help in healthcare sector's area of hospital workflow management.

7.5.2   Digital Twin for a Healthcare Facility

Healthcare facility like a hospital is always very carefully made but in a hospital there are so many things to look after and like all the arrangements, operational strategy, staffing, etc. Digital twin technology can be helpful. A digital twin of an entire hospital facility can be made. Digital twins can allow hospital to optimize resources and increase efficiency. Digital twins of hospital will help in analyzing the existing arrangements as well as in finding out if any improvements are required in the healthcare facility and testing and knowing the effects of different changes if made in the hospital. It can be extremely helpful and especially in times like pandemic where there are large number of patients visiting a hospital, this could help the hospital in various ways. By creating a digital twin of hospital, the management or staff can test different changes in operational strategy, capacities, staffing and also care delivery models so as to decide exactly which actions should be taken [21].

Thus as explained above, the digital twin for a healthcare facility can be very helpful in different ways.

GE's Hospital of Future Digital Twin
GE is working out on different new ways through which they can utilize simulation and prediction for improvement of hospital operations and patient care and in this context have come up with Hospital of Future

(HOF) digital twin. The HOF Simulation Suite has been designed especially for utilization in healthcare [21].

7.5.3   Digital Twin for Different Medical Product Manufacturing

Digital twin can help in healthcare largely. Medical products are of great importance. In healthcare various kinds of special medical products are used. Consider a medical product like vaccine. Manufacturing a medical product like vaccine requires great attention and care. Nothing should go wrong in the manufacturing process. To make sure everything goes well enough in manufacturing process, digital twin technology can be useful. Digital twin can be used for manufacturing process. It can then help in various ways like it can prevent wastage or decrease it, which is such a huge benefit. This will be very helpful. The process of manufacturing can be monitored remotely, which provides so much flexibility in work. This also will be very helpful. Similarly digital can help in more such ways when used for medical product manufacturing process.

7.5.4   Cardiovascular Digital Twin

A particular method for enabling cardiovascular digital twin by utilizing inverse analysis is suggested by [19]. The authors suggested a procedure for inverse analysis utilizing recurrent neural network for the cardiovascular system. To add to this, their procedure also suggested the use of virtual patient database which was generated, comprising of altogether 8516 patients and out of these, 4392 were abdominal aortic aneurysm (AAA) cases and 4137 were healthy cases. Through help of long short-term memory (LSTM) cells, blood pressure waveforms in different vessels of body are calculated inversely by inputting pressure waveforms from three non-invasively accessible blood vessels which are carotid, brachial arteries and femoral). Inverse analysis system which is built this way is applied to detection of AAA and its severity using neural networks [19]. On application of the proposed approach it was found that the suggested approach of inverse analysis makes development of an active digital twin, capable of continuously monitoring, and preventing medical conditions from developing or further aggravating feasible. When it comes to the case of cardiovascular system, this approach is potentially implementable in clinical environments and helps in monitoring cardiovascular parameters and critical vessels [19].

The method proposed by the authors work in [19] can perform inverse analysis with great accuracy. It found problems like AAA with high accuracy of 99.91% and classified its severity with acceptable accuracy of 97.79% [19].

7.5.5 Digital Twin Utilization for Supporting Personalized Treatment

Digital twin has the potential of being utilized to support personalized treatment of patients. There are certain cases where personalized treatment for patient can prove to be very useful. It can highly benefit the health of the patient. For example, consider the case of cancer. Here personalized treatment could be introduced with digital twin utilization for supporting personalized treatment. In this context, the authors [17] in their article, have used systems and mathematical modelling theory and on the basis of it, have put forward a classification of digital twins into different models. These different models are Grey Box model, Surrogate model and Black Box model. Then the authors explore one possible approach, namely a Black Box classification. This is for incorporating the usage of digital twins in the context of personalised uterine cancer care [17].

7.5.6 Digital Twin for Multiple Sclerosis (MS)

Authors in [18] discuss regarding the usage of digital twins for MS. They discuss about digital tool being used as a tool which can improve monitoring, diagnosis and therapy refining patients' well-being. This will save costs and allow to prevent progression of disease. Digital twins will help make care patient-centered and also make make precision medicine a reality in everyday life. According to the authors [18], with the digital twins development for Multiple Sclerosis (DTMS), it is possible to make the clinical decision-making for individual patients, shared decision-making, patient communication and thus ultimately quality of care better [18].

7.6 Digital Twin Challenges in Healthcare

There are different challenges that digital twin faces in healthcare. Some of them are as follows.

- Need of Training and Knowledge

- Cost Factor
- Trust Factor

7.6.1   Need of Training and Knowledge

During developing any medical product using digital twin or while using digital twin for any other application in healthcare, any mistake caused due to human error can have a serious negative effect.

Hence the working with digital twin and handling it requires training and knowledge. Everyone cannot work with it and handle it in a sensitive sector like healthcare. So training would be needed with detailed knowledge about it. This is also a challenge in general that digital twin faces as well as it a challenge in the healthcare applications as well to ensure that required training and knowledge is provided to the staff who will be working on digital twin.

7.6.2   Cost Factor

Creating and including digital twin in healthcare means additional increase in cost. The cost factor or expenses of creating a digital twin is also another challenge faced in general as well as in healthcare applications. As discussed above, there won't be just the cost of creating digital twin but also there will be also cost expenses in training the staff to work on digital twin and handle things related to it. So this a major challenge for digital twin.

7.6.3   Trust Factor

Every technology being introduced in healthcare which is a very important and sensitive area not only needs reliably amazing results from it but also needs trust of the people. When digital twin applications in healthcare include hospital management, help in development of medical instruments and devices, etc. the advantages of it come across as very useful and it becomes easier to trust this technology. However, when one talks of including digital twin to support personalized treatment and personalized medicine then here the trust factor could be a major challenge. Digital twins are having the ability to model individual patients with varying physiological traits and mechanistic differences. Therefore, digital twins are a natural, complementary strategy to implement personalized medicine [22]. However, it might not be easily trusted by everyone. It requires time and evidence for people to trust a technology in the case of healthcare.

At present digital twin is evolving and it is yet to be fully introduced and utilized at a large scale in healthcare sector but again here the large scale introduction and utilization of digital twin in healthcare does not guarantee that the people will trust it, especially in the case of implementing personalized medicine. Also, the data security and data privacy risk will also again come into picture here. This will further increase the issue of the trust factor. Due to this, people will find it more difficult to trust this technology in healthcare. So the trust factor is great challenge for digital twin in healthcare applications.

7.7   Conclusion

With inclusion of different technologies there have been great innovation, developments and advancements in healthcare. Along with so many advancements, introduction of digital twin and its application in healthcare can be very beneficial for this sector.

The main contributions of the chapter are as follows,

- It discusses about what is digital twin.
- The current application of digital twin not only on healthcare but also on different fields has also been discussed.
- The main focus of this chapter has been to discuss and emphasize the applications and importance of digital twin in healthcare. By utilizing digital twin, the healthcare sector can be benefitted as seen in this chapter. The chapter also explains the digital twin challenges in healthcare.

The applications of digital twin for healthcare discussed, explained and emphasized in this chapter are digital twin for hospital workflow management, digital twin for a hospital facility, digital twin for different medical product, digital twin for enabling a cardiovascular digital twin, digital twin utilization for supporting personalized treatment. And digital twin for multiple sclerosis All these applications clearly show the importance of digital twin in healthcare sector and the kind of difference its presence and utilization can make in this sector, like we saw in the case of Mater Hospital for example in Dublin.

The benefit it received from digital twin application or utilization was great. The presence of digital twin caused a great difference here. This hospital's problem of workflow management was solved efficiently with digital twin.

Likewise, in other digital twin healthcare applications also explained in the chapter, we saw that digital twin presence and utilization made such a huge difference.

The effects and results of using digital twin in different healthcare applications seen in this chapter were very phenomenal. Digital twin is yet not largely introduced and yet not implemented on large scale in healthcare sector but with digital twin showcasing great results and effects and promising of benefitting the healthcare sector its presence and application in this sector might grow further quickly.

However, there are some challenges as well which digital twin faces in this sector of healthcare which are all also discussed and explained in this chapter. Solutions need to be found and implemented for the challenges so that they can be overcome which will benefit ultimately the healthcare sector largely as it will open doors to the pathway leading to easier large scale implementation of digital twin in healthcare sector. Though digital twin has been evolving but there are still so many things related to digital twin that need to be explored in context with the healthcare sector. Therefore, the future insight of digital twin especially in healthcare is considered to be a vast area to explore.

References

1. Singh, M., Fuenmayor, E., Hinchy, E.P., Qiao, Y., Murray, N., Devine, D., Digital twin: Origin to future. *Appl. Syst. Innov.*, 4, 36, 2021, https://doi.org/10.3390/asi4020036.
2. Fuller, A., Fan, Z., Day, C., Barlow, C., Digital twin: Enabling technologies, challenges and open research. *IEEE Access*, 8, 108952–108971, 2020.
3. Najafabadi, M.M., Villanustre, F., Khoshgoftaar, T.M., Seliya, N., Wald, R., Muharemagic, E., Deep learning applications and challenges in big data analytics. *J. Big Data*, 2, Dec. 2015.
4. Grieves, M. and Vickers, J., Digital twin: Mitigating unpredictable, undesirable emergent behavior in complex systems, in: *Transdisciplinary pcerspectives on complex systems*, F.J. Kahlen, S. Flumerfelt, A. Alves (Eds.), pp. 85–113, Springer, Cham, 2017, https://doi.org/10.1007/978-3-319-38756-7_4.
5. Longo, F., Nicoletti, L., Padovano, A., Ubiquitous knowledge empowers the smart factory: The impacts of a service-oriented digital twin on enterprises' performance. *Annu. Rev. Control*, 47, 221–236, 2019.
6. Lohtander, M., Ahonen, N., Lanz, M., Ratava, J., Kaakkunen, J., Micro manufacturing unit and the corresponding 3D-model for the digital twin. *Proc. Manuf.*, 25, 55–61, 2018.

7. Josifovska, K., Yigitbas, E., Engels, G., Reference framework for digital twins within cyber-physical systems. *IEEE/ACM 5th International Workshop on Software Engineering for Smart Cyber-Physical Systems (SEsCPS)*, IEEE Xplore, pp. 25–31, 2019, https://doi.org/10.1109/SEsCPS.2019.00012.
8. Madni, A.M., Madni, C.C., Lucero, S.D., Leveraging digital twin technology in model based systems engineering. *Syst.*, 7, 2019.
9. Rosen, R.W., Lo, G.V., George, B., Kurt, D., About the importance of autonomy and digital twins for the future of manufacturing, in: *IFAC-Papersonline*, vol. 48, pp. 567–572, 2015.
10. Kaarlela, T., Pieskä, S., Pitkäaho, T., Digital twin and virtual reality for safety training, in: *Proceedings of the 11th IEEE International Conference on Cognitive Infocommunications (CogInfoCom)*, Mariehamn, Finland, pp. 115–120, 2020.
11. Jones, D., Snider, C., Nassehi, A., Yon, J., Hicks, B., Characterising the digital twin: A systematic literature review. *CIRP J. Manuf. Sci. Technol. Part A*, 29, 36–52, 2020, https://doi.org/10.1016/j.cirpj.2020.02.002.
12. Uhlemann, T.H.-J., Lehmann, C., Steinhilper, R., The digital twin: Realizing the cyber-physical production system for industry 4.0. *Proc. CIRP*, 61, 335–340, 2017.
13. Kritzinger, W., Karner, M., Traar, G., Henjes, J., Sihn, W., Digital Twin in manufacturing: A categorical literature review and classification, in: *IFAC-Papers online*, vol. 51, pp. 1016–1022, 2018.
14. Rasheed, A., San, O., Kvamsdal, T., Digital twin: Values, challenges and enablers, 2019. arXiv preprint arXiv:1910.01719.
15. Macchi, M., Roda, I., Negri, E., Fumagalli, L., Exploring the role of digital twin for asset lifecycle management, in: *IFAC-Papers online*, vol. 51, pp. 790–795, 2018.
16. Brettel, M., Friederichsen, N., Keller, M., Rosenberg, M., How virtualization, decentralization and network building change the manufacturing landscape: An industry 4.0 perspective. *Int. J. Mech. Aerosp. Ind. Mechatron. Eng.*, 8, 37–44, 2014.
17. Wickramasinghe, N., Jayaraman, P.P., Zelcer, J., Forkan, A.R., Ulapane, N., Kaul, R., Vaughan, S., A vision for leveraging the concept of digital twins to support the provision of personalised cancer care. *IEEE Internet Comput.*, 2021.
18. Voigt, I., Inojosa, H., Dillenseger, A., Haase, R., Akgün, K., Ziemssen, T., Digital twins for multiple sclerosis. *Front. Immunol.*, 12, 669811, 1–17, 2021.
19. Chakshu, N.K., Sazonov, I., Nithiarasu, P., Towards enabling a cardiovascular digital twin for human systemic circulation using inverse analysis. *Biomech. Model. Mechanobiol.*, 20, 449–465, 2021.
20. Optimizing clinical operations through digital modeling, in: *Case study*, vol. *7563*, pp. 1–6, Siemens Healthcare GmbH, 2019, https://www.siemens-healthineers.com/en-in/services/value-partnerships/asset-center/case-studies/mater-private-workflow-simulation.

21. GE Healthcare Command Centers, in: *What is a hospital of a future digital twin?*, https://www.gehccommandcenter.com/digital-twin.

22. Boulos, M.N.K. and Zhang, P., Digital twins: From personalised medicine to precision public health. *J. Pers. Med.*, 11, 745, 1–12, 2021, https://doi.org/10.3390/jpm11080745.

23. West, S., Stoll, O., Meierhofer, J., Züst, S., Digital twin providing new opportunities for value co-creation through supporting decision-making. *Appl. Sci.*, 11, 3750, 2021.

24. Romero, D., Wuest, T., Harik, R., Thoben, K.D., Towards a cyber-physical plm environment: the role of digital product models, intelligent products, digital twins, product avatars and digital shadows, in: *IFAC-Papers online*, vol. 53, pp. 10911–10916, 2020.

25. Cimino, C., Negri, E., Fumagalli, L., Review of digital twin applications in manufacturing. *Comput. Ind.*, 113, 103130, 2019.

26. Grieves, M.W., Virtually intelligent product systems: Digital and physical twins. *Complex Syst. Eng., Theory Pract.*, 175–200, 2019.

27. Glaessgen, E. and Stargel, D., The digital twin paradigm for future NASA and U.S. Air Force Vehicles, in: *53rd AIAA Structures, Structural Dynamics and Materials Conference*, American Institute of Aeronautics and Astronautics, Honolulu, Hawaii, Apr. 2012.

8

Monitoring Structural Health Using Digital Twin

Samaya Pillai[1]*, Venkatesh Iyengar[2] and Pankaj Pathak[1]

[1]Symbiosis Institute of Digital & Telecom Management, Symbiosis International (Deemed University), Pune, India
[2]Symbiosis Institute of International Business, Symbiosis International (Deemed University), Pune, India

Abstract

"Digital Twin" (DT) as a scientific paradigm offers extraordinary supremacy and dexterity both to the physical objects/systems and its digital counterparts in the backdrop of Industry 4.0 environment. Digital twin models (aka "Avatars") generate high-precision virtual replicas of physical counterparts, products, entities, and systems. The DT concept is rightfully important and useful for manufacturing, automotive, construction, etc. sectors to name a few. In this chapter, an attempt is made to understand the applicability of DT fundamentals in the Structural Health Monitoring Systems (SHMS). Application of DT in SHMS is discussed relating to damage identification in infrastructure (such as dams, bridges, power grids, port facilities, ships, aeroplanes, civil heritage structures, healthcare entities, etc.) about their structural health monitoring dimensions. The DT paradigm and its related application in SHMS discussed in this chapter offer useful in this area.

Keywords: Avatars, digital twin, emerging technologies, Industry 4.0, physical, structural health monitoring systems, virtual

*Corresponding author: samaya.pillai@sidtm.edu.in

Manisha Vohra (ed.) *Digital Twin Technology: Fundamentals and Applications,* (125–140) © 2023
Scrivener Publishing LLC

8.1 Introduction

8.1.1 Digital Twin—The Approach and Uses

Retracing its genesis from scientific literature, the concept of "Digital Twin" (DT) yet though in its infancy seems to be conceptualized initially in the aerospace domain, gradually extending beyond into several other contexts and recently much more aggressive in the manufacturing, automotive, construction, and defence industries with Industry 4.0 paradigm popularly into smart manufacturing [1].

Modern advancements in digital technology now add supreme prowess through seamless integration of interconnected and intelligent systems, into a mechanical-electric-electronic-software combine. These typically morph into amazing smart business environments, smart infrastructure, smart factories, smart cities, and several others as a viable ground for breeding Industry 4.0 product lifecycle management. The DT offers a virtual and digitalized counterpart of any physical system, which could further be simulated or synchronized using data generated in real-time environments. In other words, digital twin means digital representation of physical systems or objects. Further, modern emerging smart technologies, such as the Internet of Things (IoT), artificial intelligence (AI), machine learning (ML), virtual reality (VR), 3D modeling, and several cloud-based architectures could usefully engage with the DT paradigm for effective and efficient decision-making outcomes. In layman terms, the concept of DT helps develop virtual models and representations (simple/complex), which are replicas (i.e. digital twinning) of actual physical objects, things, entities, and systems in our real-world manifestations. DT knowledge could be largely harnessed to learn about the physical products, the virtual/digital products, and associations between the two products more precisely. The DT technology has certain characteristics distinguishable from other technologies and includes its connectivity (between the physical component and its digital counterpart; organizations, products, and their customers [2], homogenization (data/content in its identical digital form with high computing power [3], smart and reprogrammable (including automatic sensors, AI, predictive analytics, etc.), digital traces (tracking for problem traces, root-causes, and diagnostics [4], and its modularity (design/customization of product and production modules [5].

The National Aeronautics and Space Administration (NASA) in 2010 while attempting to improve upon physical model simulations of spacecraft provided a definition of DT and also subsequently using mirrored systems (namely a predecessor to the concept of DT with an objective to rescue the Apollo 13 space mission), while the conceptualization of DT is greatly attributed to Michael Grieves in 2002 [1].

The usage of DT concept can be found in many areas. One of the known application for DT is within a manufacturing setting [32]. This is widely known, as a manufacturing DT allows a detailed visualization of the manufacturing process [36]. In manufacturing, DT enables easier and safe interactions due to virtual operation, detaching the operator from the obligation to physically remain close to the industrial equipment [40]. DT concept has opportunity to change how we view system design, manufacturing and operation [33]. A comprehensive representation of a production system needs to consider several aspects [39]. Visual simulations of digital factory have a purpose i.e. to simulate operation of a factory, right from work cell, to manufacturing line and finally to the whole Factory [35]. Thanks to DT, we can simulate the manufacturing environment which creates the product, including almost each operation, be it automatic and manual that constitutes manufacturing process [34]. This technology has been used in industry, for different works like for e.g., allowing it to simulate physical environments, some specific machinery pieces in order to make decisions and assess risks in virtual environments prior to its implementation [40]. So for such work and various other work in Industry 4.0, DT technology is being used and can be used. It is viewed as cornerstone in Industry 4.0 due to its various advantages, etc. and in fact, it is now recognized as a key part of the Industry 4.0 roadmap [37, 38].

DT technology is an emerging technology towards realizing the dream of smarter cities [41]. The other areas of DT application include healthcare, structural behavior and health monitoring under multiple environmental factor conditions, monitoring crack paths, information continuity along product life cycles, fatigue-damage prediction, and many more areas.

Infrastructure in any form of engineering structures (examples such buildings, bridges, roads, aircraft, spacecraft, etc.) are highly valuable, critical, and important mankind requirements across the globe. Notably, these infrastructures are subject to risks and vagaries of our natural environment and/or manufacturing defects leading to variations, disruptions, damage or changes in its material and geometric properties in varying degrees.

Apropos to this requirement is an effective and efficient structural health monitoring system that can assist in observation, analyses, and monitoring of such systems typically through periodically sampled response measurements.

In this regard, the Digital Twin approach seems to fill the void. While the DT paradigm could be applied across diverse domains, it would be a deeper curiosity to understand its application in a critical system, such as the Structural Health Monitoring Systems (SHMS).

8.2   Structural Health Monitoring Systems (SHMS)

Structural Health Monitoring Systems (SHMS) encompasses observation and evaluation of infrastructural systems over a period of time in order to monitor and control identifiable variations to material compositions and their geometric properties.

Such infrastructure may relate to any product, systems or engineering structures to include roads, bridges, dams, power grids, tunnels, telecommunication equipment, and a host of such physical or organizational structures.

The objective of SHMS is primarily to derive periodically updated information about the characteristic performance of such infrastructure, which must perform according to its intended function. Naturally resulting operating environments, inevitable degradations, ageing and multiple environmental reasons affect the integral parameters of such infrastructure leading to issues in its performance, integrity, and life cycle.

Few health and usage monitoring systems for features comparison and contrast between serviceable and unserviceable, working and damaged infrastructure thus come in handy while resolving these issues employing select excitation methods, sensors, data management hardware and software.

SHMS could employ fatigue testing, corrosion growth, temperature cycling, induced damage testing or any correlated measured system response data points for comparison/identification of the degraded systems, operational evaluation, feature extraction, data acquisition/compression/ interpretation/diagnosis, normalization, and cleansing requirements. Structural Health Assessment data needs to employ digital signal processing and statistical classifications in order to manipulate sensed data into useful structural health status data points for further damage assessments and/or decision making. Subsequently, it also assists in statistical model development for scientific analyses.

8.2.1   Criticality and Need for SHMS Approach

Infrastructure in any part of the world normally comprises basic facilities such as transport, power supplies, communication systems, buildings, dams, bridges, roads, and a host of such systems that support humankind requirements. These infrastructures are also naturally prone to the effects of various disasters that keep occurring from time to time, such as electricity outages and breakdown, communication systems failure, collapses of buildings, dams, bridges, etc., and such damaged infrastructure leads to severe economic losses and are critical stressors to all stakeholders concerned.

As a saviour, SHMS approaches to assist in deriving usable knowledge about the integrity of serviceability of such structures on a continuous and near real-time basis. Strategic identification of damages, automated and real-time assessment, methodical approach to evaluation, monitoring, and control of structural health will help to improve the structural reliability and lifecycle management.

Such SHMS would consist of a diagnosis component at the low level, such as detection, localization, damage assessment, as well as a prognosis component at the high level to include generation of objective information for decision making upon the diagnostic observations.

8.2.2 Passive and Active SHMS

Structural health monitoring (SHM) systems could be implemented in either of these two strategies, namely

(a) passive SHM; or
(b) active SHM.

Passive SHM relates with measurement of multiple operational parameters and further inferences about the current state of such structural health status from these parameters. To cite an example, we could monitor different flight parameters of an airborne aircraft (such as airspeed, g-factors, air turbulence, vibration levels, and environmental stresses in much critical locations, etc.) and subsequently assess the aircraft design algorithms towards inferring how much of aircraft usable life is exhausted and how much more could we harness its potential.

Passive SHM systems are useful however it does not provide comprehensive solutions to all problems existing, that it does not examine all possible parameters and suggest whether the existing structure is fully damaged or not.

Active SHM systems, on the other hand, directly assess such current state of structural health by detecting all such parameters in the current state to indicate the extent to which there is structural damage.

Active SHM systems approach is almost identical to another known approach adopted by nondestructive evaluation (NDE) technique, except that active SHM moves one step further. Active SHM systems engage sensors that can perform damage detection and can be inbuilt or installed permanently onto the physical structures. These monitoring methods can provide on-demand structural health bulletins too.

Enhancing further, it would be further ideal to implement a hybrid combination of both passive and active sensing technologies for structural health monitoring, including multiple applications.

Passive sensing is different from active sensing strategies, such that in passive SHM, no energy is applied into the structure while under test and relevant sensors are deployed in a core detection mode for collecting usable dataset for assessment of structural health. Passive SHM approach use acoustic emission bases while active SHM systems use electromechanical impedance and guided ultrasonic wave signals.

Undoubtedly, structural health monitoring systems are vital in mitigating and avoidance of critical failures and related accidents. In case of proceeding with any construction activities, it would be prudent and necessary to monitor and continuously assess the construction site, as well as the assets in proximity.

8.3   Sensor Technology, Digital Twin (DT) and Structural Health Monitoring Systems (SHMS)

Using a network of sensors in a typical SHMS ecosystem will assist in remote sensing, and real-time measuring of the critical parameters relevant to the existing current state of any structure and its environment (namely strain, stress, humidity, temperature and other vital parameters) to monitor its health continuously. Smart sensing technologies including IoT helps develop automated systems rendering real-time monitoring, inspection and detection of damages to physical structures.

Alongside emerging technologies available in the marketplace, some of the following sensors are useful in the implementation of an SHMS:

- **Fiber Optic Sensors** — Measure strains, structural displacements, vibrations, frequencies, acceleration, pressure, temperature, and humidity.
- **Temperature Sensors** — Thermocouples can sense temperature variations in civil structures relating to castings and during the actual construction activity.

- **Acoustic Emission Sensor** — High-frequency energy signal measuring sensors can assess the current state of materials under stress. They are mainly used to detect the growth or onset of cracks in civil structures.
- **Accelerometer** — Measures acceleration force (dynamic or static) in multiple directions across the axis. Dynamic is when a transport vehicle crosses the bridge, while static is like the gravity acting on various components of the civil structure.
- **Vibrating Wire Transducers** — This is a wire sensor made up of tensioned steel wire, vibrating at a frequency of tensioned steel wire used to measure static strain, pressure, tilt, stress, displacement. They are used for monitoring structures, such as dams, tunnels, mines, bridges, foundations, excavations, piles, etc.
- **Tiltmeter** — Measures the inclination of a civil structure and can predict early warnings of any damages to the structure. This can measure the slope, elevation, and tilt of the object in reference to gravity. This is used in the rotation of structures like dams, walls.
- **Linear Variable Differential Transformer (LVDT)** — Measures linear displacement and can be used to measure temperature variations, and displacements due to living loads.
- **Inclinometer (Slope Indicator)** — This is a precision instrument used for deformations and subsurface movements. It can determine if the subsurface movements are constant, accelerating, or responding to any remedial measures. It can monitor settlement profiles of embankments, foundations, and other structural components. These are designed to measure horizontal subsurface deformation in a borehole when slope stability is a concern for natural slopes, constructed cut/fill slopes, and deep fill projects.
- **Load Cells** — This is a transducer used for measuring the tension, compression, pressure or torque as electrical output. They are used in many applications or even civil structures.
- **Strain Gauges** — Measures applied force on an object, monitors, and measures the strain in steel and reinforced concrete structures.

In traditional SHM systems, sensors were generally embedded into a structure. A centralized database system collected multiple sensed data relating to desired parameters of the installed structures. Key challenges involved complex installation procedures, costly erection charges, expensive maintenance, attenuation and sometimes even corruption of received data during such transmissions.

Structural health monitoring involves automated processes for sensing the loads accumulated by structures and simultaneously suggesting the diagnosis of the structural health based on the collected information if the system to monitor structural health is working in real-time and requires appropriate technologies to implement it [6].

Deep learning algorithms can be utilized for crack identification and condition assessment. The importance of control sensors and virtual reference are investigated in the naval field live monitoring of strains and damage detection is required. Structural health monitoring algorithm plays an important role for dynamic studies, like checking the design limits, sea keeping test, damage detection and life estimation of any part [7].

The heritage structures are in danger due to aggressive environmental conditions and vulnerable activities [8]. But it is also true that deploying wired or wireless sensors to monitor structural health is costly and time-consuming as well. There is a need to use a more innovative approach that can be used with engineering applications and can have different routines to research for long term and short-term structural health monitoring system. Structural health monitoring can be utilized to predict the future damage accumulation behaviour of wind turbines and ultimately the predefined service life can be achieved through a balanced power production and load reduction and it also helps in reducing the operational and maintenance costs of wind turbines [9].

Fiber optic sensors have certain characteristics like simplicity, immunity to corrosion nonintrusive sensing, which makes it a prevalent approach to structural health monitoring [10]. Railroad track are a good option of transportation. It is also requiring strong safeguarding and prevention of mishaps. Fiber optic sensors can play a very important role in developing a complete structural health monitoring system for safeguarding all components of the railroad network. IoT-based structural health monitoring devices are designed and the experimental testing and validation process has been conducted. In the study, it is found that low-cost wireless devices equipped with sensors can be deployed in the structural elements to measure the stress with acceleration. After deploying, the sensor devices can become a part of the IoT ecosystem, which can alert if the safety of the structure is compromised or diminished [11].

The research studies and works of several researchers and practitioners across the world as discussed further confirm the strong relationship between digital twin approaches integrated with SHMS. The digital twin framework is proposed to track and assess the lifetime structures. It can be functioning on two modes, i.e., online and offline and used for diagnosis, model updating, performance evaluation and data analysis. In the study, it is found that the framework is effective to predict crack growth and uncertainties through information entropy and relative entropy [12].

Including digital twin technology in the construction industry enhances the opportunity to integrate the physical world into the digital world [13].

The manufacturing and automotive industries are taking benefits of digital technologies to solve their challenges. Digital twin technologies can resolve many of the challenges of the construction industry. Machine learning tools and structural engineering collaboratively can be utilized for structural health monitoring and rapid damage detection. The proposed framework in the research is based on human-machine collaboration which can be applied on real instrumented buildings and capable to correctly identify damage and also eliminates false positive detection [14].

Review of extant literature on structural health monitoring technologies reveals that the advanced technologies which can be used for SHM relate to recent research only. It reveals that these techniques are not fully explored and implemented yet. Radar interferometry and operational model analysis by accelerometer are also important methods for structural health assessment [15].

A digital twin approach based on a nonparametric Bayesian network is proposed which can be effective for structural health monitoring, and this method can learn the number of distributions of hidden variables through data collected and is capable to establish health indicators based on modulation transfer function [16].

Cables are very crucial components in cable-stayed bridges. Monitoring of cables is very important to ensure the safety of the bridge while there are various traditional, as well as modern innovative methods for monitoring of cable force [17].

Structural repairs may alter the physical properties of any structure, and it should not be treated as the same after the repairing process. There is a change in response to structural health assessment in prerepair and postrepair data distribution [18].

Metric informed transfer learning methods can be utilized to map prerepair and postrepair data. Multipurpose sensors can be used for structural health monitoring of aerospace composites also. A review of studies upon the usage of different types of sensors, their embedding process, which is well defined could be applied to different kinds of structures whether it is a building, bridge, aircraft, or naval architecture [19].

Simulating damage evolution from the current state to failure is important while implementing structural health management or the digital twin concept [20].

Traditionally, damage diagnosis and prognosis were considered to be two different tasks, but recently these tasks are considered to be related through a stochastic feedback loop. While diagnosing the damage, it can be quantified and then fed to the prognosis component. This process of feed forwarding plays a crucial role in decision making for the structure's future operational readiness. Dynamic Bayesian networks extend standard Bayesian networks with the concept of time. This allows us to model time series or sequences [21].

Dynamic Bayesian networks (DBN) is suitable to build a health monitoring model for aircraft since its structural health status varies from one product to another. Diagnosis and prognosis both can be performed through DBN. Assessment of crack growth and its consequences is difficult through statistical methods and predicting crack growth is an important aspect of structural health monitoring systems [22].

The study proposed a framework by using advanced techniques like 3D FEA, RBF response surface and MCMC for accurate deterministic crack propagation and simulations. The traditional methods for damage detection in structures are replaced by emerging technologies viz. machine learning, IoT and big data analytics, but these technologies are not fully matured yet, hence continued exploration is required for being utilized in developing structural health monitoring [23].

A parallel development in multidisciplinary fields is the demand of time. Structural health monitoring should be united with all aspects of the digital revolution and Industry 4.0 together. Optimal deployment of microsensors is important while designing effective SHM so that a sensor network topology can be designed with improved capabilities. Signal processing is equally vital while gathering measurements data to efficiently handle the real-time estimations of structural health [24].

With advancements in recent technology, SHM is now crucial and needs to be integrated with the modern technological capabilities of machine learning and deep learning. It is interesting to note that even high-speed railroads require precise structural health monitoring systems that are capable of monitoring shallow underground environments too. Sensors can be deployed underground but large antenna elements may cause damage resulting from geological stressors [25].

Sensors deployed underground could effectively monitor different soil moisture conditions; however, it requires low-frequency wireless channels for seamless communication [26]. In the United States, SHMS integrated with digital technology has been installed and validated for digital twin on a large-scale bridge. The mechanism detects and reports changes in bridge behaviour at an early stage. The experiment done with both the mechanisms display identical behaviour and the absolute values deviate not more than 5%, which seems to be within tolerance limits. This assisted in checking the safety of construction and performances during as well as after founding alternative load paths for arch supports required for the Henry Hudson I89 Bridge [26]. The DT clearly differs from standard engineering models, since it is not simply used to assess the system safety, but also to study structural evolution in time (past and future), perform precise damage prediction or application in maintenance operations [27].

Suitable sensors are used to generate data about damage detection and its localization. An RB Model with the classification provides a good view into the damage on the entire domain. It was found that the MOR techniques in combination with decoupling tasks are based upon sensor responses for different environments, as well as operational conditions [28].

Current research also indicates high economic benefits arising from installing SHM systems for comprehensive analysis about infrastructure status, risk factor identification, and overall lifecycle management of the structure through the value of information (VoI) analysis [29].

Civil structures by natural virtues would degrade in integrity over time. Data randomness in this regard also increases over time in comparison to complete spatial randomness. Traditional analytical methods could hardly detect data anomalies as only simple single computations produced less accurate results. Spatial analysis using advanced 3D point data and longitudinal datasets help resolve complex computations and generating multilevel decision information for much better SHMS [30].

Another noninvasive and nondestructive method of Muon scattering tomography with a digital twinning approach helps improve penetration depth and precision levels about reinforcement in large concrete objects [31].

8.4 Conclusion

"Digital Twin (DT)" is a technological marvel that provides us with a virtual/digital representation counterpart of any physical object, service or process. The digital twin mimics an exact replica of a real-world entity. Such an entity could be any civil structure (like bridges, buildings, dams, jet engines or wind turbines, aeroplanes, ships, etc.), or an active system, process or activity.

Data generated from such sources can be obtained by employing sensors and real-time data can be sent to digital twin, which can give meaningful information and insights that will help in decision making.

Sensors integrated with physical infrastructure and digital twinning scientific approaches can serve mankind with quality structural health monitoring systems to effectively and efficiently manage valuable assets.

The evolving digital twin technology can be a game-changer in our lives. It can be allowed as a strategic technology in monitoring and predicting major failures and taking corrective measures in line with it.

The applicability of digital twin approach in SHMS is very helpful.

It is evident that Digital Twins as a technology can create virtual and digital replicas of small or large-scale physical objects, cities, buildings, regions and systems, and is therefore a very powerful technology. It can transform things. This transformation would certainly be a technological game-changer in the future of Industry 4.0 with adoption of smart manufacturing and monitoring strategies.

References

1. Negri, E., Fumagalli, L., Macchi, M., A review of the roles of digital twin in CPS-based production systems. *Proc. Manuf.*, *11*, 939–948, 2017.
2. Porter, M.E. and Heppelmann, J.E., How smart, connected products are transforming competition. *Harv. Bus. Rev.*, *92*, 11, 64–88, 2014.
3. Tilson, D., Lyytinen, K., Sørensen, C., Research commentary—Digital infrastructures: The missing IS research agenda. *Inf. Syst. Res.*, *21*, 4, 748–759, 2010.
4. Cai, Y., Starly, B., Cohen, P., Lee, Y.S., Sensor data and information fusion to construct digital-twins virtual machine tools for cyber-physical manufacturing. *Proc. Manuf.*, *10*, 1031–1042, 2017.
5. Rosen, R., Von Wichert, G., Lo, G., Bettenhausen, K.D., About the importance of autonomy and digital twins for the future of manufacturing, in: *IFAC-Papers online*, vol. *48*, pp. 567–572, 2015.
6. Bao, Y., Chen, Z., Wei, S., Xu, Y., Tang, Z., Li, H., The State of the Art of Data Science and Engineering in Structural Health Monitoring. *Engineering*, *5*, 2, 234–242, 2019, https://doi.org/10.1016/j.eng.2018.11.027.
7. Fanelli, P., Trupiano, S., Belardi, V.G., Vivio, F., Jannelli, E., Structural health monitoring algorithm application to a powerboat model impacting on water

surface. *Proc. Struct. Integr.*, *24*, 926–938, 2019, https://doi.org/10.1016/j.prostr.2020.02.081.

8. Gopinath, V.K. and Ramadoss, R., Review on structural health monitoring for restoration of heritage buildings. *Materials Today: Proceedings*, Vol. *43* Part-2, 1534–1538, 2020, https://doi.org/10.1016/j.matpr.2020.09.318.

9. Do, M.H. and Söffker, D., Wind turbine lifetime control using structural health monitoring and prognosis, in: *IFAC-Papers online*, vol. *53*, pp. 12669–12674, 2020.

10. Sasi, D., Philip, S., David, R., Swathi, J., A review on structural health monitoring of railroad track structures using fiber optic sensors. *Materials Today: Proceedings*, vol. *33*, pp. 3787–3793, 2020, https://doi.org/10.1016/j.matpr.2020.06.217.

11. Abruzzese, D., Micheletti, A., Tiero, A., Cosentino, M., Forconi, D., Grizzi, G., Scarano, G., Vuth, S., Abiuso, P., IoT sensors for modern structural health monitoring. A new frontier. *Proc. Struct. Integr.*, *25*, 2019, 378–385, 2020, https://doi.org/10.1016/j.prostr.2020.04.043.

12. Ye, Y., Yang, Q., Yang, F., Huo, Y., Meng, S., Digital twin for the structural health management of reusable spacecraft: A case study. *Eng. Fract. Mech.*, *234*, 1–3, 2020, https://doi.org/10.1016/j.engfracmech.2020.107076.

13. Opoku, D.G.J., Perera, S., Osei-Kyei, R., Rashidi, M., Digital twin application in the construction industry: A literature review. *J. Build. Eng.*, *40*, 1–9, 2021, https://doi.org/10.1016/j.jobe.2021.102726.

14. Muin, S. and Mosalam, K.M., Human-machine collaboration framework for structural health monitoring and resiliency. *Engineering Structures*, *235*, 1–3, 2021, https://doi.org/10.1016/j.engstruct.2021.112084.

15. Pallarés, F.J., Betti, M., Bartoli, G., Pallarés, L., Structural health monitoring (SHM) and Nondestructive testing (NDT) of slender masonry structures: A practical review. *Constr. Build. Mater.*, *297*, 1–33, 2021, https://doi.org/10.1016/j.conbuildmat.2021.123768.

16. Yu, J., Song, Y., Tang, D., Dai, J., A digital twin approach based on nonparametric Bayesian network for complex system health monitoring. *J. Manuf. Syst.*, *58*, 293–304, 2021, https://doi.org/10.1016/j.jmsy.2020.07.005.

17. Zhang, L., Qiu, G., Chen, Z., Structural health monitoring methods of cables in cable-stayed bridge: A review. *Meas.: J. Int. Meas. Confed.*, *168*, 1–2, 2021, https://doi.org/10.1016/j.measurement.2020.108343.

18. Gardner, P., Bull, L.A., Dervilis, N., Worden, K., Overcoming the problem of repair in structural health monitoring: Metric-informed transfer learning. *J. Sound Vib.*, *510*, June, 116245, 2021, https://doi.org/10.1016/j.jsv.2021.116245.

19. Rocha, H., Semprimoschnig, C., Nunes, J.P., Sensors for process and structural health monitoring of aerospace composites: A review. *Eng. Struct.*, *237*, 1–3, 2021, https://doi.org/10.1016/j.engstruct.2021.112231.

20. Leser, P.E. and Warner, J., A diagnosis-prognosis feedback loop for improved performance under uncertainties, in: *19th AIAA Non-Deterministic Approaches Conference*, p. 1564, 2017.

21. Li, C., Mahadevan, S., Ling, Y., Wang, L., Choze, S., A dynamic Bayesian network approach for digital twin, in: *19th AIAA Non-Deterministic Approaches Conference*, p. 1566, 2017.

22. Loghin, A. and Ismonov, S., Assessment of crack path uncertainty using 3D FEA and Response Surface Modeling, in: *AIAA Scitech 2020 Forum*, p. 2295, 2020.

23. Malekloo, A., Ozer, E., AlHamaydeh, M., Girolami, M., Machine learning and structural health monitoring overview with emerging technology and high-dimensional data source highlights. *Struct. Health Monit.*, 1–50, 2021, https://doi.org/10.1177/14759217211036880.

24. Mariani, S. and Azam, S.E., Health monitoring of flexible structures via surface-mounted microsensors: Network optimization and damage detection, in: *2020 5th International Conference on Robotics and Automation Engineering (ICRAE)*, IEEE, pp. 81–86, 2020, November.

25. Qiu, S., Mias, C., Guo, W., Geng, X., HS2 railway embankment monitoring: Effect of soil condition on underground signals. *SN Appl. Sci.*, *1*, 6, 537, 2019.

26. Andersen, J.E. and Rex, S., Structural health monitoring of Henry Hudson 189. *20th Congress of IABSE, New York City 2019: The Evolving Metropolis - Report*, pp. 2121–2131, 2019.

27. Angjeliu, G., Coronelli, D., Cardani, G., Development of the simulation model for digital twin applications in historical masonry buildings: The integration between numerical and experimental reality. *Comput. Struct.*, *238*, 106282, 2020.

28. Bigoni, C. and Hesthaven, J.S., Simulation-based anomaly detection and damage localization: An application to structural health monitoring. *Comput. Method. Appl. Mech. Eng.*, *363*, 112896, 2020.

29. Chadha, M., Hu, Z., Todd, M.D., An alternative quantification of the value of information in structural health monitoring. *Struct. Health Monitor.*, *21*, 1, 138–164, 14759217211028439, 2021.

30. Dargahi, M.M. and Lattanzi, D., Spatial statistical methods for complexity-based point cloud analysis, in: *ASME 2020 Conference on Smart materials, adaptive structures and intelligent systems (SMASIS)*, Vol. 84027, Paper No. SMASIS2020-2294, V001T05A007, 9 pages, American Society of Mechanical Engineers, U.S. (Verlag), 2020, September, ISBN: 978-0-7918-8402-7. https://doi.org/10.1115/SMASIS2020-2294.

31. Dobrowolska, M., Velthuis, J., Kopp, A., Perry, M., Pearson, P., Towards an application of muon scattering tomography as a technique for detecting rebars in concrete. *Smart Mater. Struct.*, *29*, 5, 055015, 2020.

32. Fuller, A., Fan, Z., Day, C., Barlow, C., Digital twin: Enabling technologies, challenges and open research. *IEEE Access*, *8*, 108952–108971, 2020.

33. Grieves, M. and Vickers, J., Digital twin: Mitigating unpredictable, undesirable emergent behavior in complex systems, in: *Transdisciplinary perspectives on complex systems*, F.J. Kahlen, S. Flumerfelt, A. Alves (Eds.), pp. 85–113, Springer, Cham, 2017, https://doi.org/10.1007/978-3-319-38756-7_4.

34. Grieves, M., Digital twin: Manufacturing excellence through virtual factory replication, in: *White paper*, vol. 1, pp. 1–7, 2014.

35. Grieves, M.W., Virtually intelligent product systems: Digital and physical twins. *Complex Syst. Eng., Theory Pract.*, 175–200, 2019.

36. Kritzinger, W., Karner, M., Traar, G., Henjes, J., Sihn, W., Digital twin in manufacturing: A categorical literature review and classification, in: *IFAC-Papers online*, vol. 51, pp. 1016–1022, 2018.

37. Singh, M., Fuenmayor, E., Hinchy, E.P., Qiao, Y., Murray, N., Devine, D., Digital twin: Origin to future. *Appl. Syst. Innov.*, 4, 36, 2021, https://doi.org/10.3390/asi4020036.

38. Mateev, M., Industry 4.0 and the digital twin for building industry. *Int. Sci. J. Ind. 4.0*, 5, 1, 29–32, 2020.

39. Terkaj, W. and Urgo, M., A virtual factory data model as a support tool for the simulation of manufacturing systems. *Proc. CIRP*, 28, 137–142, 2015.

40. Souza, V., Cruz, R., Silva, W., Lins, S., Lucena, V., A digital twin architecture based on the industrial internet of things technologies, in: *2019 IEEE International Conference on Consumer Electronics (ICCE)*, pp. 1–2, 2019, https://doi.org/10.1109/ICCE.2019.8662081.

41. Marai, O.E., Taleb, T., Song, J., Roads infrastructure digital twin: A step toward smarter cities realization. *IEEE Netw.*, 35, 2, 136–143, 2021.

9

Role and Advantages of Digital Twin in Oil and Gas Industry

Prakash J.

*Department of Computer Science & Engineering, PSG College of Technology,
Tamil Nadu, India*

Abstract

The emerging, high-level focus on utilizing simulation through means of digital twin to assist operational choices should be welcomed by simulation and automation experts. However, it is believed that critical concerns like usability, maintainability, sustainability, effectiveness, and all other aspects should be seen and evaluated if the entire potential of digital twins is to be achieved. This chapter discusses about the technology of digital twin and explains the role of digital twin in oil and gas industry by conducting a survey of the related literature.

Keywords: Digital twin, oil and gas, simulation, virtual, National Aeronautics and Space Administration (NASA), advantages

9.1 Introduction

One of the effectively growing technology is "digital twin." It was even named among first ten strategic technology trends by Gartner in the year 2017. According to Gartner, the concept of digital twin is indeed not recent, as engineering simulation has been around for at least thirty years.

They credit National Aeronautics and Space Administration (NASA) researchers with the twin notion, which dates back to the Apollo 13 mission. Gartner has also mentioned digital twin can be viewed as considered one of the milestones in the technology of simulation.

Email: jpk.cse@psgtech.ac.in

Manisha Vohra (ed.) Digital Twin Technology: Fundamentals and Applications, (141–158) © 2023
Scrivener Publishing LLC

This approach is valuable, but it obscures work done in recent decades to address localized control and monitoring problems by aligning simulations with operational data. This chapter will give an overview of the digital twin technology with its evolution and trend of research in the current era with the characteristics, advantages, and application in the various fields.

The role of the digital twin in the field of the oil and gas industry along with its benefits is been studied. This chapter is organized in different sections.

Section 9.2 to 9.3: The introduction of digital twin and evolution is explained.

Section 9.4: Discusses regarding the categories of digital twin.

Section 9.5: The advantage of digital twin are discussed in section 9.5

Section 9.6: The application of digital twin are discussed in section 9.6.

Section 9.7: The characteristics of the digital twin are discussed.

Section 9.8 to 9.9: The role of the digital twin in oil and gas industry and its role in various sectors is discussed in sections 9.8 to 9.9.

Section 9.10: The advantages of Digital Twin in the Oil and Gas Industry are discussed.

Section 9.11: Consists of the conclusion.

9.2   Digital Twin

Industry 4.0 wave is having different concepts associated with it. Among those different concepts is digital twin which is one of the main concepts associated with the wave of Industry 4.0 and in fact it is a core component of Industry 4.0 [18, 19]. Digital twin is known as a crucial part of Industry 4.0 roadmap [29].

In nowadays very competitive markets, the aspirations for reducing the time to market and for bringing an increase in the product development performance fuel the application of sophisticated virtual product models, which are frequently referred to as digital twins which are having great importance [24].

The word "digital twin" refers to or means a virtual model or virtual copy of any actual product or object. Digital twin is based on real-time data. A digital twin, according to Defense Acquisition University, is defined as "An integrated multi-physics, multi-scale, probabilistic simulation of an as-built system, enabled by digital thread that uses the best available models, sensor information, and input data to mirror and predict activities/performance over the life of its corresponding physical twin."

Digital twin is a virtual representation of a real world subject or a real world object [16]. Digital Twin technology is a concept which is emerging and it is now for the industry, a center of attention. In the past few years, digital twin is also the center of attention academia [26].

Just like a virtual prototype, digital twin is a dynamic digital representation of a physical system [8]. Based on the given definitions of a Digital Twin in any context, one might identify a commonly digital twin can be understood as digital counterparts of physical objects [11]. It is meant as a system's digital counterpart along its lifecycle [9]. It is a highly dynamic concept [12].

A digital twin can be used to understand not just how products are working now, but also how things will operate in the future. They can predict if any problem will happen.

For digital twin sensors are used which do the work of collecting data of a physical object's real-time working condition, position, or status. Since the sensors are collecting real-time data, the digital twin will behave accordingly.

The digital twin will accordingly keep updating itself in real-time. After being given the real-time information, the virtual model can carry out simulations, investigate performance concerns, and suggest changes. Digital twin gives useful insights which are very important. Digital twin lets virtual entities exist simultaneously with physical entities [3].

Digital Twin is now being more and more explored as a way to improve the performance of physical entities via leveraging computational techniques, themselves enabled through virtual counterpart [10]. A digital twin should have the ability to give assurance of services which are well defined to support activities such as management, monitoring optimization, safety, etc. [6].

Digital twin application dispenses value creation in the fields of service management and operations [14]. It has been decades since the concept of digital twin has been around [13]. The impact in real of digital twin has come into existence in recent years despite the concept being decades old [6]. Digital twin at present is an emerging trend and even an important trend in different applications [7].

Over the period of last year, most of the days there was announcement from industry announcing a new project involving digital twins or a scholarly publication with digital twin in the title [28]. Nowadays, digital twin is being developed and commercialized in order to optimize various processes of aviation and manufacturing [5].

Digital Twin is a kind of concept which has the opportunity to change how we see system design, operation and manufacturing [1].Traditionally manufacturing is defined as a process which turns raw materials into physical products [21].

Three dimensions of technology-driven service innovation are needed to be understood to provide digital services in product service system which are service ecosystem, service platform and value co-creation [17]. The rising use of information and communication technology enables digital engineering of products and production processes alike [20].

Manufacturing systems design is a complex and critical activity [23]. Determining and understanding energy use at all the stages of manufacturing process is necessary for optimising manufacturing processes and facility management to reduce the consumption of energy [25].

For the present manufacturing systems, digital twins are salient enablers [15]. Due to all the developments that are seen recently in Industry 4.0 and digital twin, there has been a growth in interest to adapt the concept of digital twin along with other concepts to get autonomous maintenance [4]. However, the actual success of the digital twin model will rest on the value it creates for manufacturers and users of their products [27].

In Industry 4.0 wave, cyber-physical systems are also of importance. The information which digital twin provides can offer different possibilities of optimization for a cyber-physical system [2]. Similarly, digital twin can be of help in various applications. Oil and gas industry which is a very crucial industry can also benefit from digital twin. Correct implementation of digital twin can offer many opportunities for the oil and gas industry [22].

9.3   Evolution of Digital Twin Technology

In 2010, in are port of NASA, digital twin was termed. It had started to evolve. Digital Twins is now looked as a great resource in manufacturing systems. Its predicting nature can benefit the manufacturing systems (Figure 9.1).

The digital twin can present a digital version of a physical manufacturing system that could help the manufacturers. They can according to the digital twins prediction, work and make adjustments or changes when manufacturing a product in reality.

The concept of the digital twin was introduced in 1960s by NASA. They used this technology on the mission Apollo 13 and in 1970.

In 2002, Dr. Grieves introduced the concept of the digital twin. Few years later, this technology got its name as digital twin and it went on progressing. With the rapid development and progress of the digital twin, it was listed as the top 10 strategic trends by Garter in 2017.

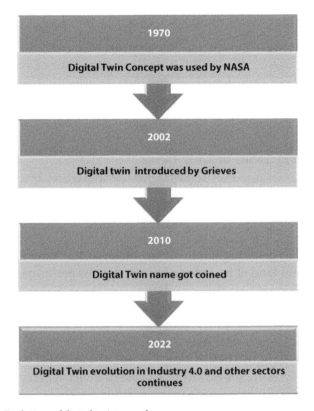

Figure 9.1 Evolution of digital twin over the years.

9.4   Various Digital Twins that Can Be Built

- Parts twins
- Product twins or Asset Twins
- System twins or Unit Twins
- Process twins

9.4.1   Parts Twins

Parts twins are the fundamental building blocks of digital twins. The physical, mechanical, and electrical properties of a part can be understood using virtual representations of the components.

9.4.2 Product Twins or Asset Twins

If more than two components are working with one and other for forming a product, it can be then called as an asset also. Asset or product twins allow to find out how those elements interact, which generates a plethora of performing data which can be analyzed and converted into useful information.

9.4.3 System Twins or Unit Twins

System twins enables engineers to manage and maintain vast fleets of diverse products that collaborate to produce a system-level outcome. Also, it allows you to observe how various products interact to build a fully functional system.

System twins give insight into different interaction of the asset and may propose certain kind of improvement related to the performance.

9.4.4 Process Twins

Process twin demonstrates how several systems interact to form a complete manufacturing facility. It may also be used to duplicate procedures and the flow of work. Process twins can aid in understanding of outcome of several systems interaction in manufacturing facility.

Thus scheduling of any scheme required for making the outcome appropriate if found to be not at par with expectations can be done seeing the results of process twins. Process twinning also allows for the optimization of the work in the refinement of raw materials and the manufacturing of final goods.

9.5 Advantage of Digital Twin

Digital twin technology has numerous advantages. The following are some of the advantages of digital twin.

- Paced prototyping
- Prediction
- Enhanced maintenance
- Monitoring
- Safety
- Reduced waste

9.5.1   Paced Prototypin

As virtual simulations allow for the examination of several possibilities, the analysis, and design phases are shortened, allowing prototype and re-designing easier and quicker.

9.5.2   Prediction

Digital twin can forecast problems for the real object or product giving the chance to make changes and develop systems accordingly. It can foresee issues at various phases of the product cycle thanks to the possible actual real-time data flow between the physical object and its digital twin.

9.5.3   Enhanced Maintenance

Existing maintenance approaches are reactive rather than proactive, as they are built on heuristic expertise and the worst scenarios rather than the unique material, structural arrangement, and usage of an individual item.

9.5.4   Monitoring

Through the digital counterpart of the physical object, it can be monitored. The process of monitoring becomes easier with digital twin.

9.5.5   Safety

The ability of the digital twin to predict problems helps minimize the likelihood of disasters and catastrophic breakdowns in sectors such as oil and gas or mines, wherein work environments are harsh and dangerous.

9.5.6   Reduced Waste

When the digital twin is used to create and test product or systems concepts in a virtual world, it can save a lot of time and money. To finalize a product before production, it can be checked and evaluated using digital twin to avoid any problems so that there is no waste by working on a problematic product for production.

9.6   Applications of Digital Twin

The different applications of digital twin are listed and explained below.

- Aerospace
- Power-generation equipment
- Structures and their system
- Manufacturing operations
- Healthcare services
- Automotive industry
- Urban planning and construction
- Smart cities
- Industrial applications

9.6.1   Aerospace

Physical twins were employed in aeronautical engineering before digital twins. With the digital twin, the NASA experts on the ground were able to mimic the aircraft state and identify solutions when significant difficulties emerged during Apollo 13 mission in 1970.

Now with advances, digital twins can be used to predict any potential problems with airframes, engines, or other components, ensuring the safety of everyone onboard.

9.6.2   Power-Generation Equipment

The digital twins can be great for heavy locomotives, such as power-generation turbines, locomotive engines and jet engines to establish their timeliness and carry the routine maintenance, making their work easier and simpler.

9.6.3   Structures and Their Systems

Digital twins can be used to improve big physical structures, such as skyscrapers or offshore drilling facilities, especially during the design phase. Also, they can be helpful in the design of systems that operate within buildings, such as heating, ventilation, and air conditioning system, etc.

9.6.4   Manufacturing Operations

In manufacturing, digital twin can mimic design of a product's full lifespan in all phases of manufacturing, leading items from concept to the final product and everything in between.

9.6.5   Healthcare Services

In the field of healthcare, using digital twins could be useful in medical developing of products for healthcare services, testing of products for healthcare services, etc. The generated data logger can be used provide critical insights here.

9.6.6   Automotive Industry

In the automotive industry, automobiles have a wide range of complex, interconnected systems, and digital twins can be widely utilized in vehicle design to enhance the performance of the vehicle and also in boosting manufacturing efficiency by monitoring.

9.6.7   Urban Planning and Construction

In the field of urban planning, the digital twins, if deployed, could help with urban strategic planning and construction substantially.

9.6.8   Smart Cities

In smart city design and implementation, the digital can enhance resource efficiency, can be employed in various activities for smart city development. It can assist urban planners, guide with traffic management, etc. for smart city development. The information from the digital twins also aids in making educated judgments about the future situation.

9.6.9   Industrial Applications

Industrial companies that implement digital twins could virtually analyze, monitor, and manage their systems well. Digital twins also can aid in the prediction of future activities and abnormalities.

9.7 Characteristics of Digital Twin

Digital Twins have the below characteristics:

- *High-fidelity*
- *Lively*
- *Multidisciplinary*
- *Homogenization*
- *Digital footprint*

9.7.1 High-Fidelity

In terms of look, contents, functioning, and so forth, a digital twin must be a relatively exact duplicate of its processes with a high degree of accuracy. Digital twin can duplicate every element of its physical counterpart in a virtual representation.

When digital twin model is created, it is provided with all available real-time data, so that they can tell about possible future scenarios, this degree of detail helps them to be more trustworthy.

9.7.2 Lively

The physical system is dynamic, which means it evolves throughout time. As a result, a digital twin must evolve in tandem with the physical system. This is accomplished by establishing a constant link between the digital and physical worlds, through which the data can be sent.

9.7.3 Multidisciplinary

A great contributor to Industry 4.0 is digital twin, which observes the fusion of multiple areas such as communication, mechanical, electronic, information technology, industrial engineering, mechatronics, electrical, and computer science and works as required.

9.7.4 Homogenization

Digital twins facilitate data homogenization and are as well the result of data homogenization. Any sort of information or material can be saved and communicated in a digital medium and due to this, it may be utilized to construct a virtual model of a product.

This breaks down the data from its actual physical reality state. As a result of this break down of data from its actual physical reality and also due to homogenization of data, digital twins have emerged.

9.7.5 Digital Footprint

Digital twin technology can generate digital footprint. The digital footprint can be useful to just go back and verify the footprint of the digital twin when a machine failed, for example, to determine where the failure occurred.

These diagnoses may be utilized by the machine's maker in the future to enhance the design of the equipment so that similar failures occur less frequently or do not occur.

9.8 Digital Twin in Oil and Gas Industry

Digital innovations can change how gas and oil firms tackle critical business challenges having the potential to generate a lot of value. There are already areas of digital competence in business, such as flow assurance and reservoir modeling.

However, there will be still enormous scope to grow further with digital technology by enabling improved collaboration among disciplines, resource groups and stakeholders of the value chain.

Digital twin technology has the potential to play a significant role for oil and gas companies. However, they need to be ready to use the technology to fundamentally change the way their companies operate.

It is estimated that digital twins will increasingly play a pivotal role in reshaping the industry's operating and business models, which includes oil and gas area industry as well. Companies can benefit from the potential of digital twins.

Oil and gas firms can ease out their work to some extent by using a viable digital twin solution. For the oil and gas industries, digital twin innovation has the capacity to provide substantial value.

They must, however, be prepared to utilize technology and transform the way their businesses function. Digital twins can play an increasingly important role in altering the industry's operational and economic structures.

Oil and gas industries can use digital twins to identify early symptoms of current equipment malfunction or deterioration by monitoring it, allowing them to prepare and perform corrective maintenance activities earlier to the failure happens, which will even reduce cost.

It can also help in design of new tools and equipments, simulate drill and extraction methods, and also it can obtain real-time data inputs from devices in an operating asset to determine its exact status and functioning, regardless of its location.

The true value of the digital twin concept is achieved when all elements of an asset are put together just to improve the asset over time. Cost considerations, logistical problems and even possible safety risks may all be put to the test.

A digital twin enables users to evaluate a variety of possible scenarios for a product and its possible effect. Most of the oil industry's digital twin work can be focused on base design and other installations, with data from both current and future setups can continually input into the simulations.

By keeping data from all around the globe in the cloud, accurate and comprehensive data may be utilized to guarantee that a new model is both correct and thoroughly tested. Although it necessitates a substantial investment in infrastructure, sensors, and analysis, many businesses think it is beneficial.

The idea of a digital twin can also be used in logistics for oil and gas industry, where it may assist in selection about creation and utilization by analyzing how activities or occurrences influence a virtual representation of an item.

The digital twin can help the operators effectively to assess the most suitable methods to achieve both efficient productivity and people's safety because it can mimic not only present conditions but also predict exceptional scenarios.

9.9   Role of Digital Twin in the Various Areas of Oil and Gas Industry

The digital twins can play a vital role in various areas of the oil and gas industry, some of the places where the digital twin can be deployed in the field of oil and gas industry are listed and discussed below.

- Planning of drilling process
- Performance monitoring of oil field
- Data analytics and simulation for oil field production
- Improving field personnel and workforce safety
- Predictive maintenance

9.9.1   Planning of Drilling Process

In modern and intricate drilling operations, the digital twin is critical. Drilling companies may use digital twin to spot possible faults and improve the efficiency of maintenance operations on drilling rigs.

It also has the ability to minimize well building time and costs while enhancing the supply chain by well services, scheduling rig movements, and other services.

9.9.2   Performance Monitoring of Oil Field

The digital twin improves a plant's growth and productivity characteristics dramatically, which may be especially beneficial for oil and gas operations. Companies can use digital twins to determine whether or not a plant is performing at its best.

It also aids in the detection of equipment concerns that might cause unexpected delay or the correction of process irregularities before they lead to rework, quality slip or trash.

9.9.3   Data Analytics and Simulation for Oil Field Production

Production facility simulators have the ability to assist workers in determining the best operating procedures. Data analytics and simulations is an integral aspect of a digital twin that evaluates existing data flows and quickly offers feasible alternatives to enable system operators make decisions when problems develop.

9.9.4   Improving Field Personnel and Workforce Safety

When it comes to protecting the safety of employees, the digital twin has numerous elements. Organizations are best placed to analyze numerous possible exposure, such as weights being lifted, radiation and fatigue prediction exposure, using the digital twin idea, and generate immediate mitigation steps as a result.

9.9.5   Predictive Maintenance

With the advent of IoT and digital twins, organizations can now create a predictive maintenance model that optimizes the maintenance cycle and strikes the ideal balance between corrective and preventative maintenance.

What is the purpose of predictive maintenance is the question that arises in the minds of many people. It employs just-in-time component replacement, which not only replaces components that are on the verge of failing, but also extends component life by minimizing unplanned maintenance and labor expenses.

9.10   The Advantages of Digital Twin in the Oil and Gas Industry

The major advantages to the operators in the oil and gas companies from the digital twin are as follows:

- Production efficacy
- Preemptive maintenance
- Scenario development
- Different processes monitoring
- Compliance criteria
- Cost Savings
- Workplace Safety

9.10.1   Production Efficacy

When strong productivity patterns are coupled with geological information, greater consistency and optimized output from reservoirs may be achieved. Digital twins are being used by businesses to help them make educated decisions and provide a digital vision for effective processes.

9.10.2   Preemptive Maintenance

A comprehensive view of maintenance and equipment data reveals preventive difficulties which can be worked on to lower the downtime expense.

9.10.3   Scenario Development

Geoscience data and equipment measurements might provide possibilities to improve drilling or simplify activities around improved, healthier extraction techniques. The digital twin is very much useful in these cases in obtaining this information.

9.10.4   Different Processes Monitoring

Many different ongoing process needs to checked and monitored in oil and gas industry. For example, the bore process, if it needs to be checked and monitored, drill operators may use actual information in seeing how the bore is doing at a particular time and make adjustments to ensure maximum performance. Digital twin can help in this as well as other processes monitoring also.

9.10.5   Compliance Criteria

Digital twin based monitoring and all the data given by digital twin could help identify and resolve compliance concerns or else they can cause harm.

9.10.6   Cost Savings

The use of digital twins can results in considerable cost savings. Oil and gas industry has a huge expenditure. Digital twins could help cut down some of the cost and result in some cost savings.

9.10.7   Workplace Safety

Oil and gas firms may develop safer work conditions by utilizing smart wearable such as a wristwatch, wearable holographic computers or smart heads-up display (HUD), Bluetooth low energy (BLE) tags, and smart work wear (biometric vests, hard helmets, and boots).

The equipment, which is backed up by a digital twin, aids in creating awareness of operator location, this will help in avoiding the operator's exposure to dangerous environments. The operator will only go at required location, eliminating operator fatigue.

9.11   Conclusion

Digital twin technology is a concept that has the interest of people from various sectors in the recent decade. This is due to the kind of advantages it can provide to in various sectors. This chapter explained digital twin in general as well as its role in oil and gas industry.

It also shed light on the various advantages and applications of digital twin. Also, a range of characteristics of digital twin was explained, along with explaining its advantages in oil and gas industry.

References

1. Grieves, M. and Vickers, J., Digital twin: Mitigating unpredictable, undesirable emergent behavior in complex systems, in: *Transdisciplinary perspectives on complex systems*, pp. 85–113, 2016.
2. Josifovska, K., Yigitbas, E., Engels, G., Reference framework for digital twins within cyber-physical systems, in: *Proceedings of IEEE/ACM 5th International Workshop on Software Engineering for Smart Cyber-Physical Systems (SEsCPS)*, pp. 25–31, 2019, https://doi.org/10.1109/SEsCPS.2019.00012.
3. Kaarlela, T., Pieskä, S., Pitkäaho, T., Digital twin and virtual reality for safety training, in: *Proceedings of the 11th IEEE International Conference on Cognitive Infocommunications (CogInfoCom)*, Mariehamn, Finland, pp. 115–120, 2020.
4. Khan, S., Farnsworth, M., McWilliam, R., Erkoyuncu, J., On requirements digital twin-driven autonomous maintenance. *Annu. Rev. Control*, 50, 13–28, 2020.
5. Barricelli, B.R., Casiraghi, E., Fogli, D., Definitions, A survey on digital twin characteristics. pp. 167653–167671, 2019.
6. Singh, M., Fuenmayor, E., Hinchy, E.P., Qiao, Y., Murray, N., Devine, D., Digital twin: Origin to future. *Appl. Syst. Innov*, 4, 36, 2021, https://doi.org/10.3390/asi4020036.
7. Rasheed, A., San, O., Kvamsdal, T., Digital twin: Values, challenges and enablers. *IEEE Access*, 8, 21980–22012, 2020.
8. Madni, A.M., Madni, C.C., Lucero, S.D., Leveraging digital twin technology in model based systems engineering. *Syst.*, 7, 1–13, 2019.
9. Macchi, M., Roda, I., Negri, E., Fumagalli, L., Exploring the role of digital twin for asset lifecycle management, in: *IFAC-Papers online*, vol. 51, pp. 790–795, 2018.
10. Jones, D., Snider, C., Nassehi, A., Yon, J., Hicks, B., Characterising the digital twin: A systematic literature review. *CIRP J. Manuf. Sci. Technol. Part A*, 29, 36–52, 2020, https://doi.org/10.1016/j.cirpj.2020.02.002.
11. Kritzinger, W., Karner, M., Traar, G., Henjes, J., Sihn, W., Digital twin in manufacturing: A categorical literature review and classification, in: *IFAC-Papers online*, vol. 51, pp. 1016–1022, 2018.
12. Rosen, R., Wichert, G.V., Lo, G., Bettenhausen, K.D., About the importance of autonomy and digital twins for the future of manufacturing, in: *IFAC-Papers online*, vol. 48, pp. 567–572, 2015.
13. David, J., Lobov, A., Lanz, M., Leveraging digital twins for assisted learning of flexible manufacturing systems. *IEEE 16th International Conference on Industrial Informatics (INDIN)*, pp. 529–535, 2018.
14. West, S., Stoll, O., Meierhofer, J., Züst, S., Digital twin providing new opportunities for value co-creation through supporting decision-making. *Appl. Sci.*, 11, 3750, 2021.

15. Pasquale, F., Sokolov, M., Sinha, S., Deep learning enhanced digital twin for closed-loop in-process quality improvement. *CIRP Ann.*, 69, 1, 369–372, 20202020, https://doi.org/10.1016/j.cirp.2020.04.110.
16. Schluse, M. and Rossmann, J., From simulation to experimentable digital twins: Simulation-based development and operation of complex technical systems. *IEEE International Symposium on Systems Engineering (ISSE)*, IEEE, pp. 1–6, 2016.
17. West, S., Gaiardelli, P., Rapaccini, M., Exploring technology-driven service innovation in manufacturing firms through the lens of service dominant logic, in: *IFAC-Papers online*, vol. 51, pp. 1317–1322, 2018.
18. Negri, E., Fumagalli, L., Macchi, M., A review of the roles of digital twin in CPS-based production systems. *Proc. Manuf.*, 11, 939–948, 2017.
19. Uhlemann, T.H.-J., Lehmann, C., Steinhilper, R., The digital twin: Realizing the cyber-physical production system for Industry 4.0. *Proc. CIRP*, 335–340, 61, 2017.
20. Brettel, M., Friederichsen, N., Keller, M., Rosenberg, M., How virtualization, decentralization and network building change the manufacturing landscape: An Industry 4.0 perspective. *Int. J. Mech. Aerosp. Ind. Mech. Eng.*, 8, 37–44, 2014.
21. Lohtander, M., Ahonen, N., Lanz, M., Ratava, J., Kaakkunen, J., Micro manufacturing unit and the corresponding 3D-model for the digital twin. *Proc. Manuf.*, 25, 55–61, 2018.
22. Wanasinghe, T.R., Wroblewski, L., Petersen, B.K., Gosine, R.G., James, L. A., De Silva, O., Mann, G, K, I., Warrian, P. J., Digital twin for the oil and gas industry: Overview research trends opportunities and challenges. *IEEE Access*, 8, 104175–104197, 2020.
23. Terkaj, W. and Urgo, M., A virtual factory data model as a support tool for the simulation of manufacturing systems. *Proc. CIRP*, 28, 137–142, 2015.
24. Schleich, B., Anwer, N., Mathieu, L., Wartzack, S., Shaping the digital twin for design and production engineering. *CIRP Ann.*, 66, 1, 141–144, 2017.
25. Mawson, V.J. and Hughes, B.R., The development of modelling tools to improve energy efficiency in manufacturing processes and systems. *J. Manuf. Syst.*, 51, 95–105, Apr. 2019.
26. Fuller, A., Fan, Z., Day, C., Barlow, C., Digital twin: Enabling technologies, challenges and open research. *IEEE Access*, 8, 108952–108971, 2020.
27. Grieves, M.W., Virtually intelligent product systems: Digital and physical twins. *Complex Syst. Eng., Theory Pract.*, 175–200, 2019.
28. Romero, D., Wuest, T., Harik, R., Thoben, K.D., Towards a cyber-physical PLM environment: The role of digital product models, intelligent products, digital twins, product avatars and digital shadows. *IFAC-PapersOnLine*, 53, 10911–10916, 2020.
29. Mateev, M., Industry 4.0 and the digital twin for building industry. *Int. Sci. J. Industr. 4.0*, 5, 1, 29–32, 2020.

10

Digital Twin in Smart Cities: Application and Benefits

Manisha Vohra

Independent Researcher, India

Abstract

Digital twin is swiftly making its way into numerous applications. It is evolving at a fast pace. Any technology is basically used to simplify things, ease out work, provide as many as possible advantages, etc. In short, each technology works towards helping in the application where it is applied. Digital twin technology also does the same. When applied in development of smart cities, it works towards helping in fulfillment of it. It has the capabilities and proficiency through which it can benefit in the work of developing smart cities. In this book chapter, the application of digital twin in smart cities is discussed. How the digital twin can help in smart cities development in different ways is stated in this chapter. Along with it, its benefits are also discussed.

Keywords: Digital twin, smart cities, healthcare, construction, structural health, traffic management, power grid, drainage system

10.1 Introduction

In today's modern world, there are rapid developments and advancements taking place. People can stay connected with each other digitally or virtually through technology even if they are located miles away in real world. Such is accelerated pace of development and advancements in today's modern world.

To keep up with pace of developments and advancements, different sectors are also advancing. For example, manufacturing sector is advancing and with the introduction of the digital twin, it is advancing greatly.

Email: manishavohra94@gmail.com

Manisha Vohra (ed.) Digital Twin Technology: Fundamentals and Applications, (159–172) © 2023
Scrivener Publishing LLC

The digital twin concept has been around for decades but only with the quick rise of the Internet of Things (IoT) is that they are more widely considered as a tool of the future [1, 4].

In different domains, digital twin is fast becoming popular tool [10]. From academic and industrial perspective, digital twin is undergoing an increase in interest from both [14].

In various applications, digital twin is now an emerging trend and important trend and combination of trusted data sharing technologies like that of blockchain, with digital twin could facilitate the way to a new wave in studies of supply chain [7, 11]. Likewise in various other applications, digital twin could be useful.

Conceptually, digital twin mimics the state of its physical twin in real time and vice versa [3]. The concept of digital twin was first utilized by National Aeronautics and Space Administration (NASA).

The digital twin concept was utilized by NASA during Apollo 13 mission which took place in the year 1970. Prior to that, in 1960's, NASA had started working on the digital twin concept but it was not utilized then. In the year 1970, NASA utilized the digital twin concept during their Apollo 13 mission which proved to be helpful for them.

Michael Grieves during conference of Society of Manufacturing Engineers in Michigan University, which was held in the year 2002 introduced the digital twin model. He introduced the digital twin model as a concept for Product Lifecycle Management (PLM).

However, the term digital twin was not mentioned for the concept back then and in fact was not even coined till that time. It was only in the year 2010, that John Vickers from NASA in roadmap report coined the term Digital Twin.

The digital twin is very useful for different kind of applications. Digital twin can very well help in different applications. The advancements which are seen in the industry 4.0 concepts have enabled digital twins growth and especially in the area of manufacturing [30].

The increasing utilization of information and communication technology lets digital engineering of products and production processes alike [19]. Digital Twin is known as an important enabler for digital transformation [2]. Digital twins are expected to enrich the already present asset information system [15].

Interest has been growing in adapting the concept of digital twin along with different concept such as machine learning to get autonomous maintenance and all this is happening due to developments that are taking place in industry 4.0 recently [12].

It is required to understand three dimensions of technology-driven service innovation which are service platform, service ecosystem and value co-creation in order to provide digital services in product service system [13].

Talking about the example of manufacturing where there is advancement seen, different opportunities are opening up for manufacturers to help them obtain a new level of productivity due to increase in digitalization in each stage of manufacturing [8].

The digitalization of manufacturing fuels the application of sophisticated virtual product models, which are referred to as the digital twins, throughout all the stages of product realization [5].

There is a great potential for analysis of energy and material flows due to capabilities of accurate machine representation and real or near-real-time process analysis because of adoption of digital twin in manufacturing facilities [9].

Digital twin should have the capability to guarantee services which are well-defined in order to support different activities like monitoring, maintenance, etc. [33]. The design of a manufacturing system is a complex as well as a critical activity entailing decisions which has an impact on a long time horizon and a large commitment of financial resources [6].

Digital twins give promise of great advantages for their different stakeholders when utilized in manufacturing to support design, management work of manufacturing, monitoring as well as control and optimisation as well of manufactured products, and production equipment and systems [21].

A manufacturing digital twin gives an opportunity to simulate and optimize the production system [1].

Digital twin allows better understanding and also prediction of performance of machines for production, flow of production and cost structure [17].

Digital twin-based approaches usage in production environments gives opportunity to make decision-making better and presents more than one perspective regarding where and how it can support decision-making [18].

Digital twin concept for production process allows coupling of production system with the digital equivalent of it as a base for optimization having minimized delay between time of data acquisition and creation of digital twin [31]. Digital twin lets all the users and stakeholders to access and as well as monitor the physical twin status, irrespective of where they are currently present [29].

Cyber-physical digital twin system are becoming popular slowly and they enact a very vital role in Industry 4.0 and cyber-physical production system (CPPS) in the context of manufacturing [32]. A reference framework for Digital Twins within a cyber-physical systems (CPS) has been established by authors in [16]. Construction sector is another sector which is advancing. The construction sector is advancing and building smart structures, healthcare sector is upgrading through technology and likewise various sectors are upgrading through technology.

Not just certain sectors are being updated and developed but along with it, cities are also getting updated and they are being developed and built as smart cities which leads to overall progress of the cities. The advancement of different sectors is in fact paving way for overall progress of the cities. It is helping the cities in getting developed and it is also in a way helping the cities to be built as smart cities.

Smart cities have a lot of benefits for the people residing in those cities. It benefits everyone in the city in some way or the other. Smart cities have enormous benefits which can reach out to the people in the city. Here again, technology plays a great role in development of the city and in building it as a smart city.

There are number of technologies which help and play a great role in development of the city and in building it as a smart city but out of the various technologies, there is one special technology which can drastically change the course of things. This one special technology is the digital twin technology. Digital twin can be very helpful when applied for smart cities.

10.2   Introduction of Digital Twin in Smart Cities

Digital twin is a digital representation of a real world object, product or process. The digital twin replicates not just the real world object, product or process but it even replicates its behavior and its details. The digital twin consist of some important parts.

Digital twin has such an in-built working functionality that makes it suitable to be applied in various applications. For it to function, it requires data. It does not remain static in nature. It can receive real-time data continuously.

After receiving the real-time data from say for example a real world object, the digital twin will change as per the changes happening in the real world object.

Along with this, digital twin has a useful ability of being able to give an estimation or prediction of what different issue or issues could turn up in an object or in anything what it is replicating. With this kind of ability, digital twin technology becomes very important. This ability of digital twin makes it favorable and highly suitable for application in different sectors.

The prediction of different issue or issues which could turn up in any object or in anything which is being replicated by digital twin is an ability or it can be even addressed as an advantage which has the potential to turn things drastically for the welfare of whatever is being replicated. Digital twin can help in various application including that of smart cities.

Smart cities concept is finding its feet and making its own place. Smart cities are being developed. Digital twin can play a great role in smart cities. They can transform functioning of many sectors in smart cities for their betterment.

In smart cities, application of digital twin can be truly of great help. A digital twin of an entire city can be made. By having a digital twin of a smart city, the what if scenarios can be simulated to be prepared for difficult situations like occurrence of floods, etc.

Digital twin technology is a technology which can help in the planning related work as well as development work of smart city. The city planners working on creating a smart city, using digital twin can test different what-if scenarios and accordingly work on it.

Digital twin can be used in various different application areas and sectors of the smart city, for example, management of traffic in a smart city can be done using digital twin. Also, digital twin can be used in construction, healthcare, etc. sectors of the smart city. Due to this, the digital twin will be able to give a lot of information regarding the application areas and sectors where it is applied which can be useful. This obtained information can be shared with different city departments which can be helpful. Seen as a basis of digital twin is linking of sensor data with city model [20].

In smart cities, digital twin application can bring transformation. It can ease out work. In smart cities, digital twin if used can thus help largely.

In smart cities, digital twin if used can help largely.

At present digital twin is already applied and used in different real world applications and it benefits them all. For example, Bridgestone Company is using digital twin technology for tire development [27] and likewise there are more such real examples of applications of digital twin where digital twin is proving to be helpful. When talking about digital twin applications in smart cities then digital twin has various different applications in smart cities, out of which some applications will be discussed in proceeding sections of the chapter.

10.3   Applications of Digital Twin in Smart Cities

Certain applications of digital twin in smart cities are mentioned and discussed as follows:

- Traffic management
- Construction
- Structural Health Monitoring
- Healthcare
- Digital Twin for Drainage System
- Digital Twin for Power Grid

10.3.1   Traffic Management

Traffic management is of utmost importance. In this fast moving world, everyone is in hurry while travelling most of the times for reaching their destination to where they are headed. There can be traffic on any given route of a city.

The number of vehicles out there on the road are growing and with the growing number of vehicles, traffic management becomes work becomes difficult. Any technology which could help in this case would be great. Digital twin can help the traffic department in this case.

Especially in development of smart cities, a resource like digital twin for traffic management would be great. Digital twin is already being utilized for traffic solutions. Consider the following example to understand how digital twin is helping in traffic management. Aimsun Company has built traffic networks digital twins. They simulate goods and people on the move. Due to this they are able to find out places in a traffic network operation which are weak and solution can be tested to get the traffic flow optimized [28].

The above example clearly shows that digital twin is very useful in traffic management by providing traffic solutions.

Some benefits of digital twin in traffic management for smart cities are as follows:

- Digital twin helps in easily finding out places that are weak in a traffic network.
- Any solution can be tested easily before implanting it.
- The traffic flow can be optimized using digital twin.
- Management of traffic for traffic department can become easier with the help of digital twin technology.

10.3.2   Construction

Construction is a very vital sector. Construction of different structures, buildings, etc. in smart cities can be done efficiently with help of digital twin. Be it the design phase, the actual construction phase or be it management of work during the construction, digital twin can pro-actively help in all these things.

In the design phase, digital twin data can be used efficiently. For example, digital can be used to test the effect and impact design changes will have and can thus make decisions on the basis of it. The design can be thus finalized accordingly.

In the construction stage, all the work being done can be monitored via the digital twin.

Monitoring of the construction work can be done using digital twin and not just monitoring but remote monitoring can be done. If anything is not as per the decided or planned process, it can be found out and corrected, thus ensuring smooth management of work.

If any errors or issues were to occur then they can be known prior to their actual occurrence and avoided with the help of digital twin. With digital twin, a lot of vital information about different parameters and aspects of the ongoing construction work can be obtained.

In modular construction work as well, digital twin can be helpful. For example, a digital twin model was recently made by Lendlease Group. It was made by them to test and know regarding feasibility of building multistory complex on a river location utilizing sustainable timber (exhibit). This timber had been utilized previously. However, it had not been tested in buildings of the height of 28- and 29-story apartment tower for building these apartment tower only the feasibility of utilizing sustainable timber (exhibit) had to be checked [24]. This was one example of application of digital twin in construction.

Another example of application of digital twin in construction is as follows. CadMakers Company successfully utilized digital twins. They used it for designing purpose. A building using digital twin was designed by them. The building is a hybrid masstimber building of 18 story [24].

Hence, for construction work in smart cities, digital twin can prove to be very advantageous.

Some of the benefits of digital twin in construction work in smart cities are as follows:

- Digital twin can help in different stages of construction work like design stage, actual construction stage, etc.

- Monitoring of the construction work will be easier with digital twin and even remote monitoring of is possible with digital twin.
- Digital twin can enable smooth management of construction work.
- Digital twin allows to find out the feasibility of materials in modular construction.

10.3.3   Structural Health Monitoring

The already built structures and the one that will be built, all require to be monitored so that the health of the structures can be known. For smart cities, the infrastructure has great value. All the structures should be in top notch condition.

Just going by the looks of any structure, its structural health cannot be precisely predicted. If the structural health is not good and if any structure like a bridge for example, consists of cracks or potholes or any other issues then it needs to be repaired and upgraded immediately. Ill health structures are a serious cause of concern and are hazards to safety of people.

Hence to avoid any bad consequences of ill structural health of any structure, timely maintenance and upgradation work needs to be performed. For this purpose, monitoring structural health is necessary and it can be done using digital twin.

The real-time data of any structure can be sent to digital twin model using sensors. The digital twin will keep on receiving real-time data and it will modify alongside changes in the digital twin. So using this digital twin, the structural health can be monitored and digital twin even allows for remote monitoring.

The digital twin can also predict and inform regarding the problems that could be faced with the structure and its structural health. Again here, the information and insights that digital twin gives are very vital. With digital twin, predictive maintenance of the structures can be carried out, which will be very beneficial. Hence, digital twin can be very effective and useful for structural health monitoring of different structures in smart city.

Some of the benefits of digital twin in construction for smart cities are as follows:

- The health of different structures built in smart cities can be easily monitored using digital twin.
- Digital twin can help with real-time monitoring of structures.

- When there is need for maintenance and upgradation of structures can be known by monitoring through digital twin remotely in real-time.
- Predictive maintenance of structures can also be carried out with digital twin.
- Safety hazards due to ill structural health can be avoided by knowing about ill health of structures timely.

10.3.4 Healthcare

Digital twin with the kind of advantages it possess, could be useful if included in healthcare. The healthcare sector is very important. Smart cities healthcare sector can benefit with application of digital twin. When a digital twin of a hospital is created, the hospital authorities can test different potential changes in various things like strategy which is operational based strategy, staffing, also capacities as well as care delivery models to find out what actions are required to be taken. For example, General Electric (GE) has introduced Hospital of Future (HoF) Digital Twin. The HoF Simulation Suite was specially designed for usage in healthcare [26].

Likewise, there are more possible applications of digital twin in healthcare. For example, digital twin can be used for workflow excellence. A private hospital in Dublin named as Mater Hospital included digital twin technology and achieved workflow excellence. They benefitted largely with digital twin application for their hospital. The hospital's management realized the urge for some kind of change in department of radiology. Certain issues such as the old becoming infrastructure, increasing patient demand, etc. was making it most difficult to provide efficient patient care. In order to get solution for these issues and to overcome them, the hospital then engaged Siemens Healthineers Value Partners for Healthcare Consulting Management who utilized digital twin technology and the resultant workflow excellence achieved thereafter was extremely useful and commendable [23].

Other than for achieving workflow excellence, digital twin can be used in manufacturing process of medical products which can be considered as a healthcare application and can be highly helpful. The time required in manufacturing the product and making it reach to the market can reduce, wastage can also be reduced, the process can be monitored remotely and more such benefits of using digital twin in manufacturing process of medical products can be gained. These are just few examples of digital twin application in healthcare. Similarly, there can be more such applications of the digital twin technology in healthcare.

Some of the benefits of digital twin in healthcare for smart cities are as follows:

- Medical product manufacturing process can be remotely monitored used digital twin to ensure the manufacturing process is going as planned.
- Digital twin can be helpful in development of medical facilities such as a hospital.
- Entire hospital's digital twin can be made to test virtually the effect of changes in operational strategy and other areas of a hospital.

10.3.5   Digital Twin for Drainage System

Drainage systems are having great importance, especially in smart cities, drainage systems should be and need to be well looked after. Digital twin can be made for drainage systems. The ones who have to manage the water i.e., water managers are always have to face water quality related challenges and flood issues which is why they are looking out for building digital twin of water systems.

These are surface water system whose digital twin will be made which will include all the data of the sensors along with online models for better understanding purpose and also to control the system dynamics. For this purpose, the authors [25] presents pipedream which is an end-to-end simulation engine. It is for real-time modeling and state estimation in natural/urban drainage networks. There are two things that the engine combines. The first one is a new hydraulic solver. This solver is based on one-dimensional Saint-Venant equations. The second one is a Kalman filtering scheme. This scheme efficiently updates hydraulic states based on observed data [25].

By utilizing sensor data from a real-world watershed, the authors find that the simulation engine is effective at both interpolating hydraulic states and forecasting future states based on current measurements. By providing a complete, real-time view of system hydraulics, the authors say that their software will enable rapid detection of flooding, improved characterization of maintenance and remediation needs, and robust real-time control for both small-scale (stormwater) and large-scale (river/reservoir) networks [25]. Thus, based on this, it can be stated that digital twin when used for drainage system can be highly beneficial and smart cities can gain all its benefits.

Some of the benefits of digital twin for drainage system in smart cities are as follows:

- Digital twin allows to look after the drainage systems in real-time.
- Digital twin will allow to better understand and control system dynamics.

10.3.6   Digital Twin for Power Grid

Digital twin can be very well used for power grid in smart cities. Power grids are very important. Digital twin application for power grid will be helpful. Digital twin is in fact already being for power grid. Hitachi Energy have recently introduced and launched IdentiQ. This is Hitachi Energy's digital twin solution for high-voltage direct current (HVDC) and power quality solutions. It will help to advance the world's energy system to be more flexible, sustainable and secure, accelerating the transition towards a carbon-neutral future [22].

The benefits of digital twin solution when used for power grid are clearly stated in this example and the biggest benefit is acceleration of the transition towards a carbon-neutral future. Digital twin functioning and benefits are such that it is found to be suitable and useful technology to be included and applied in different applications.

10.4   Conclusion

Digital twin is a technology which has the ability to bring transformation where applied. Digital twin is having various different applications in smart cities which will be very useful for the smart cities like application of digital twin in traffic management, healthcare, structural health monitoring, construction, etc. which are discussed in this chapter along with some of its benefits.

Digital twin can be truly helpful for smart cities. All the benefits that digital twin technology provides are very helpful for smart cities. Its abilities and proficiency are of great importance and use for smart cities. Digital twin thus with its functioning and benefits can transform the entire smart city and can be of great use.

References

1. Mateev, M., Industry 4.0 and the digital twin for building industry. *Int. Sci. J. Industr. 4.0*, 5, 1, 29–32, 2020.
2. Kritzinger, W., Karner, M., Traar, G., Henjes, J., Sihn, W., Digital twin in manufacturing: A categorical literature review and classification, in: *IFAC-Papers online*, vol. 51, pp. 1016–1022, 2018.
3. Singh, M., Fuenmayor, E., Hinchy, E.P., Qiao, Y., Murray, N., Devine, D., Digital twin: Origin to future. *Appl. Syst. Innov*, 4, 36, 2021, https://doi.org/10.3390/asi4020036.
4. David, J., Lobov, A., Lanz, M., Leveraging digital twins for assisted learning of flexible manufacturing systems. *IEEE 16th International Conference on Industrial Informatics (INDIN)*, pp. 529– 535, 2018.
5. Schleich, B., Anwer, N., Mathieu, L., Wartzack, S., Shaping the digital twin for design and production engineering. *CIRP Ann.*, 66, 1, 141–144, 2017.
6. Terkaj, W. and Urgo, M., A virtual factory data model as a support tool for the simulation of manufacturing systems. *Procedia CIRP*, vol. 28, pp. 137–142, 2015.
7. Rasheed, A., San, O., Kvamsdal, T., Digital twin: Values, challenges and enablers. *IEEE Access*, 8, 21980–22012, 2020.
8. Rosen, R., Wichert, G.V., Lo, G., Bettenhausen, K., About the importance of autonomy and digital twins for the future of manufacturing, in: *IFAC-Papers online*, vol. 48, pp. 567–572, 2015.
9. Mawson, V.J. and Hughes, B.R., The development of modelling tools to improve energy efficiency in manufacturing processes and systems. *J. Manuf. Syst.*, 51, 95–105, 2019.
10. Mylonas, G., Kalogeras, A., Kalogeras, G., Anagnostopoulos, c., Alexakos, c., Muñoz, l., Digital twins from smart manufacturing to smart cities: A survey. *IEEE Access*, 9, 143222–143249, 2021.
11. Longo, F., Nicoletti, L., Padovano, A., Ubiquitous knowledge empowers the smart factory: The impacts of a service-oriented digital twin on enterprises' performance. *Annu. Rev. Control*, 47, 221– 236, 2019.
12. Khan, S., Farnsworth, M., McWilliam, R., Erkoyuncu, J., On the requirements of digital twin-driven autonomous maintenance. *Annu. Rev. Control*, 50, 13–28, 2020.
13. West, S., Gaiardelli, P., Rapaccini, M., Exploring technology-driven service innovation in manufacturing firms through the lens of service dominant logic, in: *IFAC-Papers online*, vol. 51, pp. 1317–1322, 2018.
14. Jones, D., Snider, C., Nassehi, A., Yon, J., Hicks, B., Characterising the digital twin: A systematic literature review. *CIRP J. Manuf. Sci. Technol. Part A*, 29, 36–52, 2020, https://doi.org/10.1016/j.cirpj.2020.02.002.
15. Macchi, M., Roda, I., Negri, E., Fumagalli, L., Exploring the role of digital twin for asset lifecycle management, in: *IFAC-Papers online*, vol. 51, pp. 790–795, 2018.

16. Josifovska, K., Yigitbas, E., Engels, G., Reference framework for digital twins within cyber-physical systems, in: *Proceedings of the IEEE/ACM 5th International Workshop on Software Engineering for Smart Cyber-Physical Systems (SEsCPS)*, IEEE Xplore, pp. 25–31, 2019, https://doi.org/10.1109/SEsCPS.2019.00012.

17. Lohtander, M., Ahonen, N., Lanz, M., Ratava, J., Kaakkunen, J., Micro manufacturing unit and the corresponding 3d-model for the digital twin. *Procedia Manufacturing*, vol. 25, pp. 55–61, 2018.

18. West, S., Stoll, O., Meierhofer, J., Züst, S., Digital twin providing new opportunities for value co-creation through supporting decision-making. *Appl. Sci.*, 11, 3750, 2021.

19. Brettel, M., Friederichsen, N., Keller, M., Rosenberg, M., How virtualization, decentralization and network building change the manufacturing landscape: An industry 4.0 perspective. *Int. J. Mech. Aerosp. Ind. Mechatron. Eng.*, 8, 37–44, 2014.

20. Ruohomaki, T., Airaksinen, E., Huuska, P., Kesaniemi, O., Martikka, M., Suomisto, J., Smart city platform enabling digital twin. *2018 International Conference on Intelligent Systems (IS), IEEE Xplore 2019*, pp. 155–161, 2018.

21. Romero, D., Wuest, T., Harik, R., Thoben, K.D., Towards a cyber-physical plm environment: The role of digital product models, intelligent products, digital twins, product avatars and digital shadows, in: *IFAC-Papers online*, vol. 53, pp. 10911–10916, 2020.

22. Hitachi Energy launches IdentiQ™ digital twin for sustainable, flexible and secure power grids, news release, Hitachi energy. 1–4. https://www.hitachi.com/New/cnews/month/2021/11/211117.pdf.

23. Optimizing clinical operations through digital modeling, Case study, Siemens Healthcare GmbH· 7563 1019 online. 1–6, 2019. https://www.siemens-healthineers.com/en-in/services/value-partnerships/asset-center/case-studies/mater-private-workflow-simulation.

24. McKinsey & Company, Global infrastructure initiative, voices on infrastructure, scaling modular construction, voices. 1–45, September 2019. https://www.mckinsey.com/~/media/mckinsey/business%20functions/operations/our%20insights/voices%20on%20infrastructure%20scaling%20modular%20construction/gii-voices-sept-2019.pdf.

25. Bartos, M. and Kerkez, B., Pipedream: An interactive digital twin model for natural and urban drainage systems. *Environ. Model. Software*, 144, 105120, 1–11, 2021.

26. GE Healthcare Command Centers, What is a hospital of a future digital twin? https://www.gehccommandcenter.com/digital-twin.

27. Bridgestone, How Bridgestone's virtual tyre modelling revolutionalising tyre development. https://www.bridgestone.co.uk/story/mobility/how-bridgestones-virtual-tire-modelling-is-revolutionising-tire-development.

28. Aimsun, Traffic on the digital road, By Dr. Karin Kraschl-Hirschmann, Head of System Engineering and Innovation, Siemens Mobility, Austria,

GmbH, December 2020. https://www.aimsun.com/articles/traffic-on-the-digital-road/#:~:text=The%20digital%20twin%20of%2C%20for,optimisation%20parameters%2C%20and%20implementation%20options.

29. Barricelli, B.R., Casiraghi, E., Fogli, D., A survey on digital twin: Definitions, characteristics, applications, and design implications. *IEEE Access*, 7, 167653–167671, 2019.

30. Fuller, A., Fan, Z., Day, C., Barlow, C., Digital twin: Enabling technologies, challenges and open research. *IEEE Access*, 8, 108952–108971, 2020.

31. Uhlemann, T.H.-J., Lehmann, C., Steinhilper, R., The digital twin: Realizing the cyber-physical production system for industry 4.0. *Procedia CIRP*, vol. 61, pp. 335–340, 2017.

32. Lin, W.D. and Low, M.Y.H., Concept design of a system architecture for a manufacturing cyber-physical digital twin system. *IEEE International Conference on Industrial Engineering and Engineering Management (IEEM)*, pp. 1320–1324, 2021.

33. Cimino, C., Negri, E., Fumagalli, L., Review of digital twin applications in manufacturing. *Comput. Ind.*, 113, 103130, 2019.

Digital Twin in Pharmaceutical Industry

Anant Kumar Patel[1]*, Ashish Patel[2] and Kanchan Mona Patel[1]

[1]Department of Pharmacology, Swami Vivekanand College of Pharmacy, Indore, Madhya Pradesh, India
[2]Department of Medicine, M.G.M. Medical College, Indore, Madhya Pradesh, India

Abstract

The digital twin technology is a technology that can be useful for the pharmaceutical industry. Pharmaceutical industry is the one which is directly connected to healthcare. Hence, it is one of most important industry. Digital twin is a technology which can help the pharmaceutical industry. Since digital twin can help the pharmaceutical industry, application of it will be very useful for this industry. This chapter explains about the application of digital twin in pharmaceutical industry with examples. The advantages of digital twin in the pharmaceutical industry are also discussed and explained in this chapter.

Keywords: Digital twin, pharmaceutical industry, Internet of Things (IoT), digitalization, manufacturing, data, technology

11.1 Introduction

A digital twin is virtual replication or virtual copy of a physical object, product or process. Digital twin technology has existed since a very long time. In the early 1960s, the work on digital twin had started. National Aeronautics and Space Administration (NASA) had started working on digital twin technology. They were the first one to put this technology into use. It was used by them for Apollo 13 program in year 1970.

Years later, in 2010, digital twin name was given to this technology. In a report written by John Vickers from NASA, digital twin name was given to this. From there onwards, this technology was called as digital twin.

*Corresponding author: anantpatel08@gmail.com

Manisha Vohra (ed.) Digital Twin Technology: Fundamentals and Applications, (173–188) © 2023 Scrivener Publishing LLC

Digital twin technology concept had been introduced in a conference in the year 2002 at a conference in Michigan University by Michael Grieves but at that time since digital twin name was not yet coined for this technology concept, he had introduced this concept as "Conceptual Ideal for PLM." Project lifecycle management is abbreviated as PLM.

The vision of the digital twin refers to a relation between a physical artefact and set of virtual models [10]. As industry 4.0 is evolving, its evolution seems to improve the productivity of the pharma industry [12]. Digital twins act as a digital replica for the physical object or process they represent [17]. A digital twin is a digital representation of a real-world entity or system [18]. To obtain transparency, industry like manufacturing industry has to transform itself into predictive manufacturing [19]. Digital Twin is one of the enabling technologies of industry 4.0 which couples actual physical systems with corresponding virtual representation [20]. Digital twins, with the help of communication, throughout their lifecycle change and evolve along with their physical counterparts [15]. Service ecosystem, service platform and value co-creation are the three dimensions of technology-driven service innovation which are needed to be understood in order to provide smart/digital services in a product service system [34]. Digital twin is a tool which can support joint decision making by translating technical considerations into a business context and also by helping in identifying the consequences of different options [13]. The concept of digital twin is decades old but the actual impact of it has come into being in recent years [31]. Design of manufacturing system is a complex and critical activity [32]. Digital twin can help in various applications, including the manufacturing related work application. It has the potential to give real-time status regarding machines performance and production line feedback [16]. Digital twin is a vital enabler for improving system maintenance over time, on the basis of system operation and maintenance history [9]. It is expected from the digital twins that they will enrich the existent asset information system, hence enhancing the informed decision-making in asset management [29]. With the help of digital twin, stakeholders from any location can access and monitor the physical twin status [14]. Hence, due to its such various advantages, the best suitable source of knowledge within the smart factory seems to be digital twin [33]. However, from combination of technology push and market pull, recently, the need to formalize and utilize complete potential of digital twin concept has arisen [11]. Cyberphysical digital twin is also gaining attention and is being discussed about with respect to its application in Industry 4.0. With advancement of ICT technologies, it took off in recent years [28].

As mentioned earlier, digital twin can be helpful in various applications. These applications can be across different industries like oil and gas industry, healthcare industry, pharmaceutical industry, etc. and digital twin can help. However for healthcare industry, digital twin architectures need to ensure that accurate system health management predictions are made in order to avoid excessive runtime costs [30]. How digital twin can help in pharmaceutical industry, this we will be understanding in this chapter. Pharmaceutical industry is one of the most important industries as it is related to healthcare. Pharmaceutical industry develops and manufactures products which prove to be lifesaving. It develops and manufactures different medical products, such as directly consumable medicines, vaccines, etc. However, there are certain issues faced by this industry.

The issue of amount of wastage occurring when manufacturing a particular medical product, the issue of quickly getting the product being manufactured to the market, etc. are among some of the issues in the pharmaceutical industries' manufacturing process that prompt toward the urge to have some kind of improvement in the manufacturing process so that not just the issues are overcome but also certain benefits or advantages are gained, which provide an overall good effect on the manufacturing process and the product being manufactured.

Digital twin can really work greatly in the pharmaceutical industry. It can help largely in the situation of the issues in the manufacturing process. It can help overcome them and even provide benefits or advantages and also an overall good effect on the manufacturing process and the product being manufactured, just as required. It can be applied for manufacturing process as in the pharmaceutical industry. Its application in pharmaceutical industry along with examples will be explained later on in the chapter. First we will understand in detail what digital twin is exactly.

11.2   What is Digital Twin?

Digital twin is virtual replication or virtual copy of a physical object, product, or process. They replicate not only the look but also the functionality of a physical object or process. Digital twin consists of different elements. The digital twin elements are virtual space, real space, a particular link which will allow flow of data from real to virtual space, another link for flow of information from virtual to real space and virtual subspaces [23].

When a digital twin of an existing object or system is made, it remains linked or connected with its original real world counterpart throughout the lifecycle of that particular object or system. This connectivity is a great characteristic of digital twin. With the help of this connectivity, all real-time data of the real world object or system can be transmitted to the digital twin. This enables digital to update in real-time.

The changes that are happening in real world object or system those changes will also happen in digital twin. There is a virtual environment in which the digital twin works. These things are helpful. They enable monitoring real-world object or system via the digital twin. Remote monitoring through digital twin can also be done. This makes digital twin efficient. Digital twin will copy the behavior of the real world object or system. Digital twin can predict different issues or problem before it occurs in reality, i.e., before it occurs in the real-world object or system. This will prevent the loss, which could occur in the real world object or system from the different issues or problem.

There are different types of digital twin.

During defining digital twins in [23], the authors Dr. Michael Grieves and John Vickers have discussed and described types of digital twin. The first type of digital twin is DTP, which is the abbreviation for digital twin prototype. The second type of digital twin is DTI, which is the abbreviation for digital twin instance.

Digital twins (DTs) are operated on in a digital twin environment (DTE) [23].

11.2.1   Digital Twin Prototype (DTP)

As the name suggests, here this digital twin type will be describing things related to the prototype. It describes prototypical physical artifact. It has sets of information which is needed to explain and make a real version which is the replication or the twin copy of the virtual model.

11.2.2   Digital Twin Instance

Here, digital twin instance (DTI) digital twin type is the one that tells or explains a particular corresponding real-world product to which an individual digital twin stays linked throughout the lifecycle of that particular real-world product.

Digital twin environment (DTE): It is basically an integrated and multi-domain physics application space. It is for operating on digital twins for a variety of purposes. Let us understand these variety of purposes. So these purposes would actually include:

- Predictive and
- Interrogative

Now one would be wondering what do these mean. Let me explain.

- Predictive: As the name is indicating, it would be utilized for predicting purpose. So here, digital twin would be utilized for prediction of future behavior and performance of the real-world product.
- Interrogative: This would be applied to digital twin instances. There could be interrogation done from them for the history, as well as for the current things [23].

Depending upon the type of application, we can have:

- Parts twins or components twins
- Product twins,
- System twins and
- Process twins.

11.2.3   Parts Twins

Robust parts are always required. With the help of virtual representations, different characteristics like the electrical, mechanical, etc. of a part can be obtained by engineers.

11.2.4   Product Twins

Different separate parts when work together, will form a product. Product twins will enable to know the way these each different separate parts interact, and it will provide data about performance, which on processing will give some useful insights.

11.2.5   System Twins

Different products which come together to obtain a functional system can be viewed using system twins. Products interaction-related insights are given by system twins, and they can give performance improvement suggestions also.

11.2.6 Process Twins

Process twins inform how different systems work with each other for creation of a manufacturing facility. Process twins can help to find out the exact timing schemes which will eventually impact the overall efficiency.

For the pharmaceutical industry, digital twin application can be very useful and of great help.

11.3 Digital Twin in the Pharmaceutical Industry

In pharmaceutical industry, in order to make it more modern and to improve it, oral drugs which are solid, there should be continuous manufacturing (CM) of them [2]. A novel manufacturing strategy which is based on continuous processing which is integrated with online/inline monitoring tools and is coupled with an advanced control system is desired for efficient quality by design based pharmaceutical manufacturing [35]. For most of the process industries, continuous manufacturing mode offers various advantages [27]. In context of quality by design, quality risk management related to development and manufacturing of pharmaceuticals with special focus on patient health and safety is vital [3]. To get useful insights into process performance of manufacturing, pharmaceutical companies as well as regulatory bodies prefer fast, non-destructive, fast, and sensitive methods that have capability of measuring huge number of tablets to provide statistically relevant insight regarding quality of whole production-scale batch [4]. Solid oral dosage manufacturing is gradually shifting from batch to continuous processes [5]. For improving process control and to increase product quality assurance, online and real-time monitoring of product critical quality attributes is most relevant [6]. Continuous pharmaceutical manufacturing process has certain advantages, one of them being that it provides ability to monitor and rectify data or product in absolute real time [7]. Pharmaceutical companies operate in heavily regulated field, where they strive to minimise the time-to-market of new products and at the same time maintain sustainable pipelines [8]. Digital twin is a technology that can used in different industries like the construction industry, healthcare industry, oil and gas industry, etc. Pharmaceutical industry is one among the different industries where digital twin can be used. Pharmaceutical industry is an industry where work needs to be carried out efficiently.

For example, when any medical product is being manufactured in this industry, it needs to be perfect. Precision is required because it is a medical product. So the work needs to be carried out in an efficient manner. Since the product being manufactured is a medical product which needs to be perfect, it leads to increase in the responsibility of this industry to ensure work is carried out efficiently and the issues faced in the work are overcome quickly so that the results of the work are as per expectation.

In pharmaceutical industry, in the manufacturing process, there are issues faced as being discussed earlier in the chapter. Whenever any healthcare or medical product is manufactured, there is wastage of materials and resources involved. During manufacturing, sometimes due to reasons like mistakes caused in the manufacturing process, errors occurring in the manufactured product lead to the need to remanufacture the product which consumes a lot of time and results in wastage which delays the product from reaching to market. These are some serious issues faced in pharmaceutical industry's manufacturing process. To help and make things better, digital twin technology can be introduced and applied in pharmaceutical manufacturing.

In pharmaceutical manufacturing, building blocks of a digital twin, including process analytical technology (PAT) methods, data management systems, unit operations, and flowsheet models, system analyses methods, and integration approaches have all been developed in the last few years. However, there have been certain issues like gaps in accuracy of PAT, real-time model, etc. along with some concerns. With development of certain tools, methodologies and by carrying out work in the direction of overcoming the issues, all the issues can be overcome successfully and digital twin application in pharmaceutical manufacturing can emerge as a great advantage [1]. In fact, digital twin has already been applied successfully in pharmaceutical manufacturing process and the example of this along with how digital twin helps with different issues in manufacturing process of pharmaceutical industry will be explained later in the chapter.

Apart from helping in manufacturing, digital twin can help in more ways in pharmaceutical industry like it can be used for supporting scientific exchange of views with expert physicians, for letting pharmaceutical companies plan out processes, manage processes and optimize them and likewise digital twin can help pharmaceutical industry in more such different ways. We will understand digital twin applications in pharmaceutical industry further on in detail. We will also discuss the examples of use of digital twin in pharmaceutical industry.

11.4   Digital Twin Applications in Pharmaceutical Industry

Digital twin application in pharmaceutical industry can be very helpful. We will understand the applications of digital twin in pharmaceutical industry with examples. Along with it, we will even understand some real examples of use of digital twin in pharmaceutical industry.

11.4.1   Digital Twin of the Pharmaceutical Manufacturing Process

When it comes to pharmaceutical manufacturing, each and everything has to be correct and perfect because it a sector which is playing an important role in healthcare. In pharmaceutical manufacturing, different problems or issues are faced as discussed earlier in the chapter. Digital twin technology can be used here. A process digital twin will be apt here. It can really help with the issues being faced and bring great transformation and ease things out. The manufacturing process can be well managed and handled then.

To understand how process digital twin can help, consider the following example. Atos along with GlaxoSmithKline and Siemens, have come forward together and taken help of digital twin technology in manufacturing process. For manufacturing vaccines, they three together introduced and utilized digital twin technology. Sensors were utilized for data collection. Three different models were made. Digital twin of the entire manufacturing process was made. A live in-silica replica of the physical process was used. As a result batch wastage can be reduced, the product reach faster to the market and there the manufacturing process can be kept under control. So with this example, it can be rightly said that digital twin technology is beneficial for pharmaceutical industry [21].

11.4.2   Digital Twin for Pharmaceutical Supply Chains

Let us understand how digital twin for pharmaceutical supply chains can be helpful with the help of an example of a case study. In this paper [24], the authors have proposed the design and development of a digital twin. It is for a case study of a pharmaceutical company. The case study addresses the supply chain of a company in the pharmaceutical industry. Decisions are needed to locate new facilities for the production and distribution of injectable products. Similarly, different operating scenarios of the supply, manufacturing, inventory and product distribution process are modeled and analyzed. The proposed approach by the authors in Von Marmolejo-Saucedo [24] helps transparent communication, predictive analytics, which predicts disruptions or changes in the supply chain and better collaboration between its stakeholders. Some data are needed to be uploaded to the digital twin. This includes:

- customer insight,
- business processes,
- demand data,
- inventory policies,
- location of available facilities, and
- productive capacity.

The planning of the operation responds to monthly operations. However, when a trigger for a disruptive event is detected, the digital twin modifies the original planning, to simulate possible scenarios given current circumstances. The consequence of this simulation is to redefine the global operations strategy in the most resilient way [24]. This case study thus shows how digital twin for pharmaceutical supply chains can be helpful.

11.5   Examples of Use of Digital Twin in Pharmaceutical Industry

The following are some real examples of use of digital twin in pharmaceutical industry. Let us go through them one by one.

11.5.1   Digital Twin Simulator for Supporting Scientific Exchange of Views With Expert Physicians [22]

A digital twin simulator was made by Takeda Pharmaceutical Company Limited in partnership with PwC Consulting LLC. The digital twin simulator made by them is a Crohn's disease (CD) digital twin simulator. Both companies got into partnership for making this digital twin simulator. It is made so as to provide support for scientific exchange of view with expert physicians [22].

11.5.2   Digital Twin for Medical Products

Digital twin when used for medical products, can be helpful. Virtonomy, a company based in Germany is reducing time to market of medical products. They help the medical device manufacturers in the different stages of product lifecycle [25] and in doing so, they successfully make use of different resources like digital twin technology among others which proves to be very helpful.

11.5.3   Digital Twin for Pharmaceutical Companies

Kydea, a company based in Italy has developed Pharma Digital Twin which benefits the pharmaceutical companies greatly. Their developed digital twin lets pharmaceutical companies to plan out processes, manage processes and optimize them [26]. They are successfully utilizing digital twin technology.

11.6   Advantages of Digital Twin in the Pharmaceutical Industry

The following are some advantages of digital twin in the pharmaceutical industry.

- 11.6.1   Wastage Can Be Reduced
- 11.6.2   Cost Savings
- 11.6.3   Faster Time to Market
- 11.6.4   Smooth Management
- 11.6.5   Remote Monitoring

Let us understand all the advantages one by one.

11.6.1   Wastage Can Be Reduced

If anything goes wrong in a pharmaceutical process or if any problem or difficulty arises then the process might have to be started again. In doing so, different kind of materials, resources, etc. included in process would also go waste. With the help of digital twin, wastage can be reduced. To understand this better, consider the example of digital twin used in manufacturing process explained earlier in the chapter, where with the help of process digital twin which was built by Atos along with

GlaxoSmithKline and Siemens, reduction in batch wastage was one of the advantages achieved among other advantages achieved. With this example, it can be clearly understood that wastage can be reduced using digital twin.

11.6.2 Cost Savings

When there is reduction in wastage in pharmaceutical manufacturing process, there will be obviously cost savings. Hence, using digital twin, there can be cost savings.

11.6.3 Faster Time to Market

When any medical product is to be manufactured, it requires precision. If anything goes wrong in the process and the resultant manufactured product is not as desired or expected then the manufactured product will go to waste. All materials and resources involved in product manufacturing will go waste but along with this, the time involved in manufacturing of the product will also go waste and this ultimately means the product will have to be remanufactured. The work done will have to be analyzed to understand where things went wrong so that the mistakes can be avoided from getting repeated again and some solutions to get the product manufactured as desired can be worked on and applied to the process of manufacturing. However, all this will require additional time and delay will be caused. There will be ultimately delay in the time to market of the product but with digital twin this can be avoided. Digital twin enables faster time to market for pharmaceutical products. When digital twin is used in pharmaceutical manufacturing process, there will be faster time to market of the medical product being manufactured. Digital twin of the manufacturing process in the pharmaceutical industry will enable faster time to market of the medical product being manufactured.

11.6.4 Smooth Management

With digital twin technology, in pharmaceutical industry, the entire manufacturing process here can be kept in control. When digital twin is used for manufacturing application in pharmaceutical industry, i.e., digital twin of the manufacturing process is made then one can have control over the manufacturing work carried out in the manufacturing process. This will ensure a smooth management of the process.

11.6.5   Remote Monitoring

The manufacturing process is a very vital process. Monitoring this process is required and necessary to ensure everything is going in the process as needed. However, monitoring the process by always being present at the manufacturing site becomes difficult at times. Digital twin can help. When digital twin technology is used, remote monitoring can be done. When process digital twin of the whole manufacturing process is made, then the whole manufacturing process can be monitored remotely, which eases out the monitoring work to a great extent.

11.7   Digital Twin in the Pharmaceutical Industry as a Game-Changer

Digital twin technology can become the game changer in the pharmaceutical industry. The kind of issues it can solve for this industry's manufacturing process and the advantages it can provide are absolutely commendable. Along with it, real examples of use of digital twin in pharmaceutical industry shows that digital twin technology when used in the pharmaceutical industry, it can turn out to be a game changer for this industry. Digital twin can to a great extent bring gains to the pharmaceutical industry firms.

11.8   Conclusion

Pharmaceutical industry means an industry which develops and manufactures medicines, medical products, etc. healthcare related things which are having extremely high value and importance for each person. There is need for a technology, which can help with different issues in pharmaceutical industry's manufacturing process and provide advantages. Digital twin technology is the technology which can help. Digital twin is an efficient and helpful technology. Digital twin can help with the different issues in pharmaceutical industry's manufacturing process and provide advantages.

The applications of digital twin in pharmaceutical industry are discussed in this chapter along with examples. Some real examples of use of digital twin in pharmaceutical industry are also discussed. The advantages digital twin can provide in the pharmaceutical industry are stated and explained in this chapter. The advantages include wastage being reduced, cost savings, faster time to market, smooth management, and remote monitoring.

Digital twin can thus truly benefit this industry in a variety of ways. From helping with the issues in the product manufacturing process to the advantages it can provide along with the real examples of digital twin use in pharmaceutical industry in innovative ways shows that digital twin can emerge as a game changer for the pharmaceutical industry.

References

1. Chen, Y., Yang, O., Sampat, C., Bhalode, P., Ramachandran, R., Ierapetritou, M., Digital twins in pharmaceutical and biopharmaceutical manufacturing: A literature review. *Processes*, 8, 9, 1088, 2020, https://doi.org/10.3390/pr8091088.
2. Sierra-Vega, N.O., Román-Ospino, A., Scicolone, J., Muzzio, F.J., Romañach, R.J., Méndez, R., Assessment of blend uniformity in a continuous tablet manufacturing process. *Int. J. Pharm.*, 560, 322–333, 2019.
3. Rantanen, J. and Khinast, J., The future of pharmaceutical manufacturing sciences. *J. Pharm. Sci.*, 104, 3612–3638, 2015.
4. Goodwin, D.J., van den Ban, S., Denham, M., Barylski, I., Real time release testing of tablet content and content uniformity. *Int. J. Pharm.*, 537, 183–192, 2018.
5. Metta, N., Verstraeten, M., Ghijs, M., Kumar, A., Schafer, E., Singh, R., De Beer, T., Nopens, I., Cappuyns, P., Van Assche, I., Ierapetritou M., Ramachandran R., Model development and prediction of particle size distribution, density and friability of a comilling operation in a continuous pharmaceutical manufacturing process. *Int. J. Pharm.*, 549, 271–282, 2018.
6. Guerra, A., von Stosch, M., Glassey, J., Toward biotherapeutic product real-time quality monitoring. *Crit. Rev. Biotechnol.*, 39, 289–305, 2019.
7. Cao, H., Mushnoori, S., Higgins, B., Kollipara, C., Fermier, A., Hausner, D., Jha, S., Singh, R., Ierapetritou, M., Ramachandran, R.A., Systematic framework for data management and integration in a continuous pharmaceutical manufacturing processing line. *Processes*, 6, 53, 2018.
8. Lopes, M.R., Costigliola, A., Pinto, R., Vieira, S., Sousa, J.M.C., Pharmaceutical quality control laboratory digital twin—A novel governance model for resource planning and scheduling. *Int. J. Prod. Res.*, 58, 1–15, 2019.
9. Madni, A., Madni, C., Lucero, S., Leveraging digital twin technology in model—Based systems engineering. *Systems*, 7, 7, 2019.
10. Schleich, B., Anwer, N., Mathieu, L., Wartzack, S., Shaping the digital twin for design and production engineering. *CIRP Ann.*, 66, 141–144, 2017.
11. Rasheed, A., San, O., Kvamsdal, T., Digital twin: Values, issues and enablers. *IEEE Access*, 8, 21980–22012, 2020.

12. Ding, B., Pharma Industry 4.0: Literature review and research opportunities in sustainable pharmaceutical supply chains. *Process Saf. Environ. Prot*, 119, 115–130, 2018.

13. West, S., Stoll, O., Meierhofer, J., Züst, S., Digital twin providing new opportunities for value co-creation through supporting decision-making. *Appl. Sci.*, 11, 3750, 2021.

14. Barricelli, B.R., Casiraghi, E., Fogli, D., A survey on digital twin: Definitions, characteristics, applications, and design implications. *IEEE Access*, 7, 167653–167671, 2019.

15. Vrabic, R., Erkoyuncu, J.A., Butala, P., Roy, R., Digital twins: Understanding the added value of integrated models for through-life engineering services. *Proc. Manuf.*, 16, 139–146, 2018.

16. Fuller, A., Fan, Z., Day, C., Barlow, C., Digital twin: Enabling technologies, issues and open research. *IEEE Access*, 8, 108952–108971, 2020.

17. Croatti, A., Gabellini, M., Montagna, S., Ricci, A., On the integration of agents and digital twins in healthcare. *J. Med. Syst.*, 44, 161, 2020.

18. Rauch, L. and Pietrzyk, M., Digital twins as a modern approach to design of industrial processes. *J. Mach. Eng.*, 19, 1, pp. 86–97, 2019.

19. Lee, J., Lapira, E., Bagheri, B., Kao, H.-A., Recent advances and trends in predictive manufacturing systems in big data environment. *Manuf. Lett.*, 1, 38–41, 2013.

20. Melesse, T.Y., Di Pasquale, V., Riemma, S., Digital twin models in industrial operations: A systematic literature review. *Proc. Manuf.*, 42, 267–272, 2020.

21. Atos, Process Digital Twin for Pharma, Optimize operations and quality – bringing product to market faster. https://atos.net/en/industries/healthcare-life-sciences/pharma-digital-twin.

22. PwC, Takeda launches a Crohn's disease digital twin simulator using PwC's Bodylogical® use in physician engagement, Medical Science Liaisons of Takeda will use the app to support scientific discussions with expert physician, 18th May 2021 Takeda Pharmaceutical Company Limited, PwC Consulting LLC. https://www.pwc.com/jp/en/press-room/takeda-project210518.html.

23. Grieves, M. and Vickers, J., Digital twin: Mitigating unpredictable, undesirable emergent behavior in complex systems, in: *Transdisciplinary Perspectives on Complex Systems*, Kahlen F.J., S. Flumerfelt, A. Alves (Eds.), pp. 85–113, Springer, Cham, 2017, https://doi.org/10.1007/978-3-319-38756-7_4.

24. Von Marmolejo-Saucedo, J.A., Design and development of digital twins: A case study in supply chains. *Mobile Netw. Appl.*, 25, 2141–2160, 2020, https://doi.org/10.1007/s11036-020-01557-9.

25. Virtonomy, Data driven clinical trials on virtual patients. https://virtonomy.io/.

26. Kydea, Pharma digital twin, complaint & connected. https://kydea.com/.

27. Ierapetritou, M., Muzzio, F., Reklaitis, G., Perspectives on the continuous manufacturing of powder-based pharmaceutical processes. *AIChE J.*, 62, 1846–1862, 2016.

28. Lin, W.D. and Low, M.Y.H., Concept design of a system architecture for a manufacturing cyber-physical digital twin system. *IEEE International Conference on Industrial Engineering and Engineering Management (IEEM)*, pp. 1320–1324, 2021.

29. Macchi, M., Roda, I., Negri, E., Fumagalli, L., Exploring the role of digital twin for asset lifecycle management, in: *IFAC-Papers online*, vol. 51, pp. 790–795, 2018.

30. Khan, S., Farnsworth, M., McWilliam, R., Erkoyuncu, J., On the requirements of digital twin-driven autonomous maintenance. *Annu. Rev. Control*, 50, 13–28, 2020.

31. Singh, M., Fuenmayor, E., Hinchy, E.P., Qiao, Y., Murray, N., Devine, D., Digital twin: Origin to future. *Appl. Syst. Innov.*, 4, 36, 2021, https://doi.org/10.3390/asi4020036.

32. Terkaj, W. and Urgo, M., A virtual factory data model as a support tool for the simulation of manufacturing systems. *Proc. CIRP*, 28, 137–142, 2015.

33. Longo, F., Nicoletti, L., Padovano, A., Ubiquitous knowledge empowers the smart factory: The impacts of a service-oriented digital twin on enterprises' performance. *Annu. Rev. Control*, 47, 221–236, 2019.

34. West, S., Gaiardelli, P., Rapaccini, M., Exploring technology-driven service innovation in manufacturing firms through the lens of service dominant logic, in: *IFAC-Papers online*, 51, 1317–1322, 2018.

35. Singh, R., Sahay, A., Muzzio, F., Ierapetritou, M., Ramachandran, R., A systematic framework for onsite design and implementation of a control system in a continuous tablet manufacturing process. *Comput. Chem. Eng.*, 66, 186–200, 2014.

12

Different Applications and Importance of Digital Twin

R. Suganya[1]*, Seyed M. Buhari[2] and S. Rajaram[3]

[1]Department of IT, Thiagarajar College of Engineering, Madurai, India
[2]Department of IT, King Abdulaziz University, Saudi Arabia
[3]Department of ECE, Thiagarajar College of Engineering, Madurai, India

Abstract

A digital twin is a virtual copy of an entity. Digital twin is a duplicate copy of a product, process, or a system. It is updated from real-time data. It simply bridges the gap between the physical world and digital arena.

In other words, digital twin means creating an exact equivalent of a thing. It may be a chair, a building, a train, etc. Many sensors are connected to the physical things and collect real time data and transformed to virtual model. The digital twins makes, examines, and constructs the model in a virtual environment.

Internet of Things (IoT) growth helped to boost the digital twin technology as IoT helps in keeping things connected and also helps in transmission of real-time data. Digital twin is not only used to understand the present but also it helps to predict the future. In this chapter different applications of digital twin are discussed and explained and the importance of digital twin is also stated.

Keywords: Digital twin, Internet of Things (IoT), National Aeronautics and Space Administration (NASA), virtual model

12.1 Introduction

Digital was listed among top ten strategic technology trends as per Gartner in the year 2017. Usage of Digital twin is diversified in various areas. National Aeronautics and Space Administration (NASA) had first applied

Corresponding author: rsuganya@tce.edu

Manisha Vohra (ed.) Digital Twin Technology: Fundamentals and Applications, (189–204) © 2023 Scrivener Publishing LLC

digital twin concept in 1970. Inspection of the product being manufactured is one of the major applications of Digital twin.

Digital twin is a replicate or duplicate copy of a product, process or a system. Digital twin is called with a variety of names such as: parallel computational model, device optical silhouette, imitate system, maya/avatar, coordinated virtual model, etc. Digital twin not only addresses the current barriers but also assists in futuristic enhancements. Digital twin has evolved to a great extent. It is identical in appearance as well as performance of the original system or product. Digital twin supports the following value additions: real-time remote monitoring and control, efficiency and control, maintenance and scheduling, risk assessment, informed decision making, documentation and communication [1].

Digital twin can help engineers, doctors or any person working on the particular system or product whose digital twin is simulated to understand the working principles. It also predicts the future problems of that system or product. It can predict about any mishaps that could take place in that system or product. Continuous monitoring of the sensor data from the physically connected system or product as well as monitoring of the connected physical system or product is possible with digital twin. Digital twins are equipped with powerful capabilities which help in creating opportunities, brining innovation and improving system or product performance.

Many industries can make use of digital twin concepts and can learn from the data it gives out. It assists the manufacturers or the working staff achieve the following things efficiently.

- Visualizing or imagining how the products will behave.
- Analyzing/fixing bugs in the equipment easily.
- It will be easier to predict future problems in a system or product.
- Managing the product or system will become easier.
- Analyzing the risk factors earlier will be possible.

Digital twin will also help to increase the value of products and quality in the business or market. It can easily identify errors/faults and thereby improve the customer satisfaction. It can help engineers to have a thorough intricate view of the machines. Since several things or systems in the world are difficult to diagnose without examining the full structure, with the advancement of Digital twin, IoT, Augmented Reality (AR), Industry 4.0, etc. the visualization and complete things/system can be virtually seen which will help in improving systems, products, etc.

Many MNCs are doing a lot of research work, experimentation, etc. with digital twin technology. Widespread nature of digital twin in diversified fields is due to the presence of multi-discipline, multi-scale and diversified functions and digital twins are expected to enrich the existent asset information system. Digital twin are now achieving real value and presence in the industrial space [2–4]. Meanwhile, interaction of virtual and physical objects is vital for enhancement of manufacturing through various intelligent approaches [5]. Such an interaction cannot be studied using a virtual workshop approach. Digital twin handles the interaction between virtual and physical objects along with providing intelligent optimization. This intelligence relies on acquisition of data from various sensors. Furthermore, interaction between the digital twin model and physical objects is examined.

Constant learning from sensor data facilitate the digital twin to give the real-time situation, state, and/or status of the physical resources. This coupling of the physical world and the virtual world allows the working staff to supervise systems, expand strategies, and foresee harms before they occur [6].

From the perspective of data, digital twin includes:

(1)   Product design data
(2)   Process design data
(3)   Product manufacturing data that includes inspection, logistics, etc.
(4)   Product service data that includes data relevant to service, maintenance, and usage
(5)   Product scrap or recycling data.

12.2   History of Digital Twin

NASA had used digital twin in Apollo program. They were the first ones to use the digital twin technology concept. NASA was working on digital twin concept since 1960's. Then in 2002, Michael Grieves spoke about Digital Twin. Later on, after that gradually digital twin development continued and today it has developed to a great extent.

Siemens defines Digital twin as a virtual symbol of a physical object or process used to recognize and forecast the physical counterpart's performance characteristics. Digital twins are used all through the software product development phases to create, foresee and optimize the product design and production system before investing in physical prototypes [7]. The advantages of adopting digital twin technology comprise

- cost reduction
- prediction of possible problems in product or system
- efficient and effective work management, etc.

There are some misconceptions when it comes to digital twin. There are three definitions below. These three definitions help to identify the common misconceptions seen in the literature [28]. The three definitions are as follows:

- digital model
- digital shadow
- digital twin
- digital model — it is the digital model of an existing object in real world or planned real object with no automatic data transfer between real object and digital model.
- digital shadow — it is the digital version of a physical object with one way data transfer between physical object and its digital version.
- digital twin — digital twin is the one, where data flows/transfers between both directions in physical and digital entities.

12.3   Applications of Digital Twin

Digital twin can be applied in diversified areas. As an example, to prevent issues in car braking system, digital twin can be used during developing the car braking system. This will help the engineer to understand the system performance through virtual simulation easily. Digital twin and IoT are combined to converge the unimaginable things to real happenings. With IoT data, we can measure specific indicators of different things (e.g., health, soil, temperature, land, water level etc.). By combining the sensor data, processing it and modelling it into the virtual mode, engineers or doctors or working staff can have a clear picture about working principles and conditions of whatever is being modeled. This section describes various applications of digital twins in different areas which are: agriculture, education, healthcare, manufacturing and industry, modeling and simulation, network communication, security, smart cities, weather forecasting, and virtual reality.

12.3.1 Agriculture

Digital twin can be useful in agriculture. Support of digital twin in the development of agriculture at various stages is discussed by authors in their paper [11]. According to the literature survey done by them, they found digital twin could help in saving the cost and also in achieving a better improved quality of the agricultural products. Digital twin in management work of the crops was also found to be useful as stated in their literature survey. Apart from these, they also found that logistics and supply chain relevant to agriculture could also be supported using digital twin as well as some other factors involved in agriculture can also be looked after and handled well using digital twin. Thus, overall, digital twin is expected to positively impact agriculture.

12.3.2 Education

In higher learning educational systems, it is important that the curriculum be updated with the cutting edge technologies. By introducing digital twins in the educational sector, students can learn about it well. Digital twin technology is important and relevant to Industry 4.0 for example along with various other sectors where it is relevant and can be applied.

So if it is included in relevant education syllabuses, it can be helpful for students to learn about it. Apart from this, digital twin can be helpful in education in other ways as well. To understand this with an example, consider the below explained scenario.

During COVID-19 pandemic, going to school and learning in a physical environment became highly difficult and till now this difficulty is still faced by students and the staff. A digital twin acts as a bridge between physical environment and digital environment. In education, the routine conductance of classes has been hampered by the pandemic. So consider the following example of possible application of digital in education.

During regular classes, students are made to visit different industries to understand the working process and the functioning of the industries. Pandemic has made visiting different industries difficult for students and teachers. In such situation digital twin technology can be helpful. Digital twin has application in industry. Suppose in a factory some product is being made. The digital twin model created for application here can be shown to students. Through this they will even learn about the industry related working process being carried out in factory and they will also learn and see demonstration of digital twin model being used in a particular application. Digital twins can be applied in the field of education in order to enhance student learning [12].

12.3.3   Healthcare

Since healthcare is a very important sector, various criteria and specifications are evaluated before fully introducing any technology in healthcare. After evaluating all the criteria, specifications, feasibility and all the related necessary parameters, any technology is brought to implementation in the healthcare sector. Digital twin technology is a technology which is still evolving and making its way in healthcare.

Digital twins can support the healthcare sector to optimize patient care, cost and performance. Digital twins can support the healthcare sector. Applications of digital twin in healthcare are diverse. There are various suggestions of application of digital twin in healthcare, for example, it can be used in medical recommendation system, surgical risk planning and assessment, medical devices designs, etc. Modern application of digital twins can even assist the surgeon to prepare or train himself even before the actual surgery [1].

Digital Twins in healthcare can support data-driven healthcare methodologies, preparation for surgery, post-operative care and pre-operative care, etc. There are already a few implementation cases of digital twin in healthcare. For example, consider this case. At a hospital named Mater Hospital which is located in Dublin, Ireland, management recognized a need for change in the radiology department. With growing patient demand, increasing clinical complexity, ageing infrastructure and lack of space, it was becoming harder than ever to deliver efficient patient care. Rapid advances in medical technology were underlining the need for equipment modernization. Perhaps most important of all, rising waiting times, interruptions and delays were having a negative impact on patient experience. To overcome these challenges, MPH set a goal to redesign the layout and infrastructure of the radiology department. They engaged Siemens Healthineers Value Partners for Healthcare Consulting to optimize care delivery and create more value using a Digital Twin for Workflow Excellence. Shorter wait times for patients for CT scans and MRI, faster patient turnaround, Increased equipment utilization, lower staffing costs were the results and benefits obtained by using digital twin [26].

12.3.4   Manufacturing and Industry

Intelligent manufacturing can be assisted using digital twin. Digital twin use in industry is growing. Application-driven Network-aware Digital Twin Management in Industrial Edge Environments is proposed by authors in [22]. Digital Twin model needs large amounts of computing capability and information [23]. In production system's continuous improvement, digital twin is a vital tool [25]. DT aims to support decision making [10]. In a B2B context, Digital Twins of machine tools enable the customers of the products being produced to receive real-time insights in the manufacturing process [9]. Digital twin technology can be used in varied areas, like the information provided by a Digital Twin can offer various optimization possibilities for a cyber-physical system (CPS) [13]. Manufacturers making different advanced products which are having all characteristics of complex systems are having a great interest in digital twin [24]. Authors in [14] have presented and proposed a digital twin based visualized architecture for flexible manufacturing systems (FMS). They also proposed a digital twin modeling concept as GHOST (Geometric information–Historical samples–Object attribute–Snapshot collection–Topology constraint). Prototypes were developed by the authors for the general platform of the digital twin RESTful services along with cross-platform general visual mock-up software on the basis of GHOST digital twin modeling concept which was proposed. The results that the authors received showed that this particular method was quite effective in various aspects of FMS lifecycle.

Virtual workshops cannot alone have realization of the interaction between the virtual and physical or real world for smart manufacturing process, so for the much needed active connection between the real and virtual world, a digital twin workshop is proposed by authors in their paper [15]. The paper explains that digital twin programs comprise virtual program, physical events and digital twin engine to fuse the virtual and physical workshops along with optimization. The interaction among the physical and virtual workshop is both bidirectional and real-time, handled through the digital twin engine. A unified data model is proposed in Siemens' digital twin that consists of product digital twin, production digital twin and performance digital twin. Such digital twin workshops optimize the activities by suitably fusing the activities of both the virtual and physical workshops.

Electromechanical products based optimized product design, fault diagnosis and prediction using digital twins is discussed by authors in their paper [16]. Electronic accelerator pedal is used to validate the accuracy of the system. The authors have described the framework. It is designed with four layers:

- physical space layer,
- virtual space layer,
- data processing layer,
- system application layer.

Physical space layer includes various equipment, such as auto-driving instruments, connected sensors, validating instruments, etc. The network communication resources that connect various electrochemical products are also included here. Data relevant to various settings and operational conditions can be obtained at this layer. Virtual Space Layer comprises product twin model and parallel-environment model. The product twin model includes varied digital expression of the products, in terms of geometric, behavioral and state characteristics. In order to simulate with varied and diversified environments such as mechanical, climatic and electromagnetic features, parallel-environment simulation is used. Data processing layer engulfs data capturing, noise removal, feature extraction analysis, transportation and quality management. Data obtained from the physical layer are processed and fused together. Appropriate correlation analysis and other relevant approaches are applied to identify potential value from the obtained data. Knowledge mining and detection is performed in System Application Layer. This envisions the collection of suitable data to perform suitable diagnosis and predictions.

Digital twin is proposed for both machining time optimization and surface quality improvement of machine tools by authors in their paper [17]. The paper states various parameters of the controller are tuned appropriately by the digital twin to enhance production, along with enhanced speed, accuracy and surface quality. Considering various aspects of the machine, such as servo loops, feed drive system and tool center point (TCP) effects, helps in optimizing machine time and decreasing the oscillation of TCP.

At the same time, building digital copies of entire systems and process models is a complex process as there are various elements of interactions. As an example, building a cyber physical system of systems (CPSoS) and Interconnected IoT is not just about interactions but also about operational independence and goal-oriented active composition [18].

Efficient management of data in terms of sharing, storage and authenticity is vital for successful application of digital twin in industrial applications.

12.3.5 Automotive Industry

In the automotive domain, a digital twin can facilitate the union of existing gaps between physical entity and virtual entity of product working model or prototypes. Digitization in the automotive domain creates interest and challenges for vehicle software updates with respect to security guidelines.

Modern vehicles contains many electronic control units or sensors for different functions like engine control, anti-lock braking system, airbag and navigation control. Each sensor unit is computer software controlled. Many lines of code are installed in every automotive vehicle.

Monitoring the vehicle performance is very necessary so that if any errors are noticed, software updates can be prepared for fixing the problems accordingly and can be sent to the vehicles. Digital twin can be used to monitor and analyze the working model of automated vehicles. The vehicle performance can be tracked easily then with digital twin. Software updates can be then prepared accordingly, keeping in mind the noticed errors and can be sent to the vehicles to fix the errors.

The automotive industry is getting smarter and more popular because of its shared mobility, linked with devices and electric vehicles, and autonomous driving. However, the much awaited digitization and connectivity of the modern car systems point to a plethora of information that can face cyber threat. Here, digital twins can support and improve the effectiveness of cyber security. The main advantage of digital twins is that they can create a virtual process for simulations. Digital twin will be capable of creating a better and safer environment. Besides, digital twin interface can add extreme speed and precision for making decisions as they learn thousands of times faster. The essential objective of cyber security is to build processes and methods that would be able to protect your electronic gadgets and automated household devices and applications from cyber-attacks. Like mentioned above, digital twins can support and improve the effectiveness of cyber security. A cyber digital twin can be made. A cyber digital twin is a methodical representation of any automobile's software mechanism structure, including automobile versions, licenses, hardware parts, OS configuration, security mechanism, control flow, and application programming interfaces. There is already an example of cyber digital twin being utilized for automotive cyber security. The company named cybellum introduced cyber digital twin for automotive software for providing security to it from cyber threats [27].

12.3.6   Security

Digital twin can been applied in diversified areas. Considering the importance of tracking transactions, authors have studied the combination of blockchain with digital twin [19]. Building information is modeled using information obtained from IoT as part of digital twin while the updation is authenticated using blockchain. This increases the credibility of the process, by providing traceability of the data. Thus, stakeholders have access to project-related information, which provides suitable accountability.

Cyber Physical Production System (CPPS) [20] is one of the recent emphases in Industry 4.0 with regards to Cyber Physical System (CPS) based on the fourth generation of manufacturing systems. Integrating cyberspace digital models with that of physical manufacturing processes and resources is one of the core aspects of CPPS.

Appropriate handling of data with regard to various factors, like robustness, security, accuracy, and in time, are shown using visualization and intelligence layers. Such systems provide smooth transition between production database and simulation database.

Architecture of such modules could include various modules, such as:

- dashboard,
- database,
- E-scheduler,
- wireless tracking, and
- simulation modules.

Furthermore, improving the IoT security aspects of both critical and noncritical infrastructure is also studied in the literature. The need for an effective smart grid is expected to increase dramatically with the enhancing popularity of electric vehicles. The combination of IoT and energy-efficient computing devices developed the chances to enhance monitoring of smart grids. The real-time, physical-based simulation in Digital Twin is used to cater for the security and resiliency in microgrids, through regular monitoring and control. Digital Twin supports not only real-time data visualization but models both the physical and cyber layers of the Automatic Network Guardian for Electrical systems (ANGEL) [8]. Salient feature of a system like ANGEL is to be able to provide two-way coupling between simulation and physical system and helping mitigate component failures and cyber-attacks.

12.3.7   Smart Cities

Applications of digital twin are diversified. One such case is the simulation of urban scenarios [21]. Digital twin can be used in smart cities for observation and administration purpose, as well as to take significant decisions based on the data collected from digital twin to overcome any difficulty that could occur.

12.3.8   Weather Forecasting and Meteorology

Instead of relying on existing weather stations only, the widespread usage of mobile phones can be considered as minor data acquisition stations. The presence of data from billions of mobile phones could provide ample information about the atmosphere, ocean, and others. Such data could be grouped using digital twin, along with duplicating the physical system with acceptable accuracy as suggested by authors Rasheed *et al.* in their paper [1]. So, in this way, if this suggested method can be successfully implemented, digital twin could be useful in weather forecasting and meteorology.

12.4   Importance of Digital Twin

Digital twins links real space and virtual space and subspaces. Digital twin can play a vital role in various sectors, such as healthcare, manufacturing, city management, aerospace, etc. as digital twin can, through its advantages, help these sectors largely. There are different examples of successful application of digital twin which show how digital twin application is beneficial. One such example is also explained in the chapter. Various researchers have applied digital twins at different stages of their study: production phase, design phase, service phase, etc.

The prediction of possible mishaps are in an object or system is given by digital twin. Then, measures can be taken to stay clear of any mishaps in the object or system. This makes digital twin an advanced and progressive technology. This is one key importance of digital twin. It allows monitoring from any distance, i.e., remote monitoring is possible using digital twin. Digital twin provides vital information about the physical object or syst. It provides necessary insights which are applicable back to the physical object or system. These are the key points explaining importance of digital twin.

These are the key reasons why digital twin is important. There are more reasons which add to the importance of digital twin but these are the key ones being explained here. Being able to predict the possible mishaps in objects or systems and enabling of remote monitoring of any object or system will have a big positive impact on the object or system.

It will change many things for the better and provide benefits. Losses will be averted. Damages due to any mishaps will be averted. These kind of many benefits will be gained with the use of digital twin. Hence, digital twin has great importance.

12.5   Challenges

Nothing comes without challenges or limitations. Considering digital twin, challenges are seen from the perspectives of operability, security, sustainability, dependability, training.

- Operability—possibility of operability in all conditions
- Security—the security of data always
- Sustainability—sustainable in all situation
- Dependability—in all situations dependability matters
- Training—the needed training for working on digital twin

All the above points of perspective are the challenges that digital twin face.

12.6   Conclusion

The cutting edge technology ,like digital twin, is there to bring changes for the better in diverse areas as discussed in the chapter throughout. The reputation of digital twin technology is thus growing in diverse areas as it is being seen that it can bring changes for the better in the areas where it is put to use or can be put to use.

Digital twin provides several benefits. It helps to predict failures in advance. Engineers, doctors, and other professionals can take necessary preventive measures to prevent risk factors. Digital twin also enables remote monitoring of objects, systems, etc.

Digital twin has certain challenges, which need to be addressed with solutions. Efforts in the direction of overcoming the challenges will be required to in order successfully overcome them with appropriate solutions. Once these challenges are overcome, it will further boost this technology.

How digital twin is helpful can be looked at by seeing what benefits it can provide in diversified areas of healthcare, education, manufacturing and industry, etc. As seen in the chapter, the benefits of digital twin surely seem to help things change positively for the better in areas of its use. Altogether, it is a benefit providing technology for the areas where it can be used and has great importance.

References

1. Rasheed, A., San, O., Kvamsdal, T., Digital twin: Values, challenges and enablers from a modeling perspective. *IEEE Access*, 8, 21980–22012, 2020, https://doi.org/10.1109/ACCESS.2020.2970143.
2. Zhang, Y.F., Shao, Y.Q., Wang, J.F., Li, S.Q., Digital twin-based production simulation of discrete manufacturing shop-floor for onsite performance analysis, in: *2020 IEEE International Conference on Industrial Engineering and Engineering Management (IEEM)*, pp. 1107–1111, 2020, https://doi.org/10.1109/IEEM45057.2020.9309928.
3. Mateev, M., Industry 4.0 and the digital twin for building industry. *Int. Sci. J. Ind. 4.0*, 5, 1, 29–32, 2020.
4. Macchi, M., Roda, I., Negri, E., Fumagalli, L., Exploring the role of digital twin for asset lifecycle management, in: *IFAC-Papers online*, vol. 51, pp. 790–795, 2018.
5. Zhang, Z., Lu, J., Xia, L., Wang, S., Zhang, H., Zhao, R., Digital twin system design for dual-manipulator cooperation unit, in: *2020 IEEE 4th Information Technology, Networking, Electronic and Automation Control Conference (ITNEC)*, vol. 1, pp. 1431–1434, 2020.
6. Liljaniemi, A. and Paavilainen, H., Using digital twin technology in engineering education – Course concept to explore benefits and barriers. *Open Eng.*, 10, 1, 377–385, 2020, https://doi.org/10.1515/eng-2020-0040.
7. Digital Twin Siemens. (n.d.). Retrieved June 26, 2021. https://www.plm.automation.siemens.com/global/en/our-story/glossary/digital-twin/24465.
8. Danilczyk, W., Sun, Y., He, H., ANGEL: An intelligent digital twin framework for microgrid security, in: *2019 North American Power Symposium (NAPS)*, pp. 1–6, 2019, https://doi.org/10.1109/NAPS46351.2019.9000371.
9. Romero, D., Wuest, T., Harik, R., Thoben, K.D., Towards a cyber-physical PLM environment: The role of digital product models, intelligent products, digital twins, product avatars and digital shadows, in: *IFAC-Papers online*, 53, pp. 10911–10916, 2020.
10. West, S., Stoll, O., Meierhofer, J., Züst, S., Digital twin providing new opportunities for value co-creation through supporting decision-making. *Appl. Sci.*, 11, 11, 3750, 2021.

11. Pylianidis, C., Osinga, S., Athanasiadis, I.N., Introducing digital twins to agriculture. *Comput. Electron. Agric.*, 184, 105942, 2021, https://doi.org/10.1016/j.compag.2020.105942.

12. Gomerova, A., Volkov, A., Muratchaev, S., Lukmanova, O., Afonin, I., Digital twins for students: Approaches, advantages and novelty, in: *2021 IEEE Conference of Russian Young Researchers in Electrical and Electronic Engineering (ElConRus)*, pp. 1937–1940, 2021, https://doi.org/10.1109/ElConRus51938.2021.9396360.

13. Josifovska, K., Yigitbas, E., Engels, G., Reference framework for digital twins within cyber-physical systems, in: *Proceedings of the IEEE/ACM 5th International Workshop on Software Engineering for Smart Cyber-Physical Systems (SEsCPS), IEEE Xplore*, pp. 25–31, 2019.

14. Fan, Y., Yang, J., Chen, J., Hu, P., Wang, X., Xu, J., Zhou, B., A digital-twin visualized architecture for Flexible Manufacturing System. *J. Manuf. Syst.*, 60, 176–201, 2021, https://doi.org/10.1016/j.jmsy.2021.05.010.

15. Xia, L., Lu, J., Zhang, H., Research on construction method of digital twin workshop based on digital twin engine. *2020 IEEE International Conference on Advances in Electrical Engineering and Computer Applications (AEECA)*, pp. 417–421, 2020, https://doi.org/10.1109/AEECA49918.2020.9213649.

16. Lu, Y., Qiu, X., Xing, Y., Digital twin-based operation simulation system and application framework for electromechanical products, in: *2021 International Conference on Computer, Control and Robotics (ICCCR)*, pp. 146–150, 2021, https://doi.org/10.1109/ICCCR49711.2021.9349373.

17. Yu, B.-F. and Chen, J.-S., Optimizing machining time and oscillation based on digital twin model of tool center point, in: *2020 IEEE Eurasia Conference on IOT, Communication and Engineering (ECICE)*, pp. 359–362, 2020, https://doi.org/10.1109/ECICE50847.2020.9301988.

18. Maier, M.W., Architecting principles for systems-of-systems. *Syst. Eng.*, 1, 4, 267–284, 1998, https://onlinelibrary.wiley.com/doi/abs/10.1002/%28SICI%2915 20-6858%281998%291%3A4%3C267%3A%3AAID-SYS3%3E3.0.CO%3B2-D.

19. Lee, D., Lee, S.H., Masoud, N., Krishnan, M.S., Li, V.C., Integrated digital twin and blockchain framework to support accountable information sharing in construction projects. *Automat. Constr.*, 127, 103688, 2021, https://doi.org/10.1016/j.autcon.2021.103688.

20. Lin, W.D. and Low, M.Y.H., Concept design of a system architecture for a manufacturing cyber-physical digital twin system, in: *2020 IEEE International Conference on Industrial Engineering and Engineering Management (IEEM)*, pp. 1320–1324, 2020, https://doi.org/10.1109/IEEM45057.2020.9309795.

21. Lee, A., Kim, J., Jang, I., Movable dynamic data detection and visualization for digital twin City, in: *2020 IEEE International Conference on Consumer Electronics—Asia (ICCE-Asia)*, pp. 1–2, 2020, https://doi.org/10.1109/ICCE-Asia49877.2020.9277250.

22. Bellavista, P., Giannelli, C., Mamei, M., Mendula, M., Picone, M., Application driven network-aware digital twin management in industrial edge environments. *IEEE Trans. Ind. Inf.*, 17, 11, pp. 7791-7801, 2021.
23. Grieves, M. and Vickers, J., Digital twin: Mitigating unpredictable, undesirable emergent behavior in complex systems, in: *Transdisciplinary perspectives on complex systems*, pp. 85–113, Springer, Berlin, Germany, 2017.
24. Grieves, M.W., Virtually intelligent product systems: Digital and physical twins, in: Complex systems engineering: Theory and practice, S. Flumerfelt, *et al.*, (Eds.), pp. 175–200, American Institute of Aeronautics and Astronautics, 2019.
25. Melesse, T.Y., Di Pasquale, V., Riemma, S., Digital twin models in industrial operations: A systematic literature review. *Proc. Manuf.*, 42, 267–272, 2020.
26. Optimizing clinical operations through digital modeling, Case study, Siemens Healthcare GmbH · 7563 1019 online. 1–6, 2019. https://www.siemens-healthineers.com/en-in/services/value-partnerships/asset-center/case-studies/mater-private-workflow-simulation.
27. Cybellum, Automotive Product Security, Keep Cyber Risk off the Road. https://cybellum.com/automotive/.
28. Fuller, A., Fan, Z., Day, C., Barlow, C., Digital twin: Enabling technologies, issues and open Research. *IEEE Access*, 8, 108952–108971, 2020.

13

Digital Twin in Development of Products

Pedro Pablo Chambi Condori

Universidad Nacional Jorge Basadre Grohmann, Tacna, Peru

Abstract

This chapter deals with discussing and analyzing the role of digital twin technology in regard to the development of products in organizations. It also discusses and analyzes its implications. The digital twin technology is a digital representation of physical products or processes. Digital twin technology facilitates decision making in the development of products. It enables cost reduction and maximization of the benefits of the products in the world of competitiveness of different organizations. The digital twin is an ideal technology as it allows to obtain all the information of a product or production process with some great insights which can be applied it to the physical world product or process and also the best decisions can be made on the basis of it. The role and adoption of digital twin will allow organizations to avoid problems in products, will allow cost savings, will maximize efficiency, downtime avoidance, opening the way to new business opportunities, planning processes through simulation processes, product development according to consumer demands, optimization of resources, and transformation of organizations in a good way. The implications of adoption of digital twin technology in development of products in organizations are found to be encouraging and promising, which is discussed and explained in this chapter.

Keywords: Digital twin, product development, organizations, digital, production process, manufacturing, virtual, product

Email: pchambic@unjbg.edu.pe

Manisha Vohra (ed.) Digital Twin Technology: Fundamentals and Applications, (205–218) © 2023 Scrivener Publishing LLC

13.1   Introduction

Digital twin is a very potential technology. There is a rapid growth of digital twin in the technological world. Digital twin is a virtual representation of physical products or production processes.

It can be utilized for the design and development of products in organizations. It has the potential to predict about the future or upcoming obstacles or problematic issues in products or production processes, which makes it a technology having great advantages.

Digital twin is bringing a new way of working in organizations and doing business. Digital twin allows to have a data centric and data-driven decision making at workplace or different working organizations.

This is a great facility for organizations. It also provides opportunities for having collaborative environment at work, such kind of facility and opportunities help the organizations grow.

A different approach of working in different organizations can be established with digital twin technology. A new approach which includes digital twin can altogether change drastically the method of product design and development of organizations for the better.

Each and every organization has a lot of things at stake. Whenever any organization is built, right from its name, reputation of the owners, financial resources invested in building and starting the organization, time, efforts, energy, etc. are all included in the stake.

Starting an organization involves a lengthy procedure. First, to start any organization, a detailed research and survey is required to be carried out. Then all possible information needs to be gathered. After that, all aspects are required to be closely observed and studied.

All the possibilities with respect to the future of the organization need to be discussed among organization stakeholders. Merits and demerits need to be weighed. Risk factor has to be found, and calculations have to be done around it. In fact, calculations are needed to be done around each and every possible factor.

Thus, starting an organization involves a lengthy procedure. It involves a lot of work as discussed above, which is to be done before actually officially starting an organization. Financial capital is also very important. Without any financial capital, an organization cannot be started.

An organization could be any organization, e.g., it can be an organization, which manufactures electronic products, plastic products, etc. Beginning an organization is a work of great responsibility.

Organizations can either succeed or fail. Each organization's success or failure depends on how it fares in the market, among its intended customers. All organizations strive for succeeding in their work.

Organizations right from the beginning or even prior to the start of the organization try to search for techniques, ideas, technologies, etc. which could help them in their work journey.

Any organization would like to include things, which could eliminate risk and problems in their work or at least reduce it or warn about it in advance.

Digital twin technology fits the bill here. It can warn about probable problems in advance by predicting them. So, a fix can be found out for the probable problems to avoid letting them appear in reality. This will boost the efficiency of the work.

Organizations will have more confidence about their work. Organizations will largely benefit from this technology. Besides, digital twin can help benefit from digital twin in other ways as well. Digital twin can help in product development as well. Digital twin can be used for the entire lifecycle of the product made by organizations. The product performance can be also predicted using digital twin. So, altogether, organizations will benefit from digital twin. However, before discussing and understanding in detail how digital twin can help organizations in their product development and also, what will be its implications, let us try to know and understand digital twin technology in brief.

13.2   Digital Twin

Digital twin is digital representation of physical product or production process. The digital representation exactly shows the physical products or production processes as it is. It is like a same copy of the products or process but in a digital format.

In 1970, digital twin was first used for a particular mission by National Aeronautics and Space Administration (NASA). They had begun working on this technology somewhere in 1960s. However, this technology got its name quite later on in the year 2010.

In the year 2010 in one report John Vickers from NASA had given this name digital twin.

Michael Grieves from Michigan University had spoken about digital twin at a conference in the year 2002.

After that slowly digital twin started getting attention and it evolved. In the present time, this technology is growing and rising.

Digital twin can duplicate or mimic the physical product or production process very well. The physical product or production process and its digital twin both will look precisely same. The only difference will be that the digital twin of the physical product or production process will be in digital form.

Other than this difference, everything will be precisely same. Along with the look, digital twin will also duplicate all the details of the physical product or production process, whatever it is mimicking.

Digital twin of the physical product or physical process or of anything else will not remain as a still digital representation. It will go through changes precisely in the same manner as and when there will be changes in the physical product or physical process or anything else whose digital representation it is.

Commonly, digital twin is known as key enabler for digital transformation [2]. Huge amounts of information and computing capability is needed by digital twin model [1]. Physical products or systems digital representations which comprise of multiple models from various domains describing them on multiple scales are digital twins in other words [30].

Creation of virtual replicas of objects or processes which simulate behavior of their real counterparts is something digital twin technology comprises of [4]. For representing in natural way and realistic way, the current status of physical twin, and various what-if' scenarios, digital twin provides modeling and simulation applications [16].

Systems' virtual representations along their lifecycle is provided by digital twin [5]. Throughout the life cycle of the physical counterpart, digital twin evolves along with it [25]. Digital twin provides real-time information which can help in making more informed decision making and it can also make predictions about asset behavior in future and how it will evolve [26].

Move in the direction of a higher level of digitalization along with grown demand for an automated, interconnected, and completely flexible approach has shaped Industry 4.0 which is the 4th industrial revolution [22].

In the period of industry 4.0, digital twin, virtual copies of the system which are able to interact with the physical counterparts in a bi-directional way, look to be promising enablers which can replicate production systems that too in real time and along with it analyze them [29].

Manufacturing system's design is one activity which is both complex and critical complex activity and also a critical activity [20]. By traditional definition, manufacturing is a process that turns raw materials into physical products [19].

Across companies, manufacturing plants and systems vary considerably [22]. Manufactured products' virtual models which are more realistic are necessary to bridge the gap between design and manufacturing. They are also necessary to mirror real and virtual worlds [21].

There is a certain lifecycle of products. The management of it in total have been of late in focus [7]. For their different stakeholders, digital twins promise significant benefits when used to support design, manufacturing management, monitoring and control along with optimisation of manufactured products [13].

What appears to be the most suitable source of knowledge in the smart factory is digital twin [27]. Manufacturers which make advanced products that are having all characteristics of complex systems are interested in digital twin and thus digital twin it is getting a great deal of interest from these manufacturers [10].

Manufacturing system's digital twins' main objective is to facilitate decision-making process and to allow decision automation through simulation [3]. Value creation is provided in the fields of operations and service management by application of digital twins [9].

A digital twin environment allows for rapid analysis and real-time decisions which are made through accurate analytics are things which digital twin environment enables [12].

High-tech products industrial production has to be leveraged between the satisfaction of heterogeneous customer needs via individualization and also realization of scale effects along the value chain [14]. What happens in the production phase is that all production process adjustments are done and complete and the product is in full production [15].

In small and medium-sized enterprises (SME's), guidelines for implementing digital twin in production systems is proposed and along with it some other concepts are presented by authors in paper [6].

Digital twins are expected to enrich the existing existent asset information system, thereby making better the informed decision-making in asset management [18].

Interest in adapting the concepts like digital twin, industry 4.0, machine learning has been growing so as to obtain autonomous maintenance and this growth in interest is taking place due to recent developments in these concepts [8]. Digital twin is key for obtaining new level of flexibility in automation systems and hence is core enabler of autonomy [17].

If seen in the last five years across industry and academia then it can be noticed that the interest in digital twin has grown quite a lot [11]. Even for cyber-physical production system (CPPS), digital can be very helpful. For realizing digital twin contribution to development of CPPS in SME, a concept is presented by authors in paper [28].

Digital twin technology can thus benefit different organizations in more than one way especially in the design and development of products. As the chapter progresses, it will be explained that how digital twin technology can benefit the organizations in the development of products.

13.2.1   Digital Twin Types

There are two types of digital twin. The first type is digital twin prototype (DTP), and the second type is digital twin instance (DTI).

Digital twins are operated on in a digital twin environment (DTE) [1].

Digital twin prototype (DTP)—this type of Digital Twin describes the prototypical physical artifact. It contains the informational sets necessary to describe and produce a physical version that duplicates or twins the virtual version [1].

Digital twin instance (DTI)—this type of digital twin describes a specific corresponding physical product that an individual digital twin remains linked to throughout the life of that physical product [1].

Digital twin environment (DTE)—this is an integrated, multi-domain physics application space for operating on digital twins for a variety of purposes. These purposes would include:

Predictive—the digital twin would be used for predicting future behavior and performance of the physical product [1]. Interrogative—this would apply to DTI's. Digital twin instances could be interrogated for the current and past histories [1].

As seen and discussed the types of digital twin, this technology can be used in different ways. It can be used either before a product is being built or it can be used for an existing product. It will be helpful.

13.3   Different Aspects of an Organization and Digital Twin in Development of Products in Organizations

Organizations always strive for achieving their goals. They have various goals to work on for their organizations. From working on achieving progress, to finding ways for bringing profits to the organization to staying ahead from competitors are some of the examples of the goals of organizations.

With list of such goals, the basic yet the most important way of achieving the goals is by working on the development of products the organization manufactures and ensuring top most quality products are developed and manufactured. This is the key requirement for the fulfilment of any organizations goals.

For each organization to make its mark in the market or among its intended customers, it needs to build trust. Any person buying a product of any organization should be able to trust the organization.

Trust is only gained and build when there is positive feedback from users of the product. Trust of the intended customers of the organization's product, once gained, needs to be maintained as well. Be it the existing users or the new users of the product, anyone utilizing the product should themselves always have a good experience while utilizing it. In the case where any organization is new and has launched a new product, so here initially since the organization and the product, both are new so there most probably wont be record of feedback.

In such cases, the users immediate experience of the product i.e. the experience they have immediately after using the product for the first time will be the basis of their feedback for the product. It will also serve as the basis of their opinión they form for the organization.

Product quality and user experience of the product matters the most for the success of the product. Along with it, other factors, such as pricing, after sales service, shelf life of the product, etc., also matters a lot for the success of the product and the organizations as well as its reputation.

However, product quality and user experience of the product matters the most for the success of the product as stated earlier and is at the begining of the list of the things that are necessary for the product as well as the organization's success.

Building organizations name and gaining trust and ensuring that trust of intended customers is always maintained is crucial. Without this, the organization's and product's survival in the market is difficult.

There are various examples out there of different products and their organizations who have built there name and gained intended customers trust and continue to maintain the trust. For example, when someone talks about a product like cars then one of the well-trusted organization or company for cars is Tesla, Inc.

Their cars are highly trusted by its customers. This organization and their cars are highly known for the high product quality and great user experience of the product, which not only builds trust but also helps to mainatin that trust of the customers, exactly what is required for the success of the organization and the product. Besides, they even look after ensuring fulfilment of other criteria, such as after sales service, which includes sending software updates to every car when required, thus improving the overall efficiency and shelf life of the product, etc. which are also necessary for the continued trust and success and reputation of both product and organization.

When customers are happy with the product's experience they had and when trust is built and maintained for the organization who made and developed the product, the customers then dont mind spending a little more on the product. Even if a similar product is being sold at a lower price by the organization's competitors, the customers who are happy with a particular organization's product and have trust on them will spend a little more and opt to purchase the product from their trusted organization only.

This is possible due to the product quality and the user experience it could build, along with other factors like long shelf life, after sales service, which include sending of software updates, etc. which gained the customers trust and maintained it as well. For organizations to reach till such a position of success, they have to begin from scratch.

The basics of any product lies in its concept, design, and its development process. If the concept of any product is liked and approved by the organization members then only they finalize and begin their work on it.

After that the most important work is of working on the design of the product. After working on it and making changes if required, once when it is finalized, the next thing is working on the development of the product, which can be a challenging work.

Everything needs to be absolutely perfect to get the desired outcome of the product. This is very important for the organizations.

If at all anything goes wrong, it will be a huge setback for the product and largely for the organization, which is why before finalizing things during the product development, many cautions would be taken including taking references from previous similar work. Generally a, prototype of the product is made for testing the product.

However, if any error is found to have occured in the product prototype or if the performance of the product is not as per expectations then work on the product will have to be done again to get desired results. Then accordingly after making the required changes in the product, its prototype will be made again for testing, and this process will continue till the product is as desired. This will contribute to wastage of resources like materials involved in product development, increased time in development and wastage of cost involved in this work. Such situations cause a setback for the organizations. There is a need for including a technology that could help the organizations in product development. There is a technology having required potential or ability to help organizations or individuals to avoid such situations. The technology is Digital Twin technology. It is the one which can help organizations or individuals with development work of a product. Digital twin are known to run simulations and can help validate a product before it is made. Right from knowing about a product's performance by predicting about it before it is made to predicting errors in a product, digital twin has all the ability needed by organizations which could help them in product development.

For example, Bridgestone Corporation has incorporated and makes application of digital twin technology for their tyres, which proves beneficial for them.

Bridgestone Corporation uses virtual tyre modeling. What it does is, it creates a digital twin of the tyre at its development stage. This actually brings down the number of real prototype tyres that have to be made. So this automatically saves resources like materials, which are involved in making prototypes and even time is saved. Overall, the development of the product will take comparatively less time. So basically simulations that are run by digital twin are very helpful. They help to make tyre performance better, as well as tire life better [23].

Another example of use of digital twin technology for developing a product is as follows.

Siemens can greatly help in product development using the digital twin technology. Consider the example of a car. The product you want to develp is a car. Siemens NX CAD can be used for car design purpose. The digital enterprise solution portfolio of Siemens, greatly helps to create digital twin of the product which is very useful for product development and prior to the product being built in reality, there can be validation of the development work [24].

Lets consider one more real example of an organization using digital twin for their poduct. The organization is Tesla, Inc. and the product which is developed using digital twin is Tesla Cars.

Tesla, Inc. makes use of digital twin for their cars. Each and every Tesla car which is sold has its digital twin. Daily whatever data are collected by sensors from each car is taken into consideration. All these data are utilized for software update which is sent to the users of the car. The sensors give real-time data everyday so when all these data are taken into consideration, and the software is updated then the update will take care of all the requirements. Thus, the update sent will be very effective and useful. So, here clearly digital twin is proving to be very useful for Tesla cars.

Digital twin can thus help organizations in product development work efficiently.

13.4 Implications of Digital Twin in Development of Products in Organizations

Digital twin will have great implication when used in development of products in organizations. They are discussed below.

During development process of any product, organizations need to be careful and ensure everything is perfect and error free to get an error-free product.

Digital twin technology is a technology that can predict about probable errors in advance. This enables organizations to find a fix for the probable errors timely which will avert the probable errors before they come in reality. This will even help in preventing and avoiding downtime. Resources wastage will reduce significantly. Whenever errors occur in any product, then resources could be wasted which were involved in making them. The risk that the work could go wrong can reduce greatly with digital twin. This is a huge benefit of having digital twin that organizations can receive.

Digital twin can help in decision making as well increasing effeciciency and effectiveness of the products by allowing organizations to develop products in accordance with the analysis of real-time product performance and product conditions. The digital twin basically gives insights and information, which are very useful and can be applied to the product for its development and betterment.

13.5 Advantages

Digital twin has a list of many advantages for the product development in organizations. Below are some of them.

- Digital Twin Helps in Decision Making
- Avoiding Downtine
- Maximizing Efficiency
- Cost Savings
- Optimum Use of Resources

13.5.1 Digital Twin Helps in Decision Making

Digital twin helps in decision making as it allows real-time analysis of product's performance, as well as conditions and predicts about probable errors in advance, enabling organizations to make decisions for the product betterment accordingly.

13.5.2 Avoiding Downtine

Since organizations can fix probable errors and avert them before `turning up in reality using digital twin, this will avoid downtime.

13.5.3 Maximizing Efficiency

Digital twin helps in maximizing efficiency of the products by allowing organizations to develop products on the basis of analysis of real-time product performance and conditions. The digital twin basically gives information and insights which are very useful and can be applied to the product for its development and betterment. Digital twin also allows to have error free products as digital twin can predict probable errors in a product before they occur so a fix will be found by organizations timely which will avert the errors. All this will definitely help to increase and maximize the efficiency of the products.

13.5.4 Cost Savings

Digital twin will provide cost savings by allowing to timely avert errors in product before they occur in real world. This will even reduce wastage of resources, which would occur if the errors are not timely averted. This also contributes toward cost savings.

13.5.5 Optimum Use of Resources

Resources get wasted when errors occur in product. Digital twin enables reduction of resource wastage and leads to optimum use of resources.

13.6 Conclusion

In this chapter, a brief discussion about the role of digital twin technology and its implications in the development of products in organizations is done. Different aspects related to an organization are also briefly discussed.

Organizations require some technique or technology to help them lower their risk in the design and development of products and help them in ways possible. Digital twin technology can really do so and help and benefit the organizations in the development of products.

Digital twin can warn about probable problems in advance, enabling organizations to find a fix for the probable problems and helps in decision making. Organizations can have real good advantages of including digital twin technology in the development of products as discussed in the chapter.

The role of digital twin technology in the development of products seems to be beneficial, positive, and on a good note for the organizations, and its implications are also great.

References

1. Grieves, M. and Vickers, J., Digital twin: Mitigating unpredictable, undesirable emergent behavior in complex systems, in: *Transdisciplinary Perspectives on Complex Systems*, F.J. Kahlen, S. Flumerfelt, A. Alves (Eds.), pp. 85–113, Springer, Cham, 2017, https://doi.org/10.1007/978-3-319-38756-7_4.
2. Kritzinger, W., Karner, M., Traar, G., Henjes, J., Sihn, W., Digital twin in manufacturing: A categorical literature review and classification, in: *IFAC-Papers online*, vol. 51, pp. 1016–1022, 2018.
3. Kunath, M. and Winkler, H., Integrating the digital twin of the manufacturing system into a decisión support system for improving the order management process in: *51st CIRP Conference on Manufacturing Systems, Procedia CIRP*, vol. 72, pp. 225–231, 2017.
4. Marmolejo-Saucedo, J.A., Design and development of digital twins: A case study in supply chains. *Mobile Netw. Appl.*, 25, 2141–2160, 2020, https://doi.org/10.1007/s11036-020-01557-9.
5. Negri, E., Fumagalli, L., Macchi, M., A review of the roles of digital twin in CPS-based production systems. *Proc. Manuf.*, 11, 939–948, 2017.
6. Uhlemann, T.H.-J., Lehmann, C., Steinhilper, R., The digital twin: Realizing the cyber-physical production system for industry 4.0. *Proc. CIRP*, 61, 335–340, 2017.
7. David, J., Lobov, A., Lanz, M., Leveraging digital twins for assisted learning of flexible manufacturing systems. *IEEE 16th International Conference on Industrial Informatics (INDIN)*, pp. 529–535, 2018.
8. Khan, S., Farnsworth, M., McWilliam, R., Erkoyuncu, J., On the requirements of digital twin-driven autonomous maintenance. *Annu. Rev. Control*, 50, 13–28, 2020.
9. West, S., Stoll, O., Meierhofer, J., Züst, S., Digital twin providing new opportunities for value co-creation through supporting decision-making. *Appl. Sci.*, 11, 3750, 2021.
10. Grieves, M.W., Virtually intelligent product systems: Digital and physical twins. *Complex Syst. Eng., Theory Pract.*, 256, 175–200, 2019.

11. Jones, D., Snider, C., Nassehi, A., Yon, J., Hicks, B., Characterising the digital twin: A systematic literature review. *CIRP J. Manuf. Sci. Technol., 29, Part A,* 36–52, 2020, https://doi.org/10.1016/j.cirpj.2020.02.002.

12. Fuller, A., Fan, Z., Day, C., Barlow, C., Digital twin: Enabling technologies, challenges and open research. *IEEE Access,* 8, 108952–108971, 2020.

13. Romero, D., Wuest, T., Harik, R., Thoben, K.D., Towards a Cyber-physical PLM environment: The role of digital product models, intelligent products, digital twins, product avatars and digital shadows, in: *IFAC-Papers online,* vol. 53, pp. 10911–10916, 2020.

14. Brettel, M., Friederichsen, N., Keller, M., Rosenberg, M., How virtualization, decentralization and network building change the manufacturing landscape: An industry 4.0 perspective. *Int. J. Mech. Aerosp. Ind. Mechatron. Eng.,* 8, 37–44, 2014.

15. Söderberg, R., Wärmefjord, K., Carlson, J.S., Lindkvist, L., Toward a digital twin for real-time geometry assurance in individualized production. *CIRP Ann.,* 66, 1, 137–140, 2017.

16. Barricelli, B.R., Casiraghi, E., Fogli, D., A survey on digital twin: Definitions, characteristics, applications, and design implications. *IEEE Access,* 7, 167653–167671, 2019.

17. Rosen, R., Wichert, G.V., Lo, G., Bettenhausen, K.D., About the importance of autonomy and digital twins for the future of manufacturing, in: *IFAC Papers Online,* 48, 3, pp. 567–572, 2015.

18. Macchi, M., Roda, I., Negri, E., Fumagalli, L., Exploring the role of digital twin for asset lifecycle management, in: *IFAC-Papers online,* vol. 51, pp. 790–795, 2018.

19. Lohtander, M., Ahonen, N., Lanz, M., Ratava, J., Kaakkunen, J., Micro manufacturing unit and the corresponding 3d-model for the digital twin. *Proc. Manuf.,* 25, 55–61, 2018.

20. Terkaj, W. and Urgo, M., A virtual factory data model as a support tool for the simulation of manufacturing systems. *Proc. CIRP,* 28, 137–142, 2015.

21. Schleich, B., Anwer, N., Mathieu, L., Wartzack, S., Shaping the digital twin for design and production engineering. *CIRP Ann.,* 66, 1, 141–144, 2017.

22. Mawson, V.J. and Hughes, B.R., The development of modelling tools to improve energy efficiency in manufacturing processes and systems. *J. Manuf. Syst.,* 51, 95–105, Apr. 2019.

23. Bridgestone, How Bridgestone's Virtual Tyre Modelling Revolutionalising Tyre Development. https://www.bridgestone.co.uk/story/mobility/how-bridgestones-virtual-tire-modelling-is-revolutionising-tire-development.

24. Siemens, From vehicle design to multi-physical simulations. https://new.siemens.com/global/en/markets/automotive-manufacturing/digital-twin-product.html.

25. Singh, M., Fuenmayor, E., Hinchy, E.P., Qiao, Y., Murray, N., Devine, D., Digital twin: Origin to future. *Appl. Syst. Innov,* 4, 36, 2021, https://doi.org/10.3390/asi4020036.

26. Rasheed, A., San, O., Kvamsdal, T., Digital twin: Values, challenges and enablers. *IEEE Access*, 8, 21980–22012, 2020.
27. Longo, F., Nicoletti, L., Padovano, A., Ubiquitous knowledge empowers the Smart factory: The impacts of a service-oriented digital twin on enterprises' performanc. *Annu. Rev. Control*, 47, 221–236, 2019.
28. Uhlemann, T.H.-J., Lehmann, C., Steinhilper, R., The digital twin: Realizing the cyber-physical production system for industry 4.0. *Proc. CIRP*, 335–340, 61, 2017.
29. Cimino, C., Negri, E., Fumagalli, L., Review of digital twin applications in manufacturing. *Comput. Ind.*, 113, 103130, 2019.
30. Vrabic, R., Erkoyuncu, J.A., Butala, P., Roy, R., Digital twins: Understanding the added value of integrated models for through-life engineering services. *Procedia Manuf.*, 16, pp. 139–146, 2018.

14

Possibilities with Digital Twin

Vismay Shah[1] and Anilkumar Suthar[2]*

[1]Department of Civil Engineering, L.J. Institute of Engineering and Technology, LJK University, Gujarat, India
[2]New L.J. Institute of Engineering and Technology, Gujarat Technological University, Gujarat, India

Abstract

The digital twin technology is one of the fastest emerging concepts. A digital twin is a virtual replica of a real-world object. Digital twins are extremely useful for predicting future problems of the real-world object or product it is replicating. Digital twin can be used in many of applications in different sectors, including aerospace, construction, smart city development, etc. Digital twin is growing at a great speed. There are many possibilities with digital twin. In this chapter, digital twin technology concept is introduced. Along with it, different possibilities with digital twin in automotive, aviation, and supply chain sector are discussed.

Keywords: Digital twin, aviation, automotive, supply chain, Industry 4.0, technology

14.1 Introduction

As the heading suggests, in this chapter, the different possibilities, namely in the sector of aviation, automotive and supply chain, along with the concept of the digital twin technology will be explored. Technological advancement has changed things.

Technology is making various things possible. Digital twin technology is one such technology which is enabling various possibilities with its application. Digital twin technology is a technology where, in a virtual

---

*Corresponding author: sutharac@gmail.com

Manisha Vohra (ed.) Digital Twin Technology: Fundamentals and Applications, (219–232) © 2023 Scrivener Publishing LLC

environment a virtual object, which is the replica of the real world physical object is created.

Digital twin name was coined in year 2010. In one report John Vickers from National Aeronautics and Space Administration (NASA) coined this name Digital twin. NASA had begun working on digital twin quiet early.

In around the year 1960, NASA was working on Digital twin technology. In 1970 they had used this technology concept. It was used for their Apollo 13 Program. This was the first time when digital twin technology concept was put to use. In year 2002, the very famous presentation by Michael Grieves which is marked and known as the first introduction of digital twin in front of live audience was held at a conference in Michigan University. Though the presentation at the conference was not given by saying it is a presentation on digital twin, as at that time this name was also not coined.

The presentation was given regarding a concept for product lifecycle management but the concept explained had all elements of digital twin. Digital twin can bring various advantages with its possibilities. It can benefit various sectors with its possibilities.

Before understanding the possibilities with digital twin in different sectors, let us first understand in detail what digital twin technology is in brief.

14.2   What is Digital Twin Technology?

Digital twin technology means to create a virtual replica of a real world physical object in a virtual environment. In other words, digital representations of systems or physical products or systems which consist of multiple models from various domains describing them on multiple scales are digital twins [32]. This is also one way of describing or explaining digital twin. The digital twin can be explained and defined in various ways.

With the help of communication, digital twins change and digital twins evolve as well along with their physical counterparts that too not just for a certain time period but throughout their entire lifecycle [32]. Whilst physical twins have been around for some time, the first definition of a concept nowadays known as the Digital Twin first definition was made in 2002 by Michael Grieves. It was in the context of an industry presentation related to product lifecycle management (PLM) [6].

The digital twin technology concept was actually presented at a conference in the year 2002. This conference was conducted at Michigan University. The presentation was being made with reference to product lifecycle management (PLM). The presentation slide, in the conference was simply called "Conceptual Ideal for PLM." However, this presentation consisted of every element of digital twin, i.e., virtual and real space and both the links, link for flow of data from real space to virtual space and link for flow of information flow from virtual space to real space and virtual sub-spaces [12].

Digital twin by using the what-if analysis, allows simulation of different scenarios in order to optimize the performance of the physical twin [3].

In total, there are two different types of digital twin. The first type of digital twin is digital twin prototype (DTP), while the second type of digital twin is digital twin instance (DTI).

Digital twins are operated on in a digital twin environment (DTE).

- Digital twin prototype (DTP):
  This type of Digital Twin i.e. DTP describes the prototypical physical artifact. It contains the informational sets necessary to describe and produce a physical version that duplicates or twins the virtual version [12].
- Digital twin instance (DTI):
  This type of digital twin describes a specific corresponding physical product that an individual digital twin remains linked to throughout the life of that physical product [12].
- Digital twin environment (DTE):
  This is an integrated, multi-domain physics application space for operating on Digital Twins for a variety of purposes. These purposes would include:

  - Predictive
    The digital twin would be used for predicting future behavior and performance of the physical product [12].
  - Interrogative
    This would apply to DTIs. Digital twin instances could be interrogated for the current and past histories [12].

Digital Twins proliferation indicates that there can be large amounts of data that would be coming in from the system and the components of that system as well [2].

Digital twin expresses real-time data, and real-life situations which is a merit [8]. Future statuses like defects, damages, etc. are the things that a digital twin continuously predicts and allows simulating and testing novel configurations [1].

For asset lifecycle management, digital twins can be considered a concept having high potential [4]. Having plethora of advantages is the main reason digital twin technology is seen as the cornerstone in Industry 4.0 [10].

The industry is transforming currently with introduction of Industry 4.0. Digital twin technology can play a role in different applications and create different and new opportunities across various sectors in industry 4.0 period.

The technology which is at the forefront of Industry 4.0 revolution facilitated through the Internet of Things (IoT) connectivity and advanced data analytics is digital twin [9].

In industry 4.0, there is growing amount of digital product information generated and collected over entire lifecycle [26].

The growth in digital twin technology concept is greatly driven by advances in related technologies and initiatives such as IoT, real-time sensors, etc. along with a drive towards a data-driven and digital manufacturing future [15]. Digital twin adoption should make sure that it is connected to the physical twin [31].

The growing use of information and communication technology lets digital engineering of products and production processes alike [23].

Discovering and understanding energy use in manufacturing process that too at each and every stage of the manufacturing process is needed for optimising the processes of manufacturing and facility management so as to reduce the energy consumption [24]. This will be very helpful and productive.

The thing which is opening up opportunities for the manufacturers to accomplish new level of productivity is growing digitalization in every stage of manufacturing [21].

Emerging advanced analytics and systems that are presented digitally need to be embraced by the manufacturers in order to be more competitive and also to improve their efficiency and productivity [14].

Various aspects ranging from tangible to intangible, from geometric to organizational to dynamic needs to be considered by a comprehensive representation of a production system [5].

More realistic virtual models of the products which are manufactured are very necessary in order to bridge the gap between design and manufacturing and also to mirror the real world and the virtual world [19].

To reduce complexity, costs and bring growth in the effects at the same time ought to be attractive for numerous organizations [18].

However, increasing complexity of order management process reduces ability of companies to remain flexible and in profit [25].

A great way to counter these challenges, is integration of digital twin of manufacturing system in a decision support system for improving order management process [25].

Digital twin gives real-time information for more informed decision making. Digital twin can along with it make predictions regarding asset. It can predict how the asset will evolve or how the asset will behave in future [22].

The digital twin provides almost hands-on learning of various work tasks in real time is provided by digital twin, without actually going and visiting the production facility [20].

In the industry 4.0 period, cyber-physical systems (CPS) are growing. They represent systems that integrate physical units and processes with computational entities over internet and allow ubiquitous access of information and services. Different optimization possibilities for a CPS can be offered by the information provided by a digital twin [13].

Talking about industry 4.0, supply chains are very important. In order to ensure competitive costs and service level, internal and external disturbances need to be properly handled by supply chains [16]. Digital twins are changing the way supply chains do business [28].

In operations field and in service management field, value creation is provided by application of digital twins [17].

A combo of digital twins with technologies like blockchain could pave way to a new wave in the studies of supply chain [7].

The digital twins are providing a range of options in order to facilitate collaborative environments and also facilitate decision making on the basis of the data and making business processes more robust [11].

Digital twin can be helpful not just for manufacturing or supply chain, it can have a number of possibilities with it across various sectors.

Digital twin can have a number of possibilities with it across various sectors. The innovation it can bring is astonishing. It can cause great difference when used in different applications. It can benefit the different sectors where it is used. A positive difference will be noticed when digital twin is used in different applications. It can ease out work to a great extent.

In this chapter, the possibilities with digital twin in three different sectors will be discussed. Those three sectors are as follows:

- Aviation sector
- Automotive sector
- Supply chain sector

Each of this sector, be it aviation sector, automotive sector or supply chain sector, each of them is essential and has its own importance. Digital twin technology can be very well utilized in each of these sectors without any difficulties and there are different possibilities with digital twin in each of these sectors which can be very helpful for these sectors. Each sector can benefit from the different possibilities with digital twin.

14.3   Possibilities With Digital Twin in Aviation Sector

In aviation sector, not just there are various possibilities with digital twin but also there are various benefits that those possibilities can provide this sector.

14.3.1   Aviation Engineering in Combination With Digital Twin

In aviation sector, the aircraft maintenance is highly important. Also, in the aviation sector, robust engines and highly efficient maintenance practices are required and followed.

Along with it, maintenance, repair, and overhaul (MRO) for aircrafts while maintaining asset availability is also given high importance.

Despite of following highly efficient maintenance practices and having robust engines, several difficulties are faced. A lot of resources are utilized but still sometimes difficulties are faced.

To overcome the difficulties here, an advanced technology like digital twin, which is a digital replica or digital representation of a real world system or object can be used.

The aviation industry can benefit using digital twin technology. This technology can help the aviation sector with the difficulties.

The digital twin intake real-time data that can help aircraft maintenance work to be carried out preventatively. Hence, here it is possible to carry out preventative maintenance using digital twin.

Likewise, there are more possibilities with digital twin in this sector which we continue to understand. When preventative maintenance is carried out, the downtime of the aircraft will be reduced.

Most importantly, maintenance practices when carried out preventatively will not only reduce downtime but also increase the dependability on the aircraft. Any errors which can occur can be forecasted and known in advance, prior to them occurring in real world which is another great possibility with digital twin. Thus they can be prevented.

Digital twins can hence add significant value to aircraft by maximizing their dependability. The aviation sector can highly benefit from digital twin.

Let us go through examples of digital twin in aviation industry.

The Company Rolls-Royce says that by creating digital twin of their aero engines, preventive maintenance can be carried out. This will reduce downtime of the aircraft and increase the reliability. They say that using this technology will help them to maintain their very complex aero engines in a more effective way. Digital twin is part of their suite of digital models which support their vision for future [28].

GE Aviation's Digital Group is using digital twin technology. They are using Azure Digital Twin. Digital representation of aircraft and the components of the aircraft is created. The state of the aircraft and the state of the components of the aircraft can be seen at any given time. The issues can be forecasted prior to their arrival, changes or repairs can be identified and status and condition of fleets can be better understood [30]. All these benefits due to digital twin technology are very helpful.

14.3.2   Concept of Digital Twin for Aviation Components

An operational digital twin may be utilized to replicate, as well as analyze and monitor the process of operations through integrating multidimensional, context-sensitive process data like material properties, geometric alterations and process parameters.

Digital twin could be used for aircraft components as well. A typical imitation or replication would consist of the replicated behavior as well.

The replicated object would be restored in shape and behavior with astounding realism. The digital twin technology creates a digital representation using geometry, behavior, and environment.

The digital twin may be even used during manufacturing of components and help in decision-making through the whole process to avoid any problems in the components.

14.3.3   How Important is Digital Twin in the Aviation Industry?

Earlier, aircraft companies used different available techniques and technologies. Now aircraft companies have the option of using digital twin technology which provide so many possibilities. They can have prediction of any difficulties which could come and monitoring can also be carried out of the process. Through this they can reduce downtime.

There can be preventive maintenance carried out using digital twin. Through this, the lifecycle of different parts of the aircraft and its engine can be extended and managed well and the overall reliability and dependability of the aircraft will increase.

When using digital twin technology, a lot of damage that could happen is controlled and prevented by carrying out preventive maintenance. Sometimes, not carrying out maintenance timely can leave some components irreparable which would even mean increase in the overall expenses. More importantly, the risk of having some adverse ill effects by not carrying out maintenance timely is also prevented when using digital twin. These all key benefits show that how important digital twin is in aviation industry.

There can be better prediction of structural life of aircraft using Digital Twin. It may be even used to predict the fleet's sustainability needs for each aircraft in the fleet.

Hence as seen above, there are different possibilities with digital twin in aviation sector and all of them prove to be useful.

14.4   Possibilities With Digital Twin in Automotive Industry

Digital twins can help the automotive industry. There can be various possibilities with digital twin in automotive industry.

A digital twin of a vehicle tire or the entire vehicle can be made. Digital twin can help largely in automotive industry. We will understand this with the help of real examples.

14.4.1   Digital Twin in Automotive Industry

In automotive industry, digital twin can be helpful. In this sector also, there are different possibilities with digital twin which we will understand below.

In automotive industry, development of be it the vehicle or the tire used in a vehicle, is a rigorous process.

First let us consider the example of vehicle tire. During developing a product like tire of a vehicle, great precaution is taken. There are various test conducted.

This work can however be eased by a technology that can be introduced in the automotive sector i.e., the digital twin technology.

It can help not only for development of tire of a vehicle but it can also help for the development of a vehicle in the automotive industry, which is explained further on.

Continuing with the example of the tire of a vehicle, when a tire company is working on developing a new tire, it can take help of digital twin. With digital twin the tire company can work on its development which will be beneficial. Let us understand this with a real example.

When it comes to tires, who does not knows Bridgestone Corporation. It is one of the top names which comes to our minds. The high quality tires they make comprises the use of digital twin technology which is very helpful. Bridgestone Corporation uses Virtual Tire Modelling. It creates digital twin of the tire at the development stage [27].

This proves to be very beneficial as this decreases the number of actual tire prototypes that are to be made. When there is decrease in number of prototypes to be made then automatically different resources such as materials that are required in making prototype are saved [27].

Efforts required in making more number of prototypes of tires and even time involved in making more prototype are also saved because there is decrease in number of tire prototypes to be made. This means the development of tires will also need less time overall comparatively. The development of the product will take comparatively less time. The simulations that digital twin runs are of great help. They actually to achieve an improved performance for the tires and improve the life of the tire [27].

Let us go through another example of application digital twin technology in automotive industry.

Tesla, Inc. makes use of digital twin for their cars. Each and every Tesla car which is sold has its digital twin. Daily whatever data is collected by sensors from each car is taken into consideration.

All this data is utilized for software update which is sent to the users of the car. The sensors give real-time data everyday so when all this data is taken into consideration and the software is updated then the update will take care of all the requirements.

Thus, the update sent will be very effective and useful. So, here clearly digital twin is proving to be very useful for Tesla cars.

The two examples above are clearly explaining that possibilities with digital twin technology in automotive sector are amazing and digital twin is very helpful in automotive industry in different ways.

14.5 How Can Digital Twin Help in Improving Supply Chain Management?

There are different possibilities with digital twin in supply chain sector which can help in its management. Let us understand those possibilities.

Certain working processes have gotten more complicated in the supply chain businesses, making them less efficient and expensive. A digital twin may assist in supply chain business greatly.

There can be a supply chain digital twin which could help in identifying the bottlenecks which is a useful possibility with digital twin in supply chain sector. Finding out bottlenecks is a huge task and the later they are found, more damage is caused. If bottlenecks are found out early in the supply chain, solutions can be found for them.

Things can be either altered or changes can made to remove the bottlenecks and control and prevent further damage.

Digital twin can also help in testing the work process designed for the supply chain management in a virtual space, which is another possibility that will avoid any loss in the real supply chain management work. By doing so, digital twin can also help to increase the efficiency and productivity while reducing operating expenses where possible.

When there are some urgent situations like a product's demand has suddenly increased or the overall sales have suddenly increased, etc. in any such or various other urgent situations, there is a direct impact of it on the transportation facilities and the delivery of the products get delayed.

Digital twin can predict the impact such situations will cause and thus for product delivery on time, better transport options and facilities can be planned and kept in advance. Let us go through a real example of application of digital twin in supply chain management.

Capgemini presented a use case of digital twin, which it implemented for one of their global client's problem. Capgemini to help their global client took help of their transformation platform which is Digital Global Enterprise (D-GEM). They created a digital twin of their client's order management operations and this helped them greatly [29]. Digital twin thus has different possibilities in supply chain sector and proves to be helpful.

14.6   Discussion

Digital twin has so many advantages. In aviation sector, it can help in carrying out preventative maintenance, downtime of aircraft can be reduced, etc. which is very useful.

In automotive sector, digital can help in tire development and car development.

In supply chain it can help in finding out bottlenecks, testing the work process designed, etc. which is very helpful.

Overall, with some of the possibilities discussed and understood with digital twin in three sectors, namely, aviation sector, automotive sector and supply chain sector, it is safe to conclude that digital twin has great potential.

Its possibilities are not just helping them and benefitting them but also advancing these sectors towards progress. Similarly, digital twin when used in other sectors will again have different possibilities and will be of help in those sectors as well because digital twin is such a technology that if it is used in any sector, it will help and benefit that sector.

14.7   Conclusion

Digital twins can be used in many opportunities in this new industry 4.0 transformation. It initiates virtual system-based design process which is efficient.

For the aviation sector, automotive sector, supply chain sector, etc. there are various possibilities with digital twin as seen in this chapter. Digital twin is very helpful in all three sectors with its various possibilities as seen in this chapter.

The possibilities with digital twin in different sectors as seen in this chapter are very useful. Digital twin ensure that the product or service is optimally operated without problems. Thus, there is a lot of scope and possibilities with digital twin not just in aviation sector, automotive sector and supply chain sector but also in many other sectors.

References

1. Barricelli, B.R., Casiraghi, E., Fogli, D., A survey on digital twin: Definitions, characteristics, applications, and design implications. *IEEE Access*, 7, 167653–167671, 2019.

2. Grieves, M.W., Virtually intelligent product systems: Digital and physical twins. *Complex Syst. Eng., Theory Pract.*, 256, 175–200, 2019.
3. Melesse, T.Y., Di Pasquale, V., Riemma, S., Digital twin models in industrial operations: A systematic literature review. *Procedia Manuf.*, vol. 42, pp. 267–272, 2020.
4. Macchi, M., Roda, I., Negri, E., Fumagalli, L., Exploring the role of digital twin for asset lifecycle management, in: *IFAC-Papers online*, vol. 51, pp. 790–795, 2018.
5. Terkaj, W. and Urgo, M., A virtual factory data model as a support tool for the simulation of manufacturing systems. *Procedia CIRP*, vol. 28, pp. 137–142, 2015.
6. Kritzinger, W., Karner, M., Traar, G., Henjes, J., Sihn, W., Digital Twin in manufacturing: A categorical literature review and classification, in: *IFAC-Papers online*, vol. 51, pp. 1016–1022, 2018.
7. Longo, F., Nicoletti, L., Padovano, A., Ubiquitous knowledge empowers the smart factory: The impacts of a service-oriented digital twin on enterprises' performance. *Annu. Rev. Control*, 47, 221–236, 2019.
8. David, J., Lobov, A., Lanz, M., Leveraging digital twins for assisted learning of flexible manufacturing systems. *IEEE 16th International Conference on Industrial Informatics (INDIN)*, pp. 529–535, 2018.
9. Fuller, A., Fan, Z., Day, C., Barlow, C., Digital twin: Enabling technologies, challenges and open research. *IEEE Access*, 8, 108952–108971, 2020.
10. Singh, M., Fuenmayor, E., Hinchy, E.P., Qiao, Y., Murray, N., Devine, D., Digital twin: Origin to future. *Appl. Syst. Innov.*, 4, 36, 2021.
11. Marmolejo-Saucedo, J.A., Design and development of digital twins: A case study in supply chains. *Mob. Netw. Appl.*, 25, 2141–2160, 2020, doi: https://doi.org/10.1007/s11036-020-01557-9.
12. Grieves, M. and Vickers, J., Digital twin: Mitigating unpredictable, undesirable emergent behavior in complex systems, in: *Transdisciplinary perspectives on complex systems*, F.J. Kahlen, S. Flumerfelt, A. Alves (Eds.), pp. 85–113, Springer, Cham, 2017, doi: https://doi.org/10.1007/978-3-319-38756-7_4.
13. Josifovska, K., Yigitbas, E., Engels, G., Reference framework for digital twins within cyber-physical systems, in: *Proceedings of the 5th International Workshop on Software Engineering for Smart CyberPhysical Systems (SEsCPS'19)*, IEEE Press, pp. 25–31, 2019, doi: https://doi.org/10.1109/SEsCPS.2019.00012.
14. Lohtander, M., Ahonen, N., Lanz, M., Ratava, J., Kaakkunen, J., Micro manufacturing unit and the corresponding 3d-model for the digital twin. *Procedia Manufacturing*, vol. 25, pp. 55–61, 2018.
15. Jones, D., Snider, C., Nassehi, A., Yon, J., Hicks, B., Characterising the digital twin: A systematic literature review. *CIRP J. Manuf. Sci. Technol.*, 29, 36–52, 2020, doi: https://doi.org/10.1016/j.cirpj.2020.02.002.

16. Frazzon, E.M., Albrecht, A., Hurtado, P.A., Simulation-based optimization for the integrated scheduling of production and logistic systems, in: *IFAC-Papersonline*, vol. 49, pp. 1050–1055, 2016.

17. West, S., Stoll, O., Meierhofer, J., Züst, S., Digital twin providing new opportunities for value co-creation through supporting decision-making. *Appl. Sci.*, 11, 3750, 2021.

18. Lindström, J., Larsson, H., Jonsson, M., Lejon, E., Towards intelligent and sustainable production: Combining and integrating online predictive maintenance and continuous quality control, in: *Procedia CIRP*, vol. 63, pp. 443–448, 2017.

19. Schleich, B., Anwer, N., Mathieu, L., Wartzack, S., Shaping the digital twin for design and production engineering, in: *CIRP Annals*, vol. 66, pp. 141–144, 2017.

20. Kaarlela, T., Pieskä, S., Pitkäaho, T., Digital twin and virtual reality for safety training. *Proceedings of the 2020 11th IEEE International Conference on Cognitive Infocommunications (CogInfoCom)*, pp. 115–120, 2020.

21. Rosen, R., Wichert, G.V., Lo, G., Bettenhausen, K.D., About the importance of autonomy and digital twins for the future of manufacturing, in: *IFAC-Papers online*, vol. 48, pp. 567–572, 2015.

22. Rasheed, A., San, O., Kvamsdal, T., Digital twin: Values, challenges and enablers from a modeling perspective. *IEEE Access*, 8, 21980–22012, 2020, doi: https://doi.org/10.1109/ACCESS.2020.2970143.

23. Brettel, M., Friederichsen, N., Keller, M., Rosenberg, M., How virtualization, decentralization and network building change the manufacturing landscape: An industry 4.0 perspective. *Int. J. Mech. Aerosp. Ind. Mechatron. Eng.*, 8, 37–44, 2014.

24. Mawson, V.J. and Hughes., B.R., The development of modelling tools to improve energy efficiency in manufacturing processes and systems. *J. Manuf. Syst.*, 51, 95–105, Apr. 2019.

25. Kunatha, M. and Winkler, H., Integrating the digital twin of the manufacturing system into a decisión support system for improving the order management process. *Procedia CIRP*, vol. 72, pp. 225–231, 2017.

26. Mateev, M., Industry 4.0 and the digital twin for building industry. *Int. Sci. J. Industry 4.0*, 5, 1, 29–32, 2020.

27. Bridgestone, How Bridgestone's Virtual Tyre Modelling Revolutionalising Tyre Development. https://www.bridgestone.co.uk/story/mobility/how-bridgestones-virtual-tire-modelling-is-revolutionising-tire-development.

28. Rolls-Royce, How Digital Twin technology can enhance aviation. https://www.rolls-royce.com/media/our-stories/discover/2019/how-digital-twin-technology-can-enhance-aviation.aspx.

29. Capgemini, Digital twin within the supply chain- the benefits. https://www.capgemini.com/2021/03/digital-twin-within-the-supply-chain-the-benefits/.

30. Microsoft, Customer Stories, GE Aviation's Digital Group builds a holistic source of truth with Azure Digital Twins. https://customers.microsoft.com/en-us/story/846315-ge-aviation-manufacturing-azure.
31. Cimino, C., Negri, E., Fumagalli, L., Review of digital twin applications in manufacturing. *Comput. Ind.*, 113, 103130, 2019.
32. Vrabic, R., Erkoyuncu, J.A., Butala, P., Roy, R., Digital twins: Understanding the added value of integrated models for through-life engineering services. *Procedia Manufacturing*, vol. 16, pp. 139–146, 2018.

15

Digital Twin: Pros and Cons

Prakash J.

*Department of Computer Science & Engineering, PSG College of Technology,
Tamil Nadu, India*

Abstract
In this fast-moving world, technology is useful and of importance. The modern world requires technology and seeks more new technologies, which could help greatly in different industries. Prominently crucial and important industry like health, education, automotive, aviation, etc. always seeks such new technologies which can majorly help and benefit the whole industry where it will be used which is a known fact. Digital twin is a technology that can, to a great level, match the expectations of these industries, which always seeks new technology. It has pros which can help to meet and match the expectations of many industries. There are some cons also in this technology just like almost every technology. So this technology has some cons, which can be considered as potential areas for improving. In this chapter, digital twin technology is discussed and explained. Along with it, different pros and cons of digital twin are also discussed and explained. Also, some different sectors application-wise pros of digital twin are also discussed and an example of real-world application of digital twin technology is explained in this chapter.

Keywords: Digital twin, technology, pros, cons, digital twin technology, manufacturing, monitoring, real time

15.1 Introduction

In recent times, technology is used almost everywhere. From modern hi-tech sensor-based toothbrush to smart watches, technology is used everywhere where it is possible to use it.

Email: jpk.cse@psgtech.ac.in

Manisha Vohra (ed.) Digital Twin Technology: Fundamentals and Applications, (233–246) © 2023 Scrivener Publishing LLC

The gadget, which almost everyone carries along with them daily, i.e., cellphone, is also full of technology. From different gadgets to home appliances to different work sectors like health, industrial, etc., there is technology used everywhere.

Each technology has its own list of pros and cons. Each technology after being brought to use, grows, and progresses over a period of time. There will be a lot of changes in it. Some technologies get updated and stay in use in different applications, while some get replaced with some other technology that is better than it. The journey of each technology is different. In this chapter, we will be discussing and understanding the digital twin technology completely in detail first. Digital twin is a strongly emerging technology. After that, we will discuss and understand the pros and cons of digital twin technology.

15.2   Introduction to Digital Twin

Digital twin is a technology which is growing continuously. Its growth, if carefully seen, then it will be found that in the recent times, its growth has been fast paced. There is a growing focus of different sectors on this particular technology. It is gaining a lot of attention from different sectors.

Digital twin has the pros that can majorly benefit different sectors which is why there is focus of different sectors on it, and due to this, it is gaining attention from different sectors. Sectors, such as automotive, health, industrial, etc., can majorly benefit from it.

Digital twin was first used by National Aeronautics and Space Administration (NASA) in the year 1970 but the work on digital twin had started somewhere in 1960s itself. During a mission of NASA which was Apollo 13 mission, NASA had for the first time used digital twin for creating exact copy of their spacecraft.

After that, till date, the digital twin technology has progressed and grown very much. First, this technology was not much known to people, but in the recent past few years, with its growth and progress, people started knowing about this technology. As digital twin will progress and grow more, its pros and cons will keep on updating as it will be explored more, with respect to its possibilities, abilities, and so on.

Technology is required and used almost everywhere now. Take an example of industrial sector. In the industrial sector, with growing market competitiveness, industrial organizations require to shift to a smart manufacturing production paradigm for speedy product manufacturing.

Technology like digital twin can bring the desired change in the manufacturing process. Digital twin technology can largely benefit the manufacturing process. It can be of great use in the industrial sector.

One technology which has become the centre of attention for industry and is an emerging concept is digital twin [22]. There are different concepts associated to the wave of industry 4.0 and digital twin is also one of them [28].

Along with recent developments in industry 4.0, digital twin and machine learning, there has been a growth in interest in adapting these concepts [5]. It is clear that there is a growth in interest for digital twin. Not just from industrial perspective but from academic perspective as well, there is an ongoing growth in interest for digital twin [8].

Digital twin is a concept which is highly dynamic [24]. In recent competitive markets, there are aspirations for decreasing or reducing the time to market and also for bringing an increase in product development performance which fuel the application of sophisticated virtual product models, that are frequently referred to as digital twins that are having great importance [27]. Digital twin can be defined as a virtual representation of a physical asset enabled through data and simulators [2]. Digital twin is virtual representation of real world subject or real world object [29].

The digital twin refers to creating virtual model of physical objects, products, etc., where the virtual model are the exact replicate of the physical items. In other words, the creation of a virtual model (i.e., a virtual twin) of physical object, process, etc. is known as digital twinning. It connects the virtual and physical worlds.

Conceptually, digital twin mimics state of its physical twin in real time and vice versa [23]. Digital twin can also be called as digital representation of real-world entity or system [12]. Adoption of a digital twin must make sure that it is connected to the physical twin [13].

Digital twins change and evolve along with their physical counterparts throughout their lifecycle by means of communication [21]. Digital twin needs connection between the physical model and corresponding virtual model. This connection is established by utilizing sensors to generate real-time data [30]. The physical systems in the digital twin model would be in continuous communication with their digital twin [6].

The digital twin gets real-time data from the physical entity or its physical twin and it is synchronized with it. The digital twin can be then used for monitoring purpose as well. If there is any change in the physical entity then digital twin will come to know about it. Then it will also immediately go through the same change in itself.

For the concept which is now known as digital twin, the very first definition for it was made in the year 2002 by Michael Grieves in a presentation regarding product lifecycle management (PLM) [1].

Digital twin consists of virtual space, real space, link for data flow from real space to virtual space, link for information flow from virtual space to real space and virtual sub-spaces [15].

Digital twins are of two types: digital twin prototype (DTP) and digital twin instance (DTI). DTs are operated on in a digital twin environment (DTE).

Digital twin prototype (DTP)—this type of digital twin describes the prototypical physical artifact. It contains the informational sets necessary to describe and produce a physical version that duplicates or twins the virtual version [15].

Digital Twin Instance (DTI)—this type of Digital Twin describes a specific corresponding physical product that an individual Digital Twin remains linked to throughout the life of that physical product [15].

Digital twin environment (DTE)—this is an integrated, multidomain physics application space for operating on Digital Twins for a variety of purposes. These purposes would include:

Predictive—the Digital Twin would be used for predicting future behavior and performance of the physical product [15].

Interrogative—this would apply to DTIs. Digital twin instances could be interrogated for the current and past histories [15].

National Aeronautics and Space Administration (NASA) used digital twin in 1970 for the first time. When NASA had started working on digital twin in 1960s and even when NASA used it for the first time in 1970, digital twin name was not given to this technology. It was not known as digital twin back then.

In 1991, a book was published by David Gelernter named as "Mirror Worlds." In this book, David Gelernter had written about digital twins. This was a good step for digital twin technology progress as knowledge about digital twin could reach to people through this book, making people know about digital twin.

Few years later, Michael Grieves from the Michigan University talked and gave presentation on digital twin in a conference. This was in the year 2002. The conference was Society of Manufacturing Engineers. It was held in Michigan. This conference event proved to be very important for digital twin technology progress.

Through the medium of this conference, it was the first time digital twin was talked about in public. However, in this conference, digital twin concept was talked about only in a limited capacity. It was talked about only with respect to product life cycle management topic but still a talk on it for the first time in public was an important part in digital twin's evolution. John Vickers coined the word digital twin for this technology.

It was the year 2010 when John Vickers had written a report in which he had coined the word digital twin for this technology.

Now if anyone sees digital twin technology then it is still in evolving state. Since 1970 when it was used first by NASA, to this current year the growth of this technology has been tremendous.

Digital twins' core concept envisaged a system which couples physical entities to virtual counterparts, leveraging the benefits of the virtual environment as well as the physical environment to the benefit of whole system [8]. The data which digital twin produces under different what-if conditions can be used for purposes such as improving future system designs, optimization of maintenance cycles, etc. [16].

By leveraging a digital platform to speedily build high-fidelity simulations and models which can make informed decisions and along with it create the ability to analyse results, digital twin concept has gained huge traction [5].

In the design and operational phases of a factory, modelling, simulation and evaluation of manufacturing systems are relevant activities [25].

Manufacturing, can be defined in different ways. Traditionally it is defined as a process in which raw materials are turned into physical products [10].

From time to time, manufacturing businesses across the world require to innovate their manufacturing processes in order to remain in competition [26].

Similar to how eLearning has been pervasive and entrenched during the pandemic worldwide, online manufacturing operations, remote monitoring and maintenance, etc. are urgently demanded by the manufacturing industry [20].

The growth in usage of information and communication technology allows digital engineering of products [19]. Value co-creation among other few requirements is necessary to be understood to provide digital services in service system of a product [4].

Digital twin application gives value creation in the fields of operations and service management [3]. There are significant benefits promised by digital twins for their different stakeholders when digital twins are used to support different activities related to manufacturing like manufacturing management, monitoring and control of manufactured products, etc. [7]. Digital twin can enable things like remote monitoring, etc.

Digital Twin of machine tools when created in a B2B context, it lets the customers of the products which are being produced to get the real-time insights in the manufacturing process [7]. When it comes to equipment's, digital twin could let us have a correct estimate of the equipment's condition [11].

In a smart factory, digital twin seems to be most suitable source of knowledge [14]. In the operations phase, digital twin lets us understand how to more effectively and efficiently maintain the system [15].

The digital twin has the product's information throughout the product lifecycle as it the virtual representation of the real product [32]. Digital twin lets all the users and also all the stakeholders to monitor as well as access the physical twin status from any location [31].

Digital twins' role is not restricted only to some certain areas of the companies. Its ability is such that it can even integrate whole value chain in order to modify business environment for services, products, etc. [9]. There is transformation of digital twin into a strategic technology [18].

15.3   Pros of Digital Twin

There are different pros of digital twin. Some of it are as follows:

- Digital twin can forecast the problem in advance before its arrival
- Digital twin can be used in monitoring work
- Reduction in waste
- Helps avoid hazardous situations at work
- Increases speed of work

Let us discuss and understand each one of them.

15.3.1   Digital Twin Can Forecast the Problem in Advance Before Its Arrival

Digital twin has wonderful pros. One of it is that it can be known what possible problems can be caused in a product or object by using digital twin. It can actually forecast or predict about the possible problems before they arrive in reality in the physical product, object, etc. This can save a lot of trouble that could have been caused.

Any disruption or problem that could have hampered in reality the physical product, object, etc. or could have hampered the physical product, if known in advance can be prevented and can save a lot of trouble.

If suppose a company has already manufactured a product. All the instructions are well followed, each and everything was checked multiple times and all the precautions are taken while manufacturing the product.

However, despite of this, if any problems come in the product then it will cause trouble. If any technology could forecast the problem in advance before its arrival then the problem can be avoided. This will save the trouble. Digital twin technology can be used here. When digital twin of an existing real world object is made, it can help throughout the lifecycle of the product. Any problem which could occur in the product can be then forecasted by digital twin as the real world object will be connected with the digital twin for enabling real-time data transmission. Digital twin also go through the same changes as the real world object. The problem that could come in the real world product can be forecast by the digital twin in advance before its arrival. This will help to avoid the problem and thus save the trouble can could have been caused.

15.3.2   Digital Twin Can Be Used in Monitoring Work

The next in the list of pros of digital twin is that it can be used in the monitoring work. The digital twin through sensors can get real-time data. When the digital twin model will get the real-time data then it will behave, change and react same as the original object in real-time data and these real-time changes will be seen in the digital twin model.

If there would be a just a virtual model which can be made such that it looks like the original object but cannot be connected with the original real world object to receive real-time data then the virtual would remain as a fixed virtual model which does not changes and cannot update itself.

Here in digital twin, since the digital twin model can be connected with the original object and receive real-time data and change and update in the same manner as the original object, this proves to be a great advantage of using digital twin as the original object can then be monitored from anywhere using digital twin. Any change in the original real object will be mimicked in the digital twin also immediately and instantly.

Hence, digital twin can be used in monitoring work. It lets anyone remotely monitor the original object.

15.3.3   Reduction in Waste

When a particular object or product is manufactured, if something goes wrong in the manufacturing process, then the manufactured object or product would be required to be manufactured again, which leads to wastage of materials and different resources. If digital twin was used for manufacturing process, then it could help to bring reduction in waste.

To understand this better, consider and go through the following example.

Supposing there is a product which has to be manufactured. No digital twin is being used for this object manufacturing. If some problem comes and there are flaws detected and the manufactured product cannot be accepted, then this will in this case further work will have to be stopped immediately.

Then everything will have be carefully examined to find out more details about the problem and the flaws. After that it will be analyzed and maybe a strategy and solutions would be planned and finalized and then work will be done according to it. This will not just waste materials and resources but will also delay the manufacturing work.

If digital twin had been used in the above situation for the manufacturing process then it would help in reduction of wastage.

15.3.4   Helps Avoid Hazardous Situations at Work

Digital twin can be used in different sectors like oil and gas. A sector like oil and gas has safety hazards if anything goes wrong. If digital twin is used, it can forecast the future problems which will avoid anything from going wrong.

When all the work will happen as required without any problems occurring using digital twins then this will help avoid hazardous situations at work.

15.3.5   Increases Speed of Work Completion

When using digital twin, during manufacturing process of a product, it can help to complete the work faster. The product will have faster time to market.

15.4   Cons of Digital Twin

Digital twin has few cons as well. Some of them are as follows:

- Deep knowledge will be needed for creating and handling the digital twin
- Issues with sensors issue can affect the digital twin
- Complete security assurance with digital twin can be challenging

Let us discuss and understand each one of them.

15.4.1   Deep Knowledge Will Be Needed for Creating and Handling the Digital Twin

Digital twin is not simply created. All necessary things for creating the digital twin should be there and deep knowledge about it is required. Then only digital twin can be created. Even for handling the digital twin, deep knowledge of it is required.

15.4.2   Issues with Sensors Issue Can Affect the Digital Twin

The digital twin can be affected if there are issues with sensors as the incoming data from the physical object is collected and sent by the sensors.

15.4.3   Security

The security parameter is an important parameter. There should not be any data breach. The digital twin model should remain protected. If there is even the slightest of the loophole present, then the data would be at risk and eventually the connected original object could come under risk then and be affected. Hence, complete security assurance with digital twin can be challenging.

15.5   Application Wise Pros of Digital Twin

Given below are examples of some sectors. The below mentioned different sectors application wise pros of digital twin are then discussed:

- Oil and gas sector
- Industrial sector
- Automotive sector
- Construction sector

The discussion of pros of digital twin for the abovementioned sectors is as follows.

15.5.1   Oil and Gas Sector

In oil and gas sector, digital twin can help in conducting preventive maintenance, monitoring different process, providing cost savings, etc. These are some of the pros of digital twin in oil and gas sector.

15.5.2   Industrial Sector

In industrial sector also, there are different pros of digital twin. For example, for any product or object, digital twin can be used during the manufacturing process, and the process can be also monitored using digital twin. Wastage can be reduced, there will be faster time to market the product or object being manufactured.

15.5.3   Automotive Sector

In automotive sector, digital twin can help greatly. For example, Tesla, Inc. uses digital twin for all their cars which they are selling to their customers. It helps in their product development greatly. All the data which sensors on the car collect are analyzed. Every day, data are taken from each car and analyzed. All these data being the real-time data becomes all the more very useful. Since it is the real-time data, actual performance of the car can be known in different kind of environments. If any problem is being faced repeatedly which needs immediate attention can be known through this or if any immediate improvements are required then that can also be known. The software update can be prepared keeping the problems or needed improvements in mind so that they are effective enough. This way digital twin proves to be very useful.

15.5.4   Construction Sector

The pros of digital twin for the construction sector are many. They can be used during designing stage, building work stage of any structure, etc. very effectively. Also, digital twin can be useful for constructing smart cities. To support co-creation and along with it to test scenarios with city parameters, digital twin is created in smart city [17].

15.6   Conclusion

Digital twin technology in this fast moving world is evolving quickly. In this chapter, digital twin technology and its background were discussed and explained briefly. Different pros and cons of this technology were also discussed and explained in detail.

The pros we discussed and explained were digital twin can forecast the problem in advance before its arrival, digital twin can be used in monitoring work, digital twin can help to bring reduction in waste, digital twin in helps avoid hazardous situations at work and digital twin increases speed of work completion.

The cons we discussed and explained were deep knowledge will be needed for creating and handling the digital twin, issues with sensors issue can affect the digital twin, complete security assurance with digital twin can be challenging.

Along with it, different sectors application wise pros of digital twin, namely in the oil and gas sector, industrial sector, automotive sector and construction sector were also discussed in this chapter. Digital twin technology is a helping technology in this modern world. From the pros explained in this, it is visible that digital twin technology can great help different sectors. It is already applied in different sectors. An example of its application in real world was also discussed in this chapter. Though there are some cons as discussed and explained in the chapter which need to be dealt with and solutions are required to overcome those cons but still this technology with its various pros comes across as an useful and helping technology which indeed it is as we discussed and understood from one of its real world application. In the coming few years, this technology owing to its pros can rise quickly. Its application can spread across various different sectors maybe even where it has not been applied as of now but it has the potential to be applied.

References

1. Kritzinger, W., Karner, M., Traar, G., Henjes, J., Sihn, W., Digital twin in manufacturing: A categorical literature review and classification, in: *IFAC-Papers online*, vol. 51, pp. 1016–1022, 2018.
2. Rasheed, A., San, O., Kvamsdal, T., Digital twin: Values, challenges and enablers. *IEEE Access*, 8, 21980–22012, 2020.

3. West, S., Stoll, O., Meierhofer, J., Züst, S., Digital twin providing new opportunities for value co-creation through supporting decision-making. *Appl. Sci.*, 11, 3750, 2021.

4. West, S., Gaiardelli, P., Rapaccini, M., Exploring technology-driven service innovation in manufacturing firms through the lens of service dominant logic, in: *IFAC-Papers online*, vol. 51, pp. 1317–1322, 2018.

5. Khan, S., Farnsworth, M., McWilliam, R., Erkoyuncu, J., On the requirements of digital twin-driven autonomous maintenance. *Annu. Rev. Control*, 50, 13–28, 2020.

6. Grieves, M.W., Virtually intelligent product systems: Digital and physical twins. *Complex Syst. Eng. Theory Pract.*, 256, 175–200, 2019.

7. Romero, D., Wuest, T., Harik, R., Thoben, K.D., Towards a cyber-physical PLM environment: The role of digital product models, intelligent products, digital twins, product avatars and digital shadows, in: *IFAC-Papers online*, vol. 53, pp. 10911–10916, 2020.

8. Jones, D., Snider, C., Nassehi, A., Yon, J., Hicks, B., Characterising the digital twin: A systematic literature review. *CIRP J. Manuf. Sci. Technol.*, 29, 36–52, 2020.

9. Melesse, T.Y., Di Pasquale, V., Riemma, S., Digital twin models in industrial operations: A systematic literature review. *Procedia Manuf*, vol. 42, pp. 267–272, 2020.

10. Lohtander, M., Ahonen, N., Lanz, M., Ratava, J., Kaakkunen, J., Micro manufacturing unit and the corresponding 3d-model for the digital twin. *Proc. Manuf.*, 25, 55–61, 2018.

11. Aivaliotis, P., Georgoulias, K., Arkouli, Z., Makris, S., Methodology for enabling digital twin using advanced physics-based modelling in predictive maintenance. *Procedia CIRP*, Elsevier B.V, vol. 81, pp. 417–422, 2019, doi: DOI:10.1016/j.procir.2019.03.072.

12. Rauch, L. and Pietrzyk, M., Digital twins as a modern approach to design of industrial processes. *J. Mach. Eng.*, 19, 2019.

13. Cimino, C., Negri, E., Fumagalli, L., Review of digital twin applications in manufacturing. *Comput. Ind.*, 113, 103130, 2019.

14. Longo, F., Nicoletti, L., Padovano, A., Ubiquitous knowledge empowers the smart factory: The impacts of a service-oriented digital twin on enterprises' performance. *Annu. Rev. Control*, 47, 221– 236, 2019.

15. Grieves, M. and Vickers, J., Digital twin: Mitigating unpredictable, undesirable emergent behavior in complex systems, in: *Transdisciplinary perspectives on complex systems*, Kahlen FJ, S. Flumerfelt, A. Alves (Eds.), pp. 85–113, Springer, Cham, 2017, doi: https://doi.org/10.1007/978-3-319-38756-7_4.

16. Madni, A.M., Madni, C.C., Lucero, S.D., Leveraging digital twin technology in model based systems engineering. *Syst.*, 7, 2019.

17. Ruohomaki, T., Airaksinen, E., Huuska, P., Kesaniemi, O., Martikka, M., Suomisto, J., Smart city platform enabling digital twin, in: *2018 International Conference on Intelligent Systems (IS)*, IEEE Xplore, pp. 155–161, 20192018.

18. Mylonas, G., Kalogeras, A., Kalogeras, G., Anagnostopoulos, C., Alexakos, C., Muñoz, L., Digital twins from smart manufacturing to smart cities: A survey. *IEEE Access*, 9, 143222–143249, 2021, doi: 10.1109/ACCESS.2021.3120843.

19. Brettel, M., Friederichsen, N., Keller, M., Rosenberg, M., How virtualization, decentralization and network building change the manufacturing landscape: An industry 4.0 perspective. *Int. J. Mech. Aerosp. Ind. Mechatron.Eng.*, 8, 37–44, 2014.

20. Lin, W.D. and Low, M.Y.H., Concept design of a system architecture for a manufacturing cyber-physical digital twin system. *IEEE International Conference on Industrial Engineering and Engineering Management (IEEM)*, pp. 1320–1324, 2021.

21. Vrabic, R., Erkoyuncu, J.A., Butala, P., Roy, R., Digital twins: Understanding the added value of integrated models for through-life engineering services. *Procedia Manufacturing*, vol. 16, pp. 139–146, 2018.

22. Fuller, A., Fan, Z., Day, C., Barlow, C., Digital twin: Enabling technologies, challenges and open research. *IEEE Access*, 8, 108952–108971, 2020.

23. Singh, M., Fuenmayor, E., Hinchy, E.P., Qiao, Y., Murray, N., Devine, D., Digital twin: Origin to future. *Appl. Syst. Innov.*, 4, 36, 2021.

24. Rosen, R., Wichert, G., Lo, G., Bettenhausen, K.D., About the importance of autonomy and digital twins for the future of manufacturing, in: *IFAC-Papers online*, vol. 48, pp. 567–572, 2015.

25. Terkaj, W. and Urgo, M., A virtual factory data model as a support tool for the simulation of manufacturing systems. *Procedia CIRP*, vol. 28, pp. 137–142, 2015.

26. David, J. and Lanz, M., Leveraging digital twins for assisted learning of flexible manufacturing systems, in: *IEEE 16th International Conference on Industrial Informatics (INDIN)*, pp. 529– 535, 2018.

27. Schleich, B., Anwer, N., Mathieu, L., Wartzack, S., Shaping the digital twin for design and production engineering. *CIRP Ann.*, 66, 1, 141–144, 2017.

28. Negri, E., Fumagalli, L., Macchi, M., A review of the roles of digital twin in CPS-based production systems. *Procedia Manuf.*, 11, 939–948, 2017.

29. Schluse, M. and Rossmann, J., From simulation to experimentable digital twins: Simulation-based development and operation of complex technical systems, in: *IEEE International Symposium on Systems Engineering (ISSE)*, IEEE, pp. 1–6, 2016.

30. Kaarlela, T., Pieskä, S., Pitkäaho, T., Digital twin and virtual reality for safety training, in: *Proceedings of the 2020 11th IEEE International*

Conference on Cognitive Infocommunications (CogInfoCom), pp. 115–120, 2020.

31. Barricelli, B.R., Casiraghi, E., Fogli, D., A survey on digital twin: Definitions, characteristics, applications, and design implications. *IEEE Access*, 7, 167653–167671, 2019.

32. Schroeder, G.N., Steinmetz, C., Pereira, C.E., Digital twin data modeling with automation ML and a communication methodology for data exchange. *IFACPapers Online*, 49, 30, 12–17, 2016.

Index

Printed and bound by CPI Group (UK) Ltd, Croydon, CR0 4YY

27/10/2024

14580132-0001